The Patty Duke Show and
the American Sixties

The Patty Duke Show
and the American Sixties

Hot Dogs and Crêpes Suzette

CARYL FLINN AND DANA POLAN

OXFORD
UNIVERSITY PRESS

OXFORD
UNIVERSITY PRESS

Oxford University Press is a department of the University of Oxford.
It furthers the University's objective of excellence in research, scholarship,
and education by publishing worldwide. Oxford is a registered trade mark of
Oxford University Press in the UK and in certain other countries.

Published in the United States of America by Oxford University Press
198 Madison Avenue, New York, NY 10016, United States of America.

Library of Congress Cataloging-in-Publication Data
Names: Flinn, Caryl author | Polan, Dana B., 1953– author
Title: The Patty Duke Show and the American sixties : hot dogs and Crêpes Suzette /
by Caryl Flinn and Dana Polan.
Description: New York : Oxford University Press, 2026. |
Includes bibliographical references and index.
Identifiers: LCCN 2025049464 (print) | LCCN 2025049465 (ebook) |
ISBN 9780197667446 paperback | ISBN 9780197667439 hardback |
ISBN 9780197667477 | ISBN 9780197667460 epub
Subjects: LCSH: Patty Duke show (Television program) |
LCGFT: Television criticism and reviews
Classification: LCC PN1992.77.P28 F57 2026 (print) | LCC PN1992.77.P28 (ebook) |
DDC 791.45/72—dc23/eng/20251222
LC record available at https://lccn.loc.gov/2025049464
LC ebook record available at https://lccn.loc.gov/2025049465

DOI: 10.1093/oso/9780197667439.001.0001

Paperback printed by Marquis Book Printing, Canada
Hardback printed by Lightning Source, Inc., United States of America

The manufacturer's authorized representative in the EU for product safety is
Oxford University Press España S.A. of Parque Empresarial San Fernando de Henares,
Avenida de Castilla, 2 – 28830 Madrid (www.oup.es/en or product.safety@oup.com).
OUP España S.A. also acts as importer into Spain of products made by the manufacturer.

MIX
Paper | Supporting
responsible forestry
FSC® C103567

For Hudson

Contents

Acknowledgments

This book originates not only in the teamwork of Patty and Cathy—er, Caryl and Dana—but broader collaboration with friends, scholars, and librarians. Caryl and Dana want to first thank their spouses, Gary Goertz and Marita Sturken, for their patience over the many months of this project. A different sort of forbearance, but likewise essential, came from our editor, Norm Hirschy, at Oxford University Press.

We have a number of archivists to thank for their contributions to this project. Our heartfelt gratitude goes to Dana Nemeth, Reference Archivist of the Ray and Pat Browne Popular Culture Library at Bowling Green State University. Ms. Nemeth and her team responded to our requests with enthusiasm and care during our extended stay at the Archives. Thanks are due also to Phil Hallman, Head Librarian of the Donald Hall Center at the University of Michigan, who provided extensive help and support for all things Patty Duke. We likewise appreciate the help of Sandy Garcia-Meyers, head of Archival Research Services at USC's Cinematic Arts Library and Archives, for facilitating a visit by Dana to consult the Sidney Sheldon papers there, and of Mary Huelsbeck at the Wisconsin Center for Film and Theater Research, who located Duke's contract for *The Patty Duke Show*. Dr. Seonaid Valiant of ASU Library's Rare Books and Manuscripts shared documents pertaining to the show's producer, Peter Lawford. Vanessa Lee, Public Service Specialist at Columbia University's Rare Book and Manuscript Library, arranged a visit to consult Sid Ramin's scores for *The Patty Duke Show* and the papers of journalist Jane Howard. Caryl gratefully acknowledges the University of Michigan for granting extensive research support to the project, and we both express our appreciation to Sarah O'Brien for lending her expertise and eagle eyes to the first draft of the manuscript. The stills for the book were prepared by 'miracle-worker' Genevieve Havemeyer-King, formerly of the Moving Image Archiving and Preservation program at NYU. A grant from the Center for Study and Research at NYU's Tisch School of the Arts helped fund indexing: special thanks to André Lepecki and Hali Alspach for making this happen.

We want to thank a number of others for contributions—their memories, assessments, viewing and reading recommendations, and their assistance of all sorts both large and small: Bailey Apollonio; Aniko Bodroghkozy; William Boddy; Sean Donovan; Jennifer Fleeger; Krin Gabbard; Charles L. Granata; Katie Hite; David Levy; Robert Lightfoot; Cynthia Lucia; David Lugowski; William Luhr; Josh Morrison; Sarah O'Brien; Carolyn Pfeiffer; Melissa Phruksachart; James Reel; Jeff Schneider; Sally Seymor; Jack, Kathy, and Andrew Sheppard; Shawn Shimpach; Marissa Spada; Lynn Spigel; Kerry Trueman; Con Verevis; and Pamela Robertson Wojcik.

By an act of pure serendipity, Dana was at an academic conference and happened to meet William Schallert's granddaughter, Hannah Schallert, herself a graduate student in film and media studies. Afterward, she emailed us her recollections about her grandfather, including remarks from her father (Schallert's oldest son, Joseph) and his brother, Brendan. Their personal recollections confirmed and deepened our impressions of Schallert as a versatile actor and as a lovely, giving person. We are very grateful to her and her family for contributing to the project.

Actor Paul O'Keefe, who played Ross Lane on *The Patty Duke Show*, is the last surviving member of the original cast and thus holds especially up-close memories of the show's production. Mr. O'Keefe offered invaluable recollections of his work on the show and useful insights into television production at the time. And we were, of course, very grateful for the rich and affectionate memories of his famous costar, Anna Duke. We thank him deeply for his generosity and time.

Figure 0.1 The Score for "Cousins" Music by Sid Ramin Lyric by Bob Wells ©1963, 1966 (Copyright Renewed) United Artist Music Co, Inc. All Rights Controlled & Administered by EMI U Catalogue Inc. (Publishing) and Alfred Music (Print) All Rights Reserved. Used by Permission of Alfred Music.

Preface

Theme Song Themes

There is no question that the theme songs of American TV hit their stride in the Sixties, and their enduring popularity has been boosted by broadcast and cable syndication, online resources, and many a boomer dinner party.[1] Most of those theme songs came from sitcoms of the era, tunes that ritualistically eased viewers into benign, comic spaces. Even song fragments have been embedded in collective memory, decades after their original series ended, from "a three-hour tour" to "Gold, black gold, Texas Tea" to "A horse is a horse, of course, of course."

The instrumental melodies of these songs have also been committed to memory. Many Americans of a certain age will recognize the tunes for *The Andy Griffith Show*, *Bewitched*, *The Munsters*, and *Get Smart*. Many can recall how, in *The Dick Van Dyke Show*'s opening credits, a brief musical flourish effortlessly conveyed the exact moment of Van Dyke's encounter with the living room ottoman, leaving us to guess whether his pratfall would ensue or not.

Most sitcom theme songs were sung by men, either individually, as in Lester Flatt's vocals for *The Beverly Hillbillies*, or, more commonly, in small groups that prompted visions of well-scrubbed white men with short blond hair wearing matching V-neck sweaters, such as the unknown Wellingtons for *Gilligan's Island*. Most TV tunes eschewed the rock and rhythm-and-blues dominating popular music of the time, opting instead for singing styles that were typically pop-adjacent (placid, catchy, and smooth), vocalized by upbeat troubadours "telling tales" that established their series' backstories, gimmicks, and situational components.

Prominently etched in viewers' memories is "Cousins," the theme song for *The Patty Duke Show* (ABC [American Broadcasting Company], 1963–66), in which Duke plays the leading roles of identical twin cousins, American Patty Lane and Cathy Lane, the British cousin who comes to live with Patty's family in Brooklyn. In addition to introducing the series' comic premise and the themes that would be nested across its three-year run, *The Patty*

Duke Show's canonical theme song establishes the importance of twinning and pairing to the show. With images and lyrics carefully divided between Cathy and Patty, "Cousins" appears to present a pair of opposite but equal characters, "different as night and day."

"Cousins" was composed by arranger Sid Ramin (a recent Academy Award winner for co-orchestrating *West Side Story* in 1961; he had known Leonard Bernstein since childhood); lyrics were by Bob Wells. The piece was performed by a five-member group called The Skip-Jacks, also known for singing "Meet the Flintstones."[2]

The Patty Duke Show's theme song opens in near whispers. Offscreen, the three male Skip-Jacks introduce Cathy, the sophisticated "European" cousin under a series of close-ups:

> *Meet Cathy who's lived most everywhere*
> *From Zanzibar to Berk'ly Square*

Switching to the group's two female singers, the vocals increase in volume and tempo as they introduce Cathy's American cousin, also shown in smiling close-ups:

> *But Patty's only seen the sights*
> *A girl can see from Brooklyn Heights.*
> *What a crazy pair!*
> *But they're cousins, identical cousins all the way*
> *One pair of matching bookends*
> *Different as night and day.*

On the second verse, the camera pulls back to reveal a demure Cathy descending the Brooklyn homestead staircase in a slightly overwrought gown and taffeta stole, hair in a bun, pulled back with a small, ornate barrette:

> *While Cathy adores a minuet, the Ballets Russes and crêpes suzette*

The song (and camera) then pivot back to Patty, a teen coiffed in a Sixties-style flip, frenetically dancing in a room full of teens:

> *Our Patty likes to rock 'n roll; a hot dog makes her lose control.*
> *What a wild duet!*

Over the years, Wells's culinary comparison of the girls has taken up considerable real estate in the minds of viewers of the show, whether they watched it during its initial run or, later, on cable television's Nick at Night, online, or in other formats and platforms.[3] Although "Cousins" lacked some of the dynamic structures and distinct instrumentation of other sitcom themes, its catchy phrasing and lyrics solidified the series' place in popular culture then, and in the decades since. Nearly everyone familiar with the series recalls the number's slightly risqué "hot dogs" causing Patty to lose control, and the reference tends to prompt enthusiasm or contempt (or sometimes both) for the silly feminine energy that has come to define it—a silliness that continues to inflect the show's afterlife. When we mentioned our project to friends, family, and colleagues, those who knew the series, without prompting, often sang or quoted parts of the title song. In addition to the crazy-making hot dog, many cited "cousins, identical cousins" or "what a crazy pair." Indeed, many could, and did, sing the entire song. (In one rare case, though, a colleague who remembered individual plots of the show quite well had no recollection whatsoever of the theme song.)

Hot Dogs and Crêpes Suzette: The Project

Hot Dogs and Crêpes Suzette is divided into two parts. Part One, "Concocting an American Teen Icon and a Sitcom World: An Historical Account" (Chapters 1 though 3), covers the fundamental story of *The Patty Duke Show*—its production, preproduction histories and legacy and afterlives; Duke's career (and, to a lesser extent, those of her colleagues); and the series' place within a mutating and curiously demeaned moment in American sitcom history. Part Two, "Televising American Dreams and Conflicts: A Thematic Account" (Chapters 4 and 5), offers more analytical and ideological accounts of the show, positioning it alongside other obsessions and structures of the Sixties. Our focus necessarily falls on the notions of twinning and doubling, something that we trace across the country's political imagination and in mass culture and various art worlds, and then scrutinize *The Patty Duke Show*'s deep, but deeply conflicted, relationship to the youthful engagement and global cosmopolitanism that JFK's administration seemed to encourage. Yet in many ways, we argue, the series ultimately abandons such hopeful, outward-facing gestures to resecure the primacy of an insular and less pliant American ideal.

Our work starts by harvesting the twins, dyads, and pairings introduced in the show's theme song, moving outward to articulate broader cultural, ideological, and even political projects and contradictions marking the Sixties. Our Introduction examines what it might mean to deal at length with a series that media historians and cultural commentators have avoided, and how to correct that avoidance, locating *The Patty Duke Show* within the contradictory impulses of the Sixties. In Chapter 1, we present the central details of Duke's life and career; Chapter 2 covers the preproduction and production of the show, including its ancillary tie-in products (and the career imposed on Duke of becoming a pop singer) as well as its afterlives in the decades since its 1966 finale. Chapter 3 examines the series in relationship to other sitcoms of the Sixties and to the scholarship around them. Chapter 4, which opens the second part of our book, surveys discourses on twinning and doubling running across political and aesthetic realms of the time that occasionally played out through contemporary popular culture. In fact, we maintain that *The Patty Duke Show* tried to visualize possibilities for girls through its use of what we call "doubling with difference," rather than the literal twinning that grounds the premise of the series. We note how pairs and thematic oppositions of the series help illuminate some of the social and cultural concerns, fantasies, and tensions of the early to mid-Sixties.

In Chapter 5, we examine what we take to be the series' chief interaction with US culture in the Sixties. By focusing on *The Patty Duke Show*'s place in the late Camelot era of JFK's presidency, we demonstrate how that period's sense of optimism, expanded horizons, and emphasis on youth left its ideological imprint on the show and that that imprint hints at the possibility for global, cosmopolitan engagement, which various episodes tackle. Yet we also note ways in which *The Patty Duke Show* raises the potential of reaching out to difference only to shut it down, effectively exposing the US-centrism of the era's various liberal projects. The Coda returns to the show's theme song to illustrate how it, too, adumbrates and anticipates that retreat away from difference.

Our methodology is varied and strives to connect the series to diverse social, industrial, aesthetic, and ideological contexts. By considering *The Patty Duke Show*'s production history, we treat it as an industrial, ideological, and mass cultural product among others. By addressing its textual and formal details, its recurring themes, its complex position within "girl culture," we stress ways in which popular culture does not merely align itself with preoccupations of specific historical moments, but is constitutive of them.

We explore much of the era's preoccupation with doubling and dyads in our Introduction and in Chapter 4. While this obviously informs the show at large, it echoed within the career of the show's leading star. Duke was herself "split," not just in her depiction of two cousins, but in the sense that her career moved from the prior, relatively high-culture success of *The Miracle Worker* to the perceived lowbrow exploitativeness of *The Valley of the Dolls*, which followed quickly in the wake of the TV series. Moreover, Duke's long-undiagnosed struggle with bipolar disorder generates an additional, more poignant layer of doubling. Our goal, however, is not to retell her story (Duke herself produced three heartfelt memoirs) but to suggest that, even at their extreme, the confusions that she experienced as a young performer might be considered heightened versions of the tensions and divisions of identity faced by adolescents and teenage girls in a fraught period of US history.

In the pages that follow, we do not talk personally, let alone autobiographically, of our relationship to *The Patty Duke Show*. This will not be a volume of fan appreciation in which we enthuse about how fun the series was or provide gossip and speculation we've unearthed. Having said that, we both appreciate the show, especially as a refraction of its culture, and believe it has not been given its due. As scholarly friends who developed a productive exchange of emails during the COVID-19 pandemic, we welcomed the idea of a joint writing project and ultimately landed on *The Patty Duke Show*. We discovered that we both had grown up on the series and had been intrigued by its conceit of one teenage girl playing two others. Yet returning decades later to all of its 103 episodes revealed that our memories often failed to conform to the reality of the show, for a surprising number of episodes downplayed or even abandoned the basic premise of twinness. We also recognized how contradictory the ideological positions of *The Patty Duke Show* were, and remain. For instance, while it largely counters the idea of a single, defining identity for young, white, middle-class American female teenagers, it reinforces and imposes that singularity onto other groups of people, especially those from outside dominant US cultures, scoping them through a universalizing lens of exotic difference. We elaborate on these and other issues in subsequent chapters.

Figure I.1 One Pair of Matching Bookends

Introduction

Lost from History

"Methinks you are my glass, and not my brother"
Dromio of Ephesus, discovering his twin
in Shakespeare's *A Comedy of Errors*

"Wow! there's two of you! I've got my own harem!"
Richard seeing Patty and Cathy side-by-side
for the first time in *The Patty Duke Show*

The Patty Duke Show holds a critical place in television history. That's due not just for having what Tom Gliatto at *People* trumpets as "one of the best-written, best-remembered minutes of music ever to launch a subsequent twenty-three minutes of episodic television nonsense," but because Duke was, at the time, an award-winning performer who became the youngest ever to lead a series in her own name.[1]

Sid Caesar and Jack Paar had led eponymous variety shows for adults; other sitcoms titled after children featured the identities of the fictional characters they portrayed, for example, *Dennis the Menace* or *Leave it to Beaver*, and none of these figures centered the show quite like Patty Duke did, especially with her double presence as Patty and Cathy. Unlike the other young actors, Duke's offscreen, as well as onscreen, successes were credentialed enough to have had her contract worked out separately from those of the other main actors, whose work was less remunerated—and, as we'll detail, less surveilled and controlled. The credentials came from Duke's recent triumphs on Broadway and in Hollywood, where she won an Oscar for her depiction of a young Helen Keller in *The Miracle Worker*. After that, the sitcom was conceived with her specifically in mind—its creators said that they viewed her talent as outsized enough that she could play two characters (Figure I.1.).

The Patty Duke Show *and the American Sixties*. Caryl Flinn and Dana Polan, Oxford University Press.
© Oxford University Press 2026. DOI: 10.1093/oso/9780197667439.003.0001

The Patty Duke Show stands out because the series' point of view was grounded in those two teenagers, even though it was scarcely the first to have a young female lead, for example, *My Little Margie*. Other shows centering on teen girls toward the end of the Fifties and into the Sixties focused chiefly on the dating habits of their lead characters For the most part, these shows lasted but one season and have left little trace in history: few enjoy the cultural resonance that *The Patty Duke Show* maintains in popular memory.[2]

The only other long-running series that centered squarely on a teen's perspective was *The Many Loves of Dobie Gillis* (1959-63), and this was done from the vantage point of male teens.[3] In an era when many women's voices—and political critiques—were beginning to ignite in the United States, a series that concentrated on feminine points of view was quite significant. It also made it *generationally* important: *The Patty Duke Show* took teen girl viewers seriously, and though done through the prism of a light sitcom, it provided viewers with resonant stories of teen ambition and enterprise—plots that took the girls well beyond the ordeals of dating.

The Patty Duke Show made Patty Lane and, to a lesser degree, Cathy, the indisputable centers of attention; other family members and secondary characters were locked in their orbit. They lacked the teens' verve, drive, and follow through. As Moya Luckett, one of the few scholars to address the series at length, notes, "*Patty Duke* certainly highlighted the values of its female protagonist(s) by contrasting her with the awkward figures of her vapid boyfriend Richard and her 'geeky' bespectacled younger brother Ross."[4]

Patty's parents, Martin and Natalie Lane, similarly did little more than respond to her antics, rarely meting out authoritative solutions of the sort offered by most family sitcoms of the era. The antics, in short, were treated as misguided forays rather than lapses of moral judgment. The presence of Cathy, as Patty's culturally and philosophically dissimilar twin, also helped broaden the sense of possibility and dreams of teenage girls during a complex historical period. This point, we contend, is crucial to the series.

Yet, in contrast to other sitcoms of the mid-Sixties, *The Patty Duke Show* has not, theme song aside, enjoyed a robust afterlife. *The Addams Family*, *Bewitched*, *Gidget*, and even *The Beverly Hillbillies* all generated subsequent adaptations for the big screen, whereas *The Patty Duke Show* led to no theatrical films, no reboots, no musical stage adaptations. Aside from a sub-par 1999 TV reunion film and a series of PSAs for Medicare and Social Security (discussed later), its cast made few group appearances or interviews once the series was over.

Deprecating Patty

Two groups of scholars have overlooked *The Patty Duke Show* that one would have expected to address it. First, across their copious studies of the Sixties, American social historians have tended to downplay, if not out and out ignore, popular culture to prioritize instead the decade's political, legal, and military events, implying that mass culture did not impact or interact with these more serious ventures.[5] When these historians do turn their attention to TV and other mass media, it is almost always to examine journalism or news reporting, which developed in leaps and bounds over the decade; the need to expand coverage of the civil rights movement and the war in Vietnam, for instance, motivated the Columbia Broadcasting System (CBS) to lengthen its evening news report from fifteen to thirty minutes in September, 1963, the month *The Patty Duke Show* premiered, and the other networks quickly followed. Very rarely do social historians mention the fictional and variety TV shows of the Sixties, and when they do, they usually treat them as so much pablum.

The second set of writers that has bypassed the series is somewhat more surprising. This group includes cultural studies and media commentators (especially television scholars) who attend to the historical, industrial, and critical aspects of the medium. They, too, have overlooked *The Patty Duke Show*, even as they examine plenty of other series of the time: *Bewitched* for its incipient feminism; *The Mod Squad* for its attempts to deal with youth culture, protest, and integration; *Gidget* as part of an intermedial, decades-long brand; and, conversely, *The Lawrence Welk Show*, as an example of "square culture." *The Patty Duke Show* has largely been left out in the cold. (As of this writing, only a handful of articles devote themselves to it.)[6]

This oversight may owe to the common perception of the silliness of its twin-cousin premise and sadly, that judgment discourages people who might consider taking the show seriously or pursue it within the broader historical context that other sitcoms are allowed to inhabit. This neglect is arguably compounded by the fact that the show centers around and focuses on teenage girls, whom some mass culture critics dismissed as a socially insignificant group and as mindless, passive consumers, or as vulnerable creatures exploited by the culture industry, especially in girl-targeted commodities such as TV shows and their tie-in merchandise, for example, novels, toys, clothing lines, cosmetics, and records. Moya Luckett's article, "Girl Watchers: Patty Duke and Teen TV," provides a welcome cultural overview of the series, but it is very much an overview, devoted as much to girl culture in the Sixties as to the specifics of the one show. It is, to our mind, an essential and useful resource, but cannot take the place of a full-length book that considers production history, the careers of its stars, its cultural engagement, its place within TV history, its themes and structures, and that analyzes individual episodes.[7]

The scholarly neglect may also result from the fact that the series ran during what many consider a transitional moment for the Sixties, even though *Bewitched* and *Gidget* were of this same moment. *The Patty Duke Show* aired during a time that straddles (and thus problematizes) the division of the decade that historians have insisted upon: the early years, which most view as an extension of the Cold War-obsessed, conservative, and conformist Fifties, and the later years that they characterize as riven with institutional critique, social disruption, and political protest. This split relies, first of all, on sweeping generalizations of the Fifties that ignore the activities of the progressive events operating within it, such as the civil rights movement, leftist movements, global anti-colonialist uprisings, and the early stirrings of the women's movement. It also fails to consider the many Americans who did not, could not, or did not want to conform to the homogenous image of white, middle-class conservatism and compliance often depicted during the decade. For national policies and representations shunted people of color, leftists, bohemians and hipsters, immigrants, the poor, and the elderly off to the side—where many are still forced to reside.

In periodizing the decade in this fashion, historians have tended to map the disruptions of the Sixties exclusively within the decade's second half, here too disregarding the competing messaging of the time. For conservative policy makers, politicians, and pundits, for example, Barry Goldwater, George Wallace, and William F. Buckley, thrived during the "rebellious half" of the decade. In ignoring the social and political upheaval of the first half and the conservatism of the second half, those who bifurcate the decade end up homogenizing both parts. That *The Patty Duke Show* fits uneasily within the polarities attributed to the decade's two-stage trajectory may leave it hard to define and easy to dismiss.

Of course, all periodizations are fraught with problems, and it would be more accurate to cast the Sixties as riven by contradiction. The decade has often been cloaked retrospectively, and romantically, in a singular sense of rebellion, when, as we just observed, it was as strongly inflected by a conservatism whose adherents Richard Nixon infamously described as "the silent majority." Moreover, the rebelliousness associated with the Sixties was an uneven, multifaceted phenomenon itself, one that took root in the Fifties if not before, finding cultural expression in youth-oriented forms such as rock and roll, R&B, and Beat writers. In 1962, the newly formed Students for a Democratic Society (SDS) penned the Port Huron Statement (a leftist critique of the Cold War, the arms race, and the military-industrial complex's indentureship to corporate interests); civil rights actions included lunch counter boycotts, the March on Washington, D.C, Martin Luther King Jr.'s timeless speech in Selma, and so on. Betty Friedan's *The Feminine Mystique*, published in 1963, enjoyed such mainstream influence that Friedan penned a related two-part essay on women and television for *TV Guide* the following year.

Closing out the Sixties proves just as arbitrary as determining its beginnings. In some ways, the Sixties ended in the mid-Seventies, when the United States finally withdrew from Vietnam (1975); some historians, not unreasonably, place the beginning of its termination with the 1968 assassinations of Martin Luther King Jr. and Robert F. Kennedy. Those for whom the period's youth culture was most salient often set the endpoint in 1969, where their hopes and optimism were crushed when Charlie Manson's gang infamously murdered six people (including Sharon Tate, Duke's costar and friend from *The Valley of the Dolls*) in August and then, in December, a free public rock concert at California's Altamont raceway went south as Hell's Angels (hired for security detail as a PR stunt by the Rolling Stones) killed an audience member while the band performed "Sympathy for the Devil." Altamont has gone down in history as the dark underbelly to Woodstock, which just months earlier had created a hippy utopia for teens and young adults—as had the energetic Harlem Cultural Festival, often called "The Black Woodstock"—that ran across that same summer. Events at the end of the year seemed to close the door on youthful hopes, much as Nixon, who was elected President in 1968, provided an unalluring, late-decade counterpoint to JFK who beat him in the 1960 election.

Feminist media historian Susan Douglas labels 1964 the decade's "hinge year," when the purported innocence and optimism of the early Camelot era were brutally undone by Kennedy's assassination. Douglas maintains that when The Beatles made their first stateside appearance in February, 1964, teens and young adults (mostly women), were able to shift their attentions and affections onto other young male public figures. Her focus on young women's and girls' relationship to popular culture of the time was groundbreaking, and her notion of a hinge year (and by implication, *The Patty Duke Show*, although her take on it is quite different than ours) potently challenges the outmoded model of a divided Sixties. For instance, youth didn't "win out" at this or at any other point: in 1964, to take just one example, the staid cinematic adaptation of *My Fair Lady* grossed several times as much as The Beatles' more adventurous *A Hard Day's Night*. (In one of the rare episodes of *The Patty Duke Show* when Natalie and Martin Lane go out, it's to see *My Fair Lady*.)

The *Patty Duke Show* premiered two months before JFK's assassination and ended a few months shy of the Summer of Love in 1967. Yet it's safe to say that since then, when people think of the series, they usually construe it as a holdover from the Fifties that, unlike *Laugh In* or *Mod Squad*, wasn't plugged in to the zeitgeist of the time: not quite *Leave it to Beaver*, but not hip enough to merit attention. When scholars do give it a nod, it is usually to stress its preposterous premise: "identical cousins?" exclaims Douglas, "get real!"[8] And Duke herself, for nearly two decades, disowned the show for its gimmickry, and her good-natured costar William Schallert, who played Patty's father, Martin, sighed to reporters, "the problem with the show was its premise."[9]

As a "hinge show," *The Patty Duke Show* illuminated some of the tensions and preoccupations of conservative as well as progressive ideological positions and, as we'll see, those contradictions infuse some of the central themes and accomplishments of the series. During its run, from 1963 to 1966, Americans lived not only through the rise and fall of the idealized Camelot, but through growing civil rights activism, the Cuban Missile Crisis, the introduction of the Vietnam draft, the "War on Poverty," pop art, and the British invasion. What's more, and what arguably foregrounds the decade's imagination for white, middle-class Americans, is that such social and political events were made increasingly visible through mass media forms like popular mainstream magazines such as *Time*, *Newsweek*, and *Life* and, of course, television. Kennedy was dubbed the nation's first "TV president"; the Vietnam War became known as America's "televised war." A few TV shows indirectly channeled the latter, with several military sitcoms ridiculing and even condemning aspects of making war: *Hogan's Heroes* (1965–71), *F-Troop* (1965–67), *McHale's Navy* (1962–66), *Gomer Pyle* (1964–69), and, most pointedly, the later *M*A*S*H* (1972–83). To be sure, when setting their stories in past conflicts—the post-Civil War period, WWII, and the Korean War, respectively—military sitcoms muted the threat that they might pose by criticizing the country's current military engagement. (*Gomer Pyle*, though set in the present, gave no indication of Vietnam.)

We are not the first to note that, in the Fifties, mass culture often articulated Cold War (communist, nuclear war) anxieties through thematics of scale and proliferation, as exhibited in popular movies such as *The Invasion of the Body Snatchers*, *The Attack of the 50 Foot Woman*, *The Incredible Shrinking Man* and others. During the immediate postwar period, the United States tended to see the proliferating threats of nuclear war and Communism everywhere, abroad and at home. By the Sixties, though, much of popular and mass media were moving away from distortions of scale in depicting Cold War anxieties, even as they remained fascinated with proliferation. As countless "Duck and Cover" drills and instructional videos confirm, there were plenty of Cold War fears to go around. It was just one year before the premiere of *The Patty Duke Show* that the country was on its Communist-fearing edge during the Cuban Missile crisis.

Particularly during the post-war Fifties, the United States seemed to be committed to rebuilding its identity, nationhood, and normative life, including reinstalling obsolete racial and gender roles. This was something that commercial television capitalized on. Sitcoms of male authority, which Gerald Jones aptly labels "instructional sitcoms," such as *Father Knows Best*, helped reposition masculine power as part of the imputed natural order of American life along with the idealized white, middle-class families they supervised.[10] Critics of the time even noted the trend. As Leslie Raddatz wrote in 1964, "The father image show began in 1961, a date which psychologically some might find significant—it was the year that President Eisenhower, who has been called a father image, had left the White House."[11]

So, sitcoms seemed keen to shore up the authority of male-led, white, middle-class nuclear families, leaving in the dust the less atomized, ethnic sitcom communities of earlier shows such as *The Goldbergs,* which had ushered in the Fifties' golden age of television. This middle-class family was, of course, a fiction from the start, with only the thinnest of threads tying it to domestic realities of the time. It's clear that the compulsive redundancy with which those norms were produced across mass media reveals the extent to which white male authority was actually on the wane: private, independent, or family-owned businesses were giving way to gray-flannelled-suit jobs at corporations where individual breadwinners had little to no control. And female homemakers, whose labor was (then as now) unpaid, were increasingly expressing their dissatisfaction with their lot.

Gender and the Debates on Mass Culture

By the time of *The Patty Duke Show*'s debut, some national anxieties were packaged differently: while the issue of mass-scale proliferation continued to thrive, structures of scale seemed to cede to those of dyads and binarisms, in which beliefs, values, people and social groups were usually placed in opposition to one another. Although these structures are scarcely unique to the Sixties, they did seem to seep across much of the era's political, social, and media landscape. Some global examples include positioning American/democracy against USSR/Communism, but oppositional pairings organized internal tensions as well. Race relations were cast in simplified Black versus white formations, as were men against women, urban against rural, hawks against doves, the counterculture against the "establishment." Concepts such as the Generation Gap pitted parents against their children, and announcements such as LBJ's (Lyndon B. Johnson's) "war on poverty" were launched from unspoken pedestals of middle-class presumption. This book examines how popular culture took up these visions of oppositional duality and their modification.

In the Sixties, male critics of mass society often upheld a particular view of gender in their critiques, seeing women (and certainly younger females) as so vulnerable to the blandishments of empty consumerism that they were frequently blamed for their own victimization. The critical rhetoric around mass culture often feminized it, rendering it silly, unchallenging, undeveloped, seductive, etc. Female consumers could not, in these learned men's estimation, be active agents of consumption, much less emancipation.[12]

Paul Goodman, an influential promoter of youth as rebellious subjects, went so far in his widely read *Growing Up Absurd* to declare that he would not even entertain the idea of women as a force of social change because, as he saw it, they stood for nothing but a mindlessness destined for marriage.[13] Truth be told, plenty of American sitcoms of the time endorsed a similar perception of wedlock as young women's fate, with marriage as an endgame with two-parent households, children, perhaps a family dog. These families seemed so normal, even bland, that additional gimmicks or situations were needed: *single* parents, the antics of the younger generation (*Leave it to Beaver*), being set in the dad's workplace (*The Dick Van Dyke Show*), or making the family itself offbeat (*The Addams Family*). Curiously, those series that often seemed to be most "about" marriage were the ones in which a wife was made absent, such as *Bachelor Father* (1957–62), *My Three Sons* (1960–72), and *The Courtship of Eddie's Father* (1969–72)—a trend that had in fact started in the early years of television in shows like *Bonino* (1952–53) or *Wonderful John Acton* (1953). These series with single parents (usually dads) can be seen as upholding the norms of heterosexual marriage and reproduction by entertaining violations of them.

An early episode of *The Patty Duke Show* offers a soft critique of the gendered expectations built into these domestic standards and the pressure to enforce them. In "The Genius" (S1E2), a computer misclassifies Patty as a "genius," and its administrator (a hilarious Paul Lynde) instructs the family to let the girl do as she wishes in order to foster her extreme intellect (Figure I.2). They pamper Patty for a bit, but when the device's error is discovered, Patty's parents clamp down, almost vituperatively, and force their newly non-genius daughter to wash a stack of dishes at the episode's conclusion. At the bubble-filled sink, she speaks directly into the camera, "You win some, you lose some." Where one-dimensional society tries, as Herbert Marcuse lamented in 1964, to find the right slot for every individual and thereby

Figure I.2 Paul Lynde and his Malfunctioning Computer

reduce them to mere datum, "The Genius" shows how much personality classifications can fail. Although Patty is compelled to accept a normative role at the end, her declaration hints that she will be challenging these norms in future episodes.[14]

Later in the first season, "The Perfect Teenager" (S1E25) revisits the pitfalls of testing America's youth to essentially rank how normal they are or are not; like "The Genius," it dramatizes the risks of classifying moving targets such as rambunctious teenagers. Patty takes a magazine quiz to determine whether she is a "perfect" teenager after Cathy scores 85% on it. That a cultural outsider like Cathy does so well on such a quiz is an early indicator of the chasm between mainstream culture's assessments of individuals and how they fit in or don't. "Perfect" here is simultaneously defined as both top-grade *and* typical, and the episode flounders in the incompatibility between the two. Viewers have come to think of Patty as a paragon of American teenagerhood, and when she fails, her character sinks into a deep existential funk that leads her to lament to her family members, "You don't know the real me. Even I was fooled," a rather noteworthy line in a show about identical twins. But then, in the same magazine that published the damning quiz, Patty finds an ad for a finishing/modeling school that promises to enable young women to literally and characterologically "stand tall" and make a mark in the world. Patty signs up, and, when there, undergoes a series of lessons in poise and self-presentation from a snobby personality coach (played with vaudevillian relish by Kaye Ballard). Like other sitcom women before her—notably, Lucille Ball—Patty's attempts to mold herself to the seeming norms of proper feminine behavior (e.g., talking softly, enunciating carefully, walking with poise) lead to awkward and comic results.[15]

When Patty is finally selected for a modeling job at the finishing school, she is all a-twitter until she goes to work and suffers from being splashed by water and having a cream pie thrown at her face for a series of commercials. The humiliations are somewhat mitigated when she learns that the ads will be used for a public service campaign that encourages teenagers to stay in school, with captions like "Don't be all wet. Finish school." Although Patty is commended for her efforts on behalf of America's youth, by the end of the episode, she warns Cathy against taking magazine tests and simply flies off on a date with Richard. Patty may be back to where she started (a regular teenage girl who does regular things like dating), but only after she's flirted with identities beyond those norms, which in turn suggests that there is nothing inherently inevitable about these ideals for teenage girls.

Not so Normative?

In his influential manifesto, *One-Dimensional Man*, published during the run of *The Patty Duke Show*, German political theorist Herbert Marcuse voiced concern that the seeming affluence of American life would lead its citizens to lose their sense of soul and self. A member of the Frankfurt School, Marcuse was then living in the United States and deeply felt its pressures to conform. The presence of ever more mass-produced objects bound social subjects to the system, he argued, making people believe they enjoyed abundance when they in fact gained little of real value from the many commodities they welcomed into their lives. For him, television and radio were doubly commodified as technologies in the home that "one had to have" and that also championed lifestyles and objects (the products extolled in commercials) that one equally had to have. As he bluntly put it, to understand "the familiar tendencies of advanced industrial civilization ... perhaps the most telling evidence can be obtained by simply looking at television or listening to the AM radio for one consecutive hour for a couple of days, not shutting off the commercials, and now and then switching the station."[16]

For what it's worth, we did virtually that to prepare for this book—watch an hour per day of the three seasons of *The Patty Duke Show* (both the DVD box set and videos of the series posted on YouTube omit the commercials, though, which diminishes Marcuse's point). Clearly, our decision to write about a TV sitcom with a laugh-track suggests that, in contrast to Marcuse, we find something more in popular culture than an agent of the mass-instrumentalization of duped American minds. This is not to claim that *The Patty Duke Show* is revolutionary, politically or aesthetically, but that, as a key part of Sixties popular culture, it articulates hidden and overt aspects of American social life and ideology, however comically mediated. And it offers insights into how girls on the cusp of adolescence and young adulthood experienced and wondered about their lives at the time.

Theodor Adorno, another member of the Frankfurt School exiled in America, declared that US mass culture was an instrument for conformism that "offered clear-cut prescriptions of what to do and what not to do." In an article aimed specifically at television, he decried the conclusions of TV narratives in which "The outcome of conflicts is pre-established, and all conflicts are mere sham. Society is always the winner."[17] If, as Patty repeatedly shows, the idealized life of the family can be tinkered with, Adorno would likely maintain that any such deviation or experimentation only means that dominant power will come down all the more forcefully by the end of the show: "The less the message is believed," he asserts, "the more categorically it is maintained in modern culture," suggesting that dominant society reacts to deviation with "punitiveness and sadistic sternness" (64). Adorno would probably be pleased with Patty's punishment at the end of "The Genius," where her family gloats over her lost genius moniker and she is met with an overbearing normative force that pulls all eccentricity back into line.

Contrary to Adorno, though, we argue that the narrative trajectory within a sitcom episode is at least as important as its denouement. In *The Patty Duke Show*, that trajectory often hints at options and possibilities—momentary breaks from what might be simplified as "dominant ideologies," even as the endings appear to shut them down. Of course, there is a formulaic dimension to this, one even acknowledged by the show. During the brief precredit sequence of "Practice Makes Perfect" (S2E2), Patty enters the living room to proclaim, "Guess what?" Martin wryly responds, "You got involved in a new project that's going to put us all in a state of shock." As his riposte suggests, Patty regularly takes on disruptive enterprises—here the tuba, of all things. Interestingly, though, even as each episode closes out by disabusing her of her ambitions, viewers might catch glimpses into opportunities, or their possibilities, that might be available to them. As "The Genius" makes clear, both the trajectory of a narrative and its seeming closure can be fraught. Not only does its storyline play itself out as a series of contradictions (the computer determines an identity for Patty that she doesn't want to assume) but the ending also creates an expectation that subsequent episodes will reengage with experimentations with teenage norms and projects, since nothing is ever fully settled. Everyday domestic life is a juggle rather than a fixed, established fact. Countering Goodman's view that girls' marriage is their fate, *The Patty Duke Show* posits a shaky domesticity that is secured only to be challenged again and again.

In fact, a striking and persistent theme in *The Patty Duke Show* is its pronounced marriage-phobia which is articulated through multiple plotlines and dialogue, whether by Patty, Richard, or their parents. Again, in contrast to the assumption that young women's defining fate is bland matrimony, characters on the show repeatedly stress that teenage girls like Patty should "play the field" and not tie themselves to a steady boyfriend, no matter how anemically Richard serves that function. As we discuss later, several episodes explicitly and often quite critically address what marriage entails, not only as a plot or situation-altering device but as a cultural ritual with implications for real-life youth in the world beyond the show. For instance, an episode we analyze at length in Chapter 3, "Fiancée for a Day" (S3E30), even acknowledges marriage's weighty financial burdens and offers a fairly harsh assessment of the institution, especially for younger Americans.

While Patty may be far from a revolutionary agent of history, she is also not the conforming subject of complacent normativity, ready to settle into place as either a "perfect" teenager (whatever that might be) or a married woman. She may often be returned to the constraints of domesticity, yet never as a future wife or mother, but as a perpetually rambunctious teenager, ready to strike out at the next chance (or episode) she gets. In this way, *The Patty Duke Show*'s play with teenage girls' identity can take on a social or political resonance and, by splitting female teenhood into two (the cousins), it intimates that there is no singular way for female teens, or their viewers, to engage with their lives and situations.

What Betty Friedan influentially termed the "feminine mystique" entailed the social and cultural pressures on white, suburban women to accept their roles in marriage, domestic servitude, and motherhood. For every piece of pop culture that played into these pressures, it must be noted, there were others that resisted them. We believe that *The Patty Duke Show* dramatizes some of those tensions and the cultural demands placed on women and the ability to get around some of them. As Patty clomps her way through various plotlines—keeping a boyfriend, finding a more exciting new one, dreaming about jobs, or seizing business opportunities—the show activates some of the fantasies and aspirations that teenage girls might have had at the time.

In these and other ways, *The Patty Duke Show*'s engagement with its historical moment operates at the level of what Raymond Williams famously termed "structures of feeling," in which cultural phenomena, pop culture included, enact their social context in indirect, ineffable ways, rather than by directly assuming or implementing a political doctrine. For Williams, these enormously informative structures engage feelings that have not yet been addressed in extant institutions. Culture can evoke the temper of the times in citizens' sentiments—a collective sensing of an era's tenor and tone—even as it is unable to finalize or fully articulate them, or convert these feelings into an explicit political program that can be acted upon. (In a way, this describes the plotlines of many a *Patty Duke Show* episode). To be sure, Williams's assertions about structures of feeling imply more consensus and homogeneity among people's common (and perhaps unconscious) conception of life than modern social groups actually offer. For these feelings are always infused with ideological conflict and diverse ways of responding to their times—*The Patty Duke Show* is scarcely unified in the sentiments and goals in which it traffics. At the same time, Patty's desultory fixations might speak to a sense of instability in operation at the time, to an opening up of hope and opportunities for girls: the inexorability of motherhood and middle-class housewife was, in short, starting to quaver. Thus the potential identities that Patty or Cathy take up demonstrate a variety of ways girls might live, even if the options are rife with contradictions. The show enacts these tensions, and it is likely that initial audiences would have had equally varied responses. For some, it offered mindless distraction; for others, family fun; for others still, something too lowbrow to tolerate. But again, few have (especially retroactively) considered it as an engaged part of its historical, cultural moment.[18]

We noted earlier ways in which the Fifties possessed its own "structures of feeling." At the time, the country was busily at work trying to rebuild the world in its own, carefully sustained, image through political, military, and economic policies such as the Marshall Plan. But increasingly it appeared that the United States was aspiring to be a cultural leader of that world, engaging with it while also absorbing or lording over it. And it was an easy aspiration: an increasingly globalized world helped fuel that national fantasy of a colonizing metropolitanism beyond its borders. Even a seemingly silly sitcom like *The Patty Duke Show* articulates this social shift. Cathy moves to the States from the United Kingdom; three episodes embrace "Frenchness" just as real-life cultural mediators at the time were (Jacqueline Kennedy, Susan Sontag, and Julia Child, discussed below); and one episode features Patty attempting to join the Peace Corps.

More than merely participating in a period rife with gimmick-oriented sitcoms (with their memorable theme songs), *The Patty Duke Show* unlocks a uniquely wide view onto the social, cultural, and political preoccupations of the time, especially through its concern with "average" female adolescence and the period's often contradictory understandings of the nuclear family. Episodes tackle topics such as teen sexuality and relationships, entrepreneurial endeavors, class difference, international relations, even political corruption and labor activism. In "Patty, the People's Choice" (S2E7), the cousins campaign for a pair of political candidates. One is respectable and well educated in the issues, the other corrupt and opportunistic, and the contrast teaches the girls crucial civics lessons. In "Patty the Organizer" (S2E4), Patty forms the United Association for Unprotected Minors to demand greater rights and allowances from the children's parents. (This may well be the only moment in a Sixties sitcom to give mention, and positively, of Samuel Gompers!) Obliquely perhaps, such episodes engage with concerns animating the United States during the decade, gently extending some of the ambitions and the anxieties of the Fifties, adding new ones, and anticipating others still.

It is not our intention (or interest) here to argue for the "greatness" or innovation of *The Patty Duke Show*. We do, however, maintain that the series' connections to Sixties American culture offer insights into contemporary issues, such as the hypocrisies of American cosmopolitanism, the corporatization of the workplace, the commodification of "girl culture," American exceptionalism, race relations, class, wealth, and poverty, among others. In the following chapters, we elaborate on this assertion by delving into the particularities of *The Patty Duke Show* that confirm its place as a vital participant in American popular culture of the time.

We do find that its connections to Sixties US culture were often more far-reaching than those of its peers. *Gidget*, for instance, another contemporaneous "girl culture" show with a bubbly, young star (Sally Field), seldom strayed beyond the beach or home. *The Patty Duke Show* also differed from other sitcom forms in its attention to social and political ground: *The Munsters* spoofed the domestic sitcom, *F Troop* the heroes of the Wild West, *Get Smart* the smooth spy moves of James Bond, and so on. *The Patty Duke Show* wasn't a sendup of anything; its gimmick was its twinning and its use of an established girl star. Because it doesn't use the distortions of parody or satire, it seemed able to point, gingerly, to social debates, fads, and trends of the time.

PART I
CONCOCTING AN AMERICAN TEEN ICON AND A SITCOM WORLD

An Historical Account

1

Patty Duke

Life and Career

In 1963, Patty Duke won the Academy Award for Best Supporting Actress for her role as Helen Keller in *The Miracle Worker*, Arthur Penn's adaptation of the 1959 Broadway hit drama, which he had also directed and she had starred in. Duke's costar in both was Anne Bancroft as Keller's "teacher," Annie Sullivan, and Bancroft also garnered an Oscar, for Best Actress. At only sixteen, Duke won her supporting award against not only accomplished Oscar contenders like Thelma Ritter (*Birdman of Alcatraz*) and Angela Lansbury (*The Manchurian Candidate*) but also Mary Badham, who depicted the young Scout in *To Kill a Mockingbird*. Duke accepted her award with the shortest speech possible—a polite "Thank you."

Although Duke's work in the entertainment industry did not begin with *The Miracle Worker*, it certainly took off from there. Her handlers, primarily her Svengali managers and nightmarish stand-in parents John and Ethel Ross, wondered how they could widen their young star's reach and marketability. The theatrical and cinematic versions of *The Miracle Worker* were seriously themed and upscale, geared for thoughtful, adult audiences. The Rosses wanted to expand Duke's ascending popularity into a new arena: mass-targeted popular culture. Her eponymous TV series would provide the launching pad for their efforts. It also capitalized on the girl culture that was trending for teens and preteens in the early and mid-Sixties.

Duke had been acting since she was a young girl, mainly in television commercials and live TV productions, comic and dramatic, and she had played minor film roles as well, sometimes uncredited. Although she was a young teen by the end of the Fifties (she was born in 1946), Duke was overwhelmingly typecast as a child of around ten, in large part because Ethel and John Ross fed producers false ages to make their talented charge appear precocious. Her small size was also a factor: even as an adult, she reached no more than 5'0." (A *Woman's Day* article later noted that, "At 16, PD is still so small that she looks younger than her years.")[1]

The Patty Duke Show *and the American Sixties*. Caryl Flinn and Dana Polan, Oxford University Press.
© Oxford University Press 2026. DOI: 10.1093/oso/9780197667439.003.0002

Two of Duke's commercials from the period—one for a Remco drive-in theater toy set and another for a Remco Coney-Island penny arcade game—survive on YouTube. In both, Duke sits next to a young boy who plays with the toy set. After he says that boys will love the toys, Duke jauntily adds "and girls, too," winking.[2] She did ads for a cleanser called Lestoil, Minute Maid orange juice (vomiting after four glasses during takes under hot set lights), and Van Camp's Beanie-Weanies, "a canned frankfurter beans combination" that "was really disgusting."[3] As an adult, Duke openly expressed her contempt for her work in commercials and said she had been no less repulsed at the time. Duke had to feign enthusiasm for products she deemed stupid and degrading.

The commercials were only one aspect of a life lived damagingly in fakery, and one wonders whether the duplicity she experienced may have compounded her own sense of selfhood played out as a lie, however young she was. Duke did not have, nor was she permitted to have, an average childhood or adolescence. Taking cues demanded by the Rosses, she lived a series of fabrications: lying about her name, her age and life story and the amount of her professional experience. She was even forced to misrepresent her experience on a rigged quiz show, the very public 1959 scandal of *The $64,000 Challenge*.

Many television critics read this scandal as evidence of the new medium's ability to corrupt. What happened was that the adults involved in producing *The $64,000 Challenge* gave Duke and Eddie Hodges, the other child-actor contestant, correct answers to questions they would later be asked on air. This ultimately drew the attention of the New York District Attorney's office and grand jury. When first interviewed by the legal authorities, Duke attested that she had never been coached, just as the Rosses had prompted (they also urged Duke to pretend not to understand the questions posed to her). In her second interview, however, in Washington, DC, conducted by the House Special Committee on Legislative Oversight, the terrified child came clean, displeasing the Rosses.

Despite these deceits, Duke's television and film work started to cement her endearing image as a wholesome young girl. She epitomized the media's relentless demand for cute kids in double ponytails, sometimes precocious but usually just regular young girls or preteens. In the low-budget sci-fi film, *The 4-D Man* (1959), for example, Duke depicts Marjorie, a young girl being watched by a distracted babysitter (the film's heroine). She is sent to bed and her character fades for a long time from the film, later emerging pushing a toy baby carriage outdoors and stumbling into the "4-D man," whose body emanates a growing energy forcefield due to a scientific accident. What follows echoes the monster's playful encounter in *Frankenstein* (1931) with a little girl whom he inadvertently drowns: the scene ends with Duke's Marjorie innocently encouraging the 4-D man to play with her (fade-out), the implication being that she will become one more victim of his atomic powers. Such were the anxieties of Cold War America.

The 4-D Man shows Duke taking on the image her managers wanted: a cute kid with stereotypic simplicity and innocence. Unless one knew otherwise (and the Rosses did their utmost to suppress that knowledge), people would assume that Duke was playing someone like herself: a sweet girl in pigtails, nearly identical to the image of girlhood honed by Angela Cartwright in the Sixties in *The Birds*, *Lost in Space*, and *The Sound of Music*.

Duke's turn that same year as Tootie in a television remake of the classic MGM musical *Meet Me in St. Louis* was slightly edgier. As scholars have noted, the film's Tootie is not the adorable kid she might appear to be. Just under the surface, she is fascinated with violence and harbors a penchant for dire troublemaking, as evident in her attempt to derail a trolley car and when she decapitates her family of snowmen in the back garden. Duke, however, evinces none of the devilish or grotesque qualities that Margaret O'Brien famously brought to the original film (1944). Whereas O'Brien had been playing a Tootie who was too grown up for her age, Duke was, as usual, playing a girl younger than her years. Unsurprisingly, perhaps, Duke is at her best in a Halloween scene where her cuteness is obscured by her costume and she doesn't seem to be the typical darling she was supposed to be.

Duke had a strong, inexplicable fondness for her early role in a 1958 film, *The Goddess*, a somewhat fictionalized biography of Marilyn Monroe. Duke depicts the star as a child; the adult is portrayed by Kim Stanley. Duke's section of the film is set during the Depression. She plays Emily Ann Faulkner, the result of an affair by a dissolute mother who now wants to unload her on her sanctimonious brother and his wife so she can enjoy a more frivolous lifestyle. The mother's gambit doesn't work out and she must labor at a burdensome job, made bearable only by leaving her daughter to her own devices all day. Poor Emily Ann can't get her mother to look at her report card or even respond to the news that she was promoted to the next grade at school. She wanders despondently and then, at home alone, mopes and pours herself a glass of milk. A stray cat enters their bare-bones lodging, and Emily

Ann gives it some of the milk, sharing the good news her mother wouldn't pay attention to. The scene fades on Emily Ann with the cat as her sole confidant, and the film leaves the girl behind to jump years later, when Emily Ann has become an adult and Duke is literally out of the picture. Overall, her moments in *The Goddess* are brief but poignant. In her first autobiography, Duke plaintively stresses Emily Ann's final scene, noting that the role echoed her own life, as her largely absent mother handed her off to the overbearing Rosses.

Anna: A Lost Name and Stolen Childhood

Patty Duke was born Anna Marie Duke to Catholic parents on New York's Lower East Side. She spent most of her childhood in a rough and tumble working-class Irish and Italian neighborhood, where she played with her older brother, Raymond, and sister, Carol. Ethel and John Ross, a middle-aged couple known for promoting the entertainment careers of young actors, including Raymond, lived on Manhattan's tony Riverside Drive. Raymond had enjoyed an active career as a child actor in what Patty recalled were "dozens and dozens of shows and commercials."[4] (Unlike her, Raymond would continue to live at home.) Patty was seven when she met the Rosses. At the time, she was hardly impelled by a desire to act but didn't have much of a choice: her father, a heavy drinker, had left the family, and her mother, whose severe depressive spells exacerbated the family's financial precarity, eventually relinquished her daughter to the Rosses. She visited her daughter quietly, often tearfully, and the couple assigned her demeaning chores, such as doing Patty's laundry or signing autographs on her behalf. Duke was quick to perceive the Rosses as odd, noting that although only John knew anything about acting and "Ethel knew only results," Ethel ultimately proved to be the more dominant and crueler of the pair.[5]

In *Call Me Anna*, the first of her autobiographies, Duke recounts the abuses she suffered under their control and that were kept from everyone in her circle for years, including costars and family. Published in 1987, when she was almost forty, the memoir was the first time the public learned about Duke's bipolarism, which had been diagnosed at the somewhat mature age of thirty-five, and her scarring mistreatment by the hard-drinking Rosses, which took emotional and verbal forms—and from John, sexual forms as well. (Duke recalls throwing up when he made one such advance.)

The couple was constantly critical of Duke. Once she entered their charge, they worked her over, changing her hairstyle, her working-class New York accent ("I sounded like a young Jimmy Cagney"), even her name. Deeming "Anna" insufficiently "perky,"[6] the Rosses told her, "Anna Marie's dead, you're Patty now" (28). That symbolic death inaugurated what Duke would call a "little by little murder" (24) as the couple transformed her into "the perfect Stepford child" (26).

"Patty" was made to feel completely dependent upon the Rosses, forced to please them and do everything as they wanted. They prepped her for interviews by giving her lines to memorize. Of her laconic Oscar acceptance, Duke confessed to *Woman's Day* that, "I only said 'Thank you,' because the Rosses felt that preparing a speech in advance would add to my disappointment if I lost."[7] John Ross maintained an office on the set of *The Patty Duke Show* where he kept a vigilant eye on her, typing up extensive dictums that, among other things, forbade her to whistle (considered too vulgar). The expectation in the Ross household was that the young Duke should be eternally grateful: "If it wasn't for us," they informed her, "you'd be a hooker or you'd work in a five and dime."[8] Later, Duke learned that her surrogate parents had instructed her brother and sister to avoid her, leaving her to feel all the more abandoned. It is scarcely surprising that the moment she turned eighteen, Patty left the Rosses and never looked back and, later, reclaimed the name Anna for friends and family, retaining Patty for professional reasons only.

Reading Duke's accounts of the abuse is heart-wrenching. John Ross nearly always handled press interviews: he was the one to grant reporters access, and his young star's lines reek of memorized platitudes, which reporters essentially played back to their readers. She was forced to play "Patty," a perky "average" young teen, and interviewers, especially those for young people's publications, followed along. In *Calling All Girls*, the writer pondered "What is Patty Duke like? Well, she's a thoroughly nice girl who likes to have fun with boys and girls her age. Swimming, riding, ice skating, and boating are her favorite activities, and she enjoys doing them with her friends."[9] In a *TV Guide* article, the interviewer relays that the Ross home had several pull-out sofa beds and that "the children they manage are welcome to visit as often as they wish, and to sleep over, too, if their parents agree."[10] That Duke was actually not permitted to see friends, much less cultivate new ones, was but the tip of the iceberg.

The ugly reality is on more telling display in the drafts of an unpublished 1963 interview with Duke and John Ross by journalist and writer Jane

Howard (author of a Margaret Mead biography, among other things) for *Life* magazine. Howard was trying to construct the Patty Duke who embodied everyday teendom and who offered up a certain role model. Howard even quoted a curious line from Duke about contemporary pressures on America's youth: "It's too bad we have to worry about war, but I guess most teenagers think as I do that there isn't too terribly much we can do about it." Yet Howard also observed that Duke had not been allowed to be a regular teen herself: "Her only awareness of things like the friendships, rivalries, intrigues, delights and agonies known to ordinary adolescents comes through the scripts for her show."[11]

Ross's control of Duke is evident throughout Howard's notes. "Though Ross has other child clients, Patty is quite evidently the brightest star in his firmament. He seldom leaves her side . . . She rarely has dates," and, in Duke's words, "It's kind of our policy for me not to watch the show. . . I saw myself just once, in 'Miracle Worker,' and I laughed in all the wrong places." In a note appended to the piece, photographer David Schermer wrote that he'd be sending Howard's interview to story editor Ralph Green, but that he was clearly displeased with Howard's sugarcoating and "would have preferred a more flat-footed statement that this kid is in the middle of a first-rate dilemma. She has sold herself to a couple of promoters and cannot call her life her own. . . . She has lost her freedom." Ralph's handwritten reply is even more blunt: "Dave—I agree completely. This is so much on the surface, so uncommented on as to be quite unusable."[12]

Like Howard's probable superiors, an unnamed *TV Guide* reporter was flatly uncharmed by the young actor, wondering if she had been "groomed by John Ross to be nothing but sweetness," describing Duke as "long on acceptability and short on originality" and as "the kind of girl who just isn't there." "Happy," this journalist declares, "is the word she uses to describe everything."[13]

The Rosses determined which jobs Duke would take and claimed that they turned down the role of Liesl in the stage production of *The Sound of Music* while she was busy preparing for *The Miracle Worker*. To ready her for her dual television roles, the couple made Duke behave as Cathy on one day, and Patty on another, and, as one journalist reported, "would nag her every time she made a slip."[14] When *The Patty Duke Show* aired, they forbade her to watch it for fear it would "swell her head." (To further discourage any head swelling, they demanded that she wash the household's dishes after returning home from her twelve-hour workdays.) In ironic contrast to Patty Lane's love of dancing to "rock 'n roll," Duke was not allowed to listen to rock records, nor did she know how to dance when, at sixteen, she started the series. As she later revealed, "I had no more idea than the middle-aged screenwriters what someone my age should say, so what I was speaking [on the show] was a Writers Guild idea of teenage talk. It had nothing to do with kids of my generation."[15] Some critics, as we shall see, would assign this out-of-touchness to the series itself. The star's isolation from the outside world was so extreme that the Rosses installed a disconnected phone in her room as a prop for her photo-interviews. At times, their maltreatment of Anna/Patty reads nearly like a gothic novel.

John and Ethel Ross had spent the better part of a year preparing Patty for *The Miracle Worker* tryouts. They blindfolded her and watched her fumble around the apartment and, to mimic the experience of Deafness, subjected her to sudden, raucous blasts of noise (clanging pot covers, dropping hammers on the floor) to train her not to react to sound. The couple concocted a point system for her successes and failures. Duke recalls her confusion when the Rosses ordered her to do something during this phase. Were they testing her preparations or giving her an actual command? Responding incorrectly meant punishment and demerits.

This extreme preparation for the hotly anticipated Broadway show paid off, as Duke was selected over scores of other wannabes to play the young Helen Keller on stage. For her, working on the show would be a positive, even life-changing experience. Unlike her feigned appreciation of the Rosses, Duke was truly grateful for the professional and personal rewards derived from participating in the show. Over the course of its run, she developed a close personal bond with Anne Bancroft, who treated her with respect and affection. (Suzanne Pleshette later replaced Bancroft.) Duke treasured her mentorship and was especially proud when her name was given billing, after Bancroft's, on the theater marquee. Duke shines in the film adaptation (reviews insisted she had been no less astounding on stage) in a performance that mixes rich emotions, vibrant physicality, and complex intimations of psychological vulnerability, rebellion, and longing, all at once. One rather humorous breakthrough she cited was when she was having difficulty with the show's climatic moment at the water pump when Keller finally understands Annie Sullivan's hand spelling of "w-a-t-e-r" to mean water (Figure 1.1). Director Penn told the young girl to vocalize the word "as if she were constipated." Later, Duke would repeatedly claim that her theatrical and film experiences on *The Miracle Worker* led her to realize that, hot

Figure 1.1 Struggling to Get It Out

dog ads and the Rosses' maniacal pressure aside, she genuinely wanted to become an actor.

The Miracle Worker endures as a work of earnest uplift, first with its Broadway pedigree, and then with Penn's art-cinema style—the film shows looming faces in deep focus against backgrounds, uses handheld camera, most notably in the real-time fight scene between Helen and Annie, and deploys artsy flashbacks and dream sequences. Penn began his career in live television drama and likely considered Broadway and the art film as a step up in artistic quality. Duke's own path took the reverse course, moving from what many consider the "highbrow culture" of *The Miracle Worker* to the massified world of TV sitcoms and, throughout much of her later career, TV movies.

While there is no smoking-gun memo to reference, it seems likely that Duke's star turn in the productions of *The Miracle Worker* convinced the Rosses that her best path to success would, unlike her work in the Fifties, entail *not* playing what she superficially appeared to be. Instead of being an adorable kid, she would now be extending her reach by projecting personae divergent from whatever Duke might be—or might be said to be. She was thus moved to the popular art of television in a twinned teenage guise that it was believed would expand her range.

Duke's ability to portray a distinctive individual—rather than a generic type—with a richness of identity is worth acknowledging. After all, Duke, a sighted, hearing girl, had compellingly played the Deaf and blind American icon Helen Keller. While today's cultural politics might lead us to object to non-disabled people depicting disabled ones, *The Miracle Worker* nevertheless confirmed Duke's ability to play unique characters who had little in common with how the young girl was perceived to be.

So, as distinct as her roles in *The Miracle Worker* and *The Patty Duke Show* were, both relied on Duke's skill at inhabiting identities that deviated from her own yet still presented a rounded, convincing personality. Because her series required her to depict two personalities with very different features, Duke's efforts effectively became allegories of performance, expanding her repertoire of identities. Duke also endowed the cousins with a depth of emotion, making each character seem to be emanating from herself rather than an impersonation or replication of the other. For instance, in "The Best Date in Town" (S2E13), Cathy watches as Patty breaks down in tears when her dad tells her an upcoming job assignment will cause him to miss the father-daughter dance that she expected would be a highpoint of her life. Little seems comic or playfully performative in this moment, which comes off as quite genuine and heartfelt, especially for a sitcom sitting on a foundation of floating identities.

"The Glint"

When Duke is absorbed in a character like Keller and struggling toward the emotional and cognitive breakthrough that Helen both desires and resists, her eyes have a special, lovely sparkle. It seems to signal the vitality within a character whose external world has been curtailed. We see hints of that in a publicity photograph taken of Patty Duke, not in character, when she met Keller, with whom she was able to communicate in ASL (American Sign Language). The photo hardly gives the impression of a put-on, performed sense of joy, but rather a deeply felt admiration: Duke's eyes hold a quiet gleam of delight (Figure 1.2).

One sees that twinkle in *The Patty Duke Show* too, often in pronounced fashion. We catch it in the freeze frames that end each episode's precredit sequence, when Patty responds with sparkling, sometimes devious, enthusiasm

Figure 1.2 Meeting Helen Keller: "I'm an Actress Because of Helen Keller"

to whatever conundrum or opportunity the sequence presents (Figure 1.3). Years later, in 1972, that twinkle returns when Patty Duke appeared as the mystery guest on the TV game show *What's My Line?* Showcasing her ability to create rich identities, Duke assumed a smart-aleck persona, perhaps

Figure 1.3 Duke Twinkles as Patty Lane

channeling the New Yawwk accent that the Rosses had drummed out of her. She was clearly delighted by the act, her eyes sparkle with the complicity of it all. Even as she assumes a persona, she is authentically enjoying herself and the gleam encapsulates her delight.[16]

In addition to her engaging sparkle, one of Duke's patented acting traits is to squint her eyes, usually when her character seems to be burrowing into her psyche. The squint is at work in *The Miracle Worker* as Duke's Helen valiantly but, until the end, vainly tries to bring some buried knowledge and connections to the surface. What has Annie been trying to get Helen to do with her constant hand signing? The squint appears just as Helen lets out the constipated "Waaah waaah." By contrast, *The Patty Duke Show*'s narrative and emotional conventions rendered the acting tic unnecessary: as interesting as the show is, bringing inchoate sentiments to the surface is not one of its defining features. Yet it isn't altogether buried. In "Do You Trust Your Daughter?" (S3E25), Patty's father thinks his daughter has arrived home late from a date—with an older boy, no less, spiking his anxiety. Patty in fact had not broken curfew, but a farcical mix-up convinces Martin that she had, and she can't convince him otherwise. As Patty pleads her case, the ingenuousness of her performance approaches a degree of pathos that is seldom called for elsewhere in her series. She squints her eyes at the effort.

Splitting Patty Duke

Duke's skill at melting into her characters has an ominous, dark corollary to it that shadowed her ability to move between identities throughout her career. After her bipolar diagnosis was made public knowledge, series writer Sidney Sheldon claimed retroactively that he had noticed a dual nature to her personality when he worked with the young star. Sheldon asserted that Duke's early visit to his and his wife's home as he was trying to imagine her in the dual roles showed him that those two sides could be captured and exploited through the twinning motif. (Duke would describe herself as "schizoid" in her memoir, "a perky me and a corporate executive me.")[17]

It's hard to say whether Duke manifested diverging personality traits at this early age. She states that her depressive symptoms didn't appear until she was about fifteen or sixteen, at the time of her show, but never while working on the series itself (no one was aware that she spent Friday through Mondays in bed). She notes that her mania, by contrast, began *at work* in her late teens.[18] She always wondered whether a paranoid incident involving Anne Bancroft during the stage run of *The Miracle Worker* had been an early sign of her mania.

Whatever the timeline of her biological symptoms, John and Ethel Ross had already accomplished much to "split" Patty, the starlet they had formed out of Anna Marie Duke. In fact, when William Asher, cocreator of *The Patty Duke Show*, met them on the East Coast, he recalled that John "really managed her *very* closely. Her [biological] mother . . . was just out of the picture because of the Rosses . . . and she [Anna/Patty] moved in with them. That part of it was a little bit strange. . . . They were arranging all her dates and social life; it was not good." It is impossible to gauge how much Asher relies on hindsight here, but he claims to have advised the young girl that "They're holding you back and not really doing you any good. I think you should go back to your mother."[19]

In addition to her struggle with (at this point, undiagnosed) bipolar disorder and its uncontrollable behavioral oscillations, and her performance as the Rosses' "perfect Stepford child," Duke's public image vacillated between lionized achievements to gossip-inducing embarrassments as she transitioned from award-winning child actor to troubled young adult in overwrought, salacious roles such as *The Valley of the Dolls* and in her calamitous marriage to Harry Falk Jr., an assistant director on *The Patty Duke Show*. Duke would find balance only in the second half of her life.

Most viewers, unaware that the Rosses had deprived her of a regular life, likely would have felt that the star of the show more closely resembled Patty Lane, the active American teenager always thanking her "can-do spirit!" rather than cousin Cathy. Simply calling the series *The Patty Duke Show* encouraged audiences to be more invested in Patty, and Duke herself maintained that viewers would be more likely to identify with the upbeat, irrepressible Patty, even though she felt closer to the introverted Cathy. During the run of the series, however, she was dutifully careful to tell interviewers that she had no preference for one twin over the other and that she shared features of both Lane girls. Two sons of William Schallert (Patty's father on the series) confirmed that young girls tended to identify profoundly with the star in general.

One can speculate that Duke's long-held contempt for her television show might have derived from her lack of control over the series or having been forced into it, not to mention the absence of praise she received at home for her work in it. Duke was increasingly unhappy having to play someone younger than herself again, although ironically in the case of her work in the subsequent *The Valley of the Dolls*, Duke admits that she didn't look old enough to play a woman in her mid-twenties. (As we'll discuss, twenty-nine-year-old Eddie Applegate, the ever-cheerful Richard, also resented playing Patty's seventeen-year-old beau.) In *Call Me Anna*, Duke makes her initial contempt for *The Patty Duke Show* emphatically clear. In contrast to *The Miracle Worker*, she opines, the series didn't enable her to develop as an actor, and she acerbically calls Patty and Cathy "two halves that equaled less than one."[20] As the decades went by, however, she came to appreciate the show and what it meant to fans worldwide.

But, initial demurring aside, Duke's ability to engage the performative acting style required by the series is impressive as she slides across multiple identities, a talent woven into the premise of a number of episodes. In "The Wedding Anniversary Caper" (S1E27), her younger brother Ross surreptitiously enters Patty into *New York Metropolitan*'s "beautiful teen" contest. The first prize is a television set, which Ross wants to give his parents as a surprise twentieth-anniversary gift, instead of the unsightly clay ashtrays he has been crafting for them year after year. Along with his sister's photo,

Ross submits a brief biography that fabricates her special talents and backstory: "born in Paris, France, her father was an ace pilot shot down over Normandy who escaped prison camp, meeting her mother, a baroness who was working as a spy in the French resistance . . . ."

When Patty learns she is one of the finalists and is required to meet the judges, Ross comes clean to Patty, who at first is furious but acquiesces in hopes of winning the TV for their parents. We see Patty standing on a small stage facing representatives of *Metropolitan*. All goes swimmingly until the talent portion of the competition, for Ross had failed to mention that Patty would have to showcase the skills he had attributed to her in his letter. First up: singing an "American song." Duke, in her own warbly (prerecorded) voice, performs an inconsequential pop tune, "Tell Me Mama," which had recently enjoyed success in the United Kingdom. The tension escalates when the head judge then requests that Patty then sing "something operatic," another ability created by Ross. Patty dashes into the wings, where she and Cathy exchange outfits and redo their hairstyles, and Cathy goes onstage to deliver a brief, slightly painful aria as Patty. The judges next demand that Patty display her tap dancing, so Cathy runs back and sends Patty onstage, where, after some hammed-up tapping, a fatigued Patty switches places with Cathy to "say a few lines to us in Italian, French, and Spanish." This final display shows off Patty Duke's rather respectable skills with foreign accents.

However transparently executed, "The Wedding Anniversary Caper" stages key distinctions between Patty and Cathy. Patty is predictably aligned with the ostensibly low forms of American mass culture (tap dancing, pop songs), whereas Cathy is linked to the more elevated European forms of opera and foreign languages. Once the performances end, the Lane children return home clutching Patty's first-prize trophy; the television is to be delivered the next day. Yet the trio is wrought with guilt about having cheated to win ("we stole it"), and so, as good sitcom kids, they fess up to Natalie and Martin, who endorse their plan to return the trophy and appreciatively accept the more modest anniversary gifts of the kids, including another ashtray. The episode also contains an intriguingly self-conscious line of dialogue: a judge greets Patty Lane with, "It isn't often you come across so much talent in one person," suggesting audiences reflect on Patty Duke's own outsized skills as an actor.

For its first two years, *The Patty Duke Show* was shot in New York City, where most broadcast television programs had been produced during the Fifties. By the early Sixties, though, most TV production had moved to Los

Angeles and *The Patty Duke Show* was somewhat of a novelty for staying behind. While its adult cast members William Schallert and Jean Byron had to relocate from California, the east coast location made things easier for NY child actors Duke and Paul O'Keefe. Since California labor laws determined the maximum number of hours young actors could work daily, after having made the show's pilot there, Asher moved production to New York "where there were no rules," a claim repeated by O'Keefe and nearly everyone else connected to the show. O'Keefe was still a preteen when, after a full day at *The Patty Duke Show* (starting at around eight a.m. and ending at five or six p.m.), he would be whisked off for his role in *Oliver!* where he "work[ed] until midnight." (Wednesdays, he said, were especially taxing, since Broadway runs included, then as now, matinee and evening performances).[21]

When the show moved to Los Angeles for its third season, the most important thing for Duke was that she had turned eighteen. Officially an adult, she was now legally and geographically separated from the Rosses, despite their attempts to still hold sway over her. Before moving west, the seventeen-year-old star had surreptitiously started dating thirty-one-year-old Falk, newly separated from his wife. Their relationship continued on the West Coast and the two soon married, in part, Duke later acknowledged, to assert her independence from the Rosses.

Singing and the Self

Duke's career was launched in other directions during the run of *The Patty Duke Show*. By 1964, teen stars were expected to develop a pop music career. Television companies and music producers exploited their young stars across various media platforms, sometimes within single, synergistic businesses (Duke recorded for United Artists' record division and UA produced her TV series as well). *The Patty Duke Show* not only accommodated this new branch of Duke's celebrity but advertised it, something noted in her abbreviated performance of "Tell Me Mama" in the talent contest. It's not as if Duke had never sung publicly before: her 1959 role in the musical of *Meet Me in St. Louis* intimated that, even as a young girl, being the kind of versatile, profitable talent the Rosses wanted required singing. But neither she nor the Rosses ever saw singing as her top talent. On this point, the Rosses were right.

Other singing sitcom teens included Shelley Fabares, who had combined a successful role as the precocious teenage daughter on *Father Knows Best* with a reasonably successful recording career (her hit was "Johnny Angel"); Ricky Nelson from *Ozzie and Harriet*; Paul Peterson from *The Donna Reed Show*; and Sally Field of *The Flying Nun*, which banked on Debbie Reynolds's upbeat hit single "Dominique" from the 1966 film, *The Singing Nun* (unfortunately, Field's voice was little more than a warble). Even Peggy Lipton, of the slightly later and hipper *The Mod Squad* released several pop tunes.

The entertainment industry clearly recognized the growing economic power of teenage girl consumers. By the Sixties, exploitable heartthrobs like Bobby Sherman, Paul Peterson, and other ostensibly singing male teenage TV stars were immensely successful, and Lipton's coolness was no turnoff either. Magazines targeting girl fans such as *Tiger Beat* (started in 1965) and variety TV shows oriented around teens emerged in this period, and both phenomena were in their prime when *The Patty Duke Show* ran. *Hullabaloo, Shindig,* and the long-running *American Bandstand* showcased TV stars' attempts at conquering the world of popular music.[22]

And so, Duke added pop singer to her repertoire in 1964. Conveniently, her persona as Patty Lane was already linked to contemporary pop music since "our Patty loves to rock 'n roll." The Lane girls promoted guest singers such as real-life duo Chad and Jeremy as "Patrick and Nigel," and interacted with clean-cut vocalists such as Frankie Avalon and Frank Sinatra Jr. in cameos, although Duke never dueted with them. These singers were worlds away from The Beatles, rock and roll, or R&B and soul performers, a detail William Schallert claimed made the series out of step with teen life of the time. Patty Duke did duet with cornpone Jimmy Dean on his TV variety show in 1963, around the time her own show debuted. (ABC produced Dean's show as well as Duke's, and he had a cameo on hers, enabling the network to cross-promote its offerings.) They sing "Bushel and a Peck," from *Guys and Dolls*, as a rousing love song. Duke plays her part with some maturity, although her diminutive height is striking next to the 6'3" Dean—and her gingham and lace outfit does nothing to make her appear remotely adult (Figure 1.4). The duet ends chastely as Dean, bending down, plants a kiss on Duke's forehead before straightening back up—way up.

In the first season of *The Patty Duke Show*, Duke sings in several scattered moments. In addition to the pop song and operatic arias of "The Wedding Anniversary Caper," she performs in "The Songwriters" (S1E13) as Cathy, who has set to music an ostensible songwriting effort by Patty, a plagiarism

Figure 1.4 Two Bushels and a Peck

actually, for yet another contest. Indicating what is to come in Duke's own career, when Cathy sings the ballad, a sudden reverb takes over, making her voice less a modest, homespun effort than an industrially backed one, orchestrated (in several senses of the word) by ABC. This time, it's Richard, not Ross, who enters their work into a local songwriting contest in which the cousins, once more, win first place. The accomplishment is announced on a show hosted by none other than Duke's off-show singing partner, Jimmy Dean, who performs the piece to great applause. In a detail that illustrates how formulaic *The Patty Duke Show* could be, the cousins' accomplishment is tempered when, as in "The Wedding Anniversary Caper," it is revealed that Patty cheated, in this case taking the song's lyrics from an old book of poetry, setting the stage for a set of moral and legal questions. All ends happily in this case although, given the repeated cycle of Patty's adventures, it's unlikely the character has learned anything.

Some episodes of the second season were also premised on Patty (Lane or Duke) embarking on a pop-singing career. In "Patty the Folk Singer" (S2E32), she sets out to be a folk singer in a local beatnik coffee shop called the Pink Percolator. To look the part, Patty wears a lot of eye makeup, but the reality of the job is less glamorous and largely entails bussing tables ("Are you sure this is the way The Beatles started?" she wonders aloud). Patty is finally permitted to perform onstage the one evening her parents decide to go out to "see what a typical coffee house is like." As her parents enter, Patty chokes, exhibiting a stage fright that other episodes (and the series reunion decades later) capitalize on. While the detail humanizes Patty Lane as a character, the exaggerated manifestations of her stage fright showcase Duke's acting chops.

By the show's final year, Patty is allowed full-blown pop-music performance, beginning in "Partying Is Such Sweet Sorrow" (S3E3), on the heels of installments featuring Frankie Avalon (who doesn't sing in his episode) and Troy Donohue (who didn't have a very successful pop career). "What's the one thing you want more than anything else in the world?" Richard asks Patty in "Partying." Functioning as a manager of sorts, he answers his own question, "The chance for you to sing with a band!" He lands Patty a gig as singer for The Shindogs, a band in search of a lead vocalist. Rehearsing at the Lane family home (with predictable parental jokes about their noise), the Shindigs provide backup for Patty, who sings a complete rendition of "Funny Little Butterflies," about a teenage girl experiencing feelings of blossoming love and desire. When The Shindogs perform at Patty's rival Monica's party, Patty, who has sneaked in disguised as Cathy, joins them onstage for a rousing cover of Herman's Hermits' "Henry the Eighth" (a then-current hit on the pop charts), gleefully doing an overblown cockney accent. (This cover did not appear on any of Duke's LPs.) With one notable exception that we'll discuss in Chapter 5, neither Duke nor her guest stars sing live on the show, and the dubbed performances add another layer of doubling to the show, and to Duke.

The Shindogs were the house band on *Shindig*, a music show broadcast from 1964 to 1966—and, for part of that time, immediately after *The Patty Duke Show* in ABC's Wednesday night line-up. One of Duke's first pop performances outside her sitcom was on the show in June 1965, "launching," as the emcee says, "a whole new phase of her career as a singer and a recording artist." Seated on a stool, Duke performs her first single, "Don't Just Stand There." Her next piece, "Say Something Funny to Me," is culled from her first LP, and recounts the story of a girl asking the boy who has broken up with her to keep up appearances in front of her peers. A heavily made-up Duke valiantly emotes, closing her eyes in anguish, forcefully pleading, raising her hand as a chorus of square-jawed white men and another one of pert female African Americans sing backup. After an interlude in which

The Zombies (of "Season of Loving" fame) perform, Duke returns to encore "Funny Little Butterflies" with the same background singers. The song anticipates her performance of it in the film *Billie* (discussed below), released mid-September 1965.

Duke's first album, *Don't Just Stand There*, collects some of the songs she performed on *Shindig*, in her TV series, and in *Billie*. A few had modest success as singles, including "Don't Just Stand There," which made it to number eight on *Billboard*'s pop charts (Figure 1.5). As her series was winding down in 1966, she released a second album, *Patty*, featuring a more mature pants-suit look on the cover. Both LPs combined original material along with covers from contemporary pieces, from "Yesterday" to "(Don't They Know It's) The End of the World." She would later release a folk album and a collection of songs for *The Valley of the Dolls* (whose main theme was performed by Dionne Warwick in the film).

Figure 1.5 Popstar Patty

When Duke acts on her show and variously has to "be" Cathy or Patty (as well as a few other related characters), she offers multiple identities. But when she sings, by contrast, the songs avoid that sense of expansion and point only to the fact that Patty Duke is singing as herself. She downplays the signs of performative labor and highlights (even exaggerates) those of "authenticity" and "expressivity," closing her eyes, for instance, to signal heartfelt emotion, in contrast to the ingenuous twinkling eyes so charming in her acting.

In this way, Duke's vocal performances worked assiduously to publicize the new direction her career was taking and were offered as a natural extension of who she was as a teen celebrity rather than who she was as a character. For her performances to be successfully marketed as pop songs in their own right, there could be no suspicion of masquerade or fakery. Patty Lane might join The Shindogs at a high school party in the fictional world of her TV series, but when she does so and sings, audiences recognize her as Patty Duke, performing herself as a pop singer outside the fictional realm of either TV cousin.

In a move that recalls her presence as a generic cute girl in the Fifties, the singer Patty Duke inhabits the role of a white middle-American teenage girl singer singing about the things that white middle-American teenage girls were supposed to sing about in the early to mid-Sixties: Does he love me? How strong is our love? Has he fallen out of love with me? The sound, it must be said, is generic. Duke herself never expressed much faith in her singing abilities and acknowledged it was all about marketing. Truth be told, she doesn't have much dynamic range, her tonalities are limited, and her vocals are often reduced to breathy whispers, occasionally falling back into childish warbles. (Her cover of "Yesterday" bears a slight English accent, as if Duke were channeling Cathy Lane.) Most of her renditions display an earnest, if undistinguished, effort. But that didn't deter producers from trying to fit her in. "Don't Just Stand There" owes a clear debt to the reverb sound that surrounded Lesley Gore (a great singer, actually) in her 1963 hit, "You Don't Own Me." Duke's version is stuffed with wall-of-sound echoes and overdubbing; accompanied by lachrymose strings, her voice is buried beneath layers of acoustic effects.

Yet quality may not have been the primary concern for female teenagers eager to accept the media-industry attention and consume the commodities aimed at them. Duke's albums and singles sold rather well and were essential to her expanding popularity and branding. The industry was well aware of the purchasing power of the teen or youth market; *Variety*, for instance, heralded the release of *Billie* with the revealing title "Patty Duke Film Due for Slotting in Teen-Wake of Beatles Release," referring to the Fab Four's "big teenage grosser" *Help*.[23] Such moves to sell Duke to an older teen market were confined to material outside of the show itself, which refused to age the Lane girls (they are perennially 15) or to stay abreast of youth culture and music as they evolved in the world beyond the show.

When Duke tried to move beyond the calculated teen image of her sitcom, especially in the brash *The Valley of the Dolls*, she was clearly trying to establish a new public persona as a young woman. In taking on such a self-deprecating role, Duke was participating in a long, ongoing pattern of young female celebrities who revolt against their G-rated cuteness by diving headfirst into adult, often risqué roles, behaviors, or styles. Duke later described her internal cheerleading as she naïvely accepted the role in *The Valley of Dolls*: "I'll make the transition to adult roles overnight!"[24]

But she followed other, less controversial paths to guide her star image into more adult territory. One of her post-series LPs consisted of folk tunes, a genre ostensibly marked by non-commodified authenticity and maturity. The political urgency of songs such as "Blowin' in the Wind," which Duke included in her LP, only enhanced that view. Ironically, in this new quest for musical authenticity, the songs belted out by Duke's character in *The Valley of the Dolls* were dubbed by an uncredited singer.

Billie

After shooting on Season 2 of *The Patty Duke Show* wrapped, Duke was cast as the lead in *Billie*, a barely remembered and very odd film from 1965. *Billie* was based on a Fifties play, "Time Out for Ginger," about a tomboy, that had first been mounted on Broadway, then made into a TV movie, and then later a pilot for a TV series that never got off the ground. The medium-budget film musical (half a million dollars) was produced by Chrislaw, the same company that made *The Patty Duke Show*, and its shoot was scheduled for a speedy fifteen days in Los Angeles. As we chronicle in Chapter 2, Chrislaw was run by Peter Lawford, who was then married to John F. Kennedy's sister Patricia. Don Weis, who had helmed nine episodes of *The Patty Duke Show* and was expected to become the primary house director for Chrislaw productions, directed, and his presence on *Billie* comforted Duke.

Along with Lawford as executive producer, John Ross was credited as producer, indicating that arrangements for the project began when Duke was still under the Rosses' control prior to her turning eighteen. Intriguingly, the year before *Billie*, *TV Guide*'s listing for the May 13, 1964 episode of *The Patty Duke Show*, "The Working Girl," in which Patty becomes exhausted in her job as a soda jerk, included an unusual description that melded character and actor: "Tonight's script parallels Patty Duke's own life: the fatigue of a full TV season has caused her to cancel plans to do the movie version of the 1953 Broadway play 'Time Out for Ginger.'" (Typically *TV Guide* only listed plot summaries and guest stars.) Was Duke finally playing herself?[25]

Billie was supposed to be Duke's transitional film in which she moved from "child star to full-fledged adult actress."[26] There was some hope that it might lead to a sequel, to be written by the author of "Time Out for Ginger." However, unlike *Inside Daisy Clover*, a similar 1965 film about a tomboy with a young Natalie Wood making her own attempt at more mature roles, *Billie* failed to render Duke more adult and, if anything, reinforced her image as a perennial teenager. "Adulthood" for Duke would come, with its heavy baggage, two years later, in *The Valley of the Dolls*.

In *Billie*, Duke portrays Billie Carol, a fifteen-year-old tomboy (once again, someone younger than her own age) who can outrun all the boys on the high school track and decathlon team. Her secret, she tells her friend and fellow athlete Mike Benson, is that she runs to "the beat" in her head, which she can speed up whenever she needs to go faster (Figure 1.6). (Later, Billie teaches "the beat" to her fellow students as a dance craze, as if she were Patty Lane still loving to rock 'n roll.) *Billie* sets up its central narrative tension

Figure 1.6 Duke as Billie with the Beat

in its opening sequence, cutting between scenes of Billie demonstrating her athletic prowess and gaining the attention of the track coach ("Who's that boy?" he asks from a distance), and scenes of her father, Howard Carol (Jim Backus), delivering a mayoral campaign speech in which he decries the erosion of gentility and femininity in today's women. One of these two characters will have to cave. In the end, both do.

The film is quick to contrast Billie's femininity, at once butch and oddly desexualized, to that of her high-femme older sister Jean, who looks a full generation older. Early on, Jean returns home to announce she's quitting college, much to her father's delight, for he believes this also means she is no longer going steady with Bob, her Harvard beau (played by Ted Bessell, best known as Donald, the lackluster boyfriend of *That Girl* [1966–71]). Echoing the same parental anxiety about marriage that permeates *The Patty Duke Show*, Howard lectures Jean, "You're a young girl. Plenty of time to play the field." It turns out, however, that Jean has secretly married Bob and is pregnant, a condition that a loose-lipped nurse, thinking Jean is single, relays to Howard's political rival. At a campaign debate, this opponent vaguely mentions that Howard's "progressivism at home will create bedlam," threatening to expose what he thinks is the Carols' dirty laundry of an unmarried, pregnant daughter. Meanwhile, Billie repeatedly sticks up for her rights to participate in the school track team, grandly referencing the Bill of Rights' guarantee of "life, liberty and the pursuit of happiness."

Halfway through the film, Howard inexplicably has a change of heart and defends his daughter's right to try out for the team, where her successes, along with her magical "beat," attract the attention of *Life* magazine. She makes the front cover. Despite these accomplishments and attention, however, Billie has inner conflicts that she reveals in two songs, sung to no one except the movie audience from the privacy of her bedroom: "In-Between" and "Butterflies."

Today, filmgoers would easily interpret Billie's struggles as those of a gender nonconforming person, but in 1965, the character's "in-betweenness" presented itself as a *narrative* problem in need of resolution (or what might be more crudely called "fixing"). And so Billie's downfall into generic heterosexuality begins. Her mother, played by Jane Greer (the femme fatale from 1947's *Out of the Past*, here largely confined to the sidelines of her suburban family), tells her daughter that "Being a girl is an easy adjustment to make." As the film motors along, and once Billie's friend Mike holds her hand, she admits (again, through song) that the moment gave her "little butterflies."

As her romantic feelings for Mike develop, Billie loses a track race to him, whether deliberately or due to a diminished "beat" is left for the viewer to decide. By this point, the movie is painting heterosexuality in such thick, ubiquitous strokes as to be almost queer. In the all-male locker room, the high school boys perform "A Girl Is a Girl Is a Girl," a lowbrow version of *South Pacific*'s campy "There Ain't Nothing Like a Dame," and Mike, now Billie's beau, asks her to quit the team. His request sparks a fight, after which an angry Billie magically beats him at the next track meet. Mike turns to Howard for advice, and ends up apologizing to Billie, "You were right. You're not my equal. You're my better."

The happy ending is as fast as it is multidirectional. Howard is elected mayor after his elder daughter publicly announces her marriage at his final debate, before Howard's rival can smear him with the news of her "unwed" pregnancy. Mike and Billie, heading out for the prom, announce that both will be giving up track, and Billie's mother reveals her own pregnancy to Howard ("Maybe this time, it'll be a boy," she says, hopefully). The film concludes in song: "I am a girl/am a girl/just as proud as I can be/Just to be glad to be a girl/is my greatest victory."

This cinematic curiosity is striking, first of all, in its function as an extension of *The Patty Duke Show*, that is, as a family-friendly piece of media aimed at the series' teen and tween female fans, potentially grappling with their own coming-of-age struggles, and as a musical, advertising Duke's branching out into the realm of pop singing. Its gender dynamics are also quite striking. At once a proto-feminist call for women's equality in sports (Title IX would not be passed until 1972) and a decidedly queer coming-of-age story, *Billie* grappled with gender and, to a lesser extent, sexuality far more than *The Patty Duke Show* ever did. Despite her relentless vitality, her averred boy craziness, and her relationship with Richard, Patty never oozed teenage sexual energy.

Much the same can be said of Duke's star image, which, even for an adult, was strikingly lowkey as a gendered or sexualized persona. This may have been part of the problem of her being cast in *The Valley of the Dolls*, a tale to which salacious sexuality was critical. Duke was never a glamour icon. (She later joked that she was never invited on the *Johnny Carson Show* because she lacked the large breasts Carson seemed to demand of female guests.)[27] Even in non-*Patty Duke Show* efforts, Duke comes off as a regular teenager; her imprint as a "womanly star" is far less forceful.

Billie's unconventional gender dynamics are underscored when Billie sings of herself as an "in-between" ("I should have been a boy/But here I am a girl . . . I'm an in-between/A lonely little in-between"), reframing the split identity Duke had enacted in *The Patty Duke Show*. Her father is no help: at one point, Billie says, "I wish I'd been born a boy," and Howard blurts out, "So do I," much to everyone's embarrassment, including his own. Billie repeatedly asserts that she doesn't want to be a boy but an "equal," and, as her classmates put it, "She's discovered a whole new sex: boys, girls, and equals." Even the opening chorus plays with the idea of a newly created gender category in lyrics such as "she walks like a Billie should walk/She talks like a Billie should talk."

In a relatively recent book on the movie, a pair of writers maintain that, "even the most progressive critics [at the time of the film's release] were oblivious to what was bubbling just below the [tomboy] surface."[28] (One would imagine that LGBTQ audiences of the time would have had quite different responses; some fifty years later, a woman told us that Patty Duke had been her first childhood crush.) From a twenty-first-century vantage point, the film's queer dimensions are patently obvious from its narrative themes and musical numbers to Billie Carol's first and last names and her slightly butch, slightly androgynous look. (Duke complained that *Billie*'s producers were "too cheap" to buy a wig and, to her considerable discomfort, bleached her hair twice weekly, resulting in a short, bowl-cut coiffure that transformed her hair into a white helmet, pleasing her no more than the wigs on *The Patty Duke Show* had.) Throughout most of the movie, Duke wears an unbearably generic, sleeveless top and a *very* short pair of athletic shorts; toward the finale, when her character is clad in an unsightly prom dress, she looks like a little girl playing dress-up (Figure 1.7).

Figure 1.7 Billie attempts femininity

Billie might not have given Duke the transitional role into adulthood she craved, but it burnished her image with queer gender attributes that would periodically resurface throughout her career. Most of all, her turn in the campy *The Valley of the Doll*s would garner her a strong queer following.

Decades later, Duke guest starred as a lesbian in "All or Nothing," an episode of the fourth season of the musical show *Glee* that garnered a robust queer following. There were discussions that the couple she and Seventies/Eighties TV star Meredith Baxter played would become regular characters on the show, but it never came to pass.

The two aforementioned authors observe that *Billie* "is essentially a big screen sitcom" (65) complete with a gimmick (the "beat" in Billie's head) and comically exaggerated secondary characters, such as the uptight school principal. In fact, the film boasts a compendium of character actors from sitcom television (Jim Backus, Ted Bessell, and others) and offers a facile, slapdash resolution to the narrative/familial disruption caused by Billie's tomboy-ness. As in *The Patty Duke Show*, Duke portrays a split character, although here she is forced to "take sides," something the series appreciably does not demand of her. And the meaningful eye squint that was so powerful in *The Miracle Worker* becomes cloying here, deployed when Billie conjures up the beat to spur her to athletic victories, not emotional expressivity. At the same time, much like the historical positioning of *The Patty Duke Show*, *Billie* also straddled the "hinge years" of the Sixties, with the cowriters of the book about it calling the film itself an "in-between" phenomenon with "*Gidget*-like pleasures of a simpler time just before Vietnam exploded" (xiv–xv).

In California

Billie was shot in California where Duke was experiencing more manic incidents. And although she always claimed that her behavior never interfered with her work, problems were rising to the surface. Duke herself recalls being nicknamed the "little shit," especially toward the end of the show when, in Los Angeles, she started hanging out with Peter Lawford and Sammy Davis Jr., both heavy drinkers. The young Paul O'Keefe, by contrast, remembers things differently. For him, the show's move to Los

Angeles created a special bond between the two, as young actors and displaced New Yorkers left relatively on their own in a new world. He fondly recalls driving around the city in Duke's new Mustang as she was learning to drive (by all accounts, not well). Due to her newfound adulthood and indispensability to the show, Duke was able to enlist husband Harry Falk Jr. as director, not just assistant director, on several episodes. (Ironically, one was the blisteringly anti-marriage "Fiancée for a Day" which we discuss in Chapter 3.) Privately, their life was a mess, and between his infidelities and her problems with prescription medications, suicidal thoughts, and manic behavior, their marriage was short-lived.

Although *The Patty Duke Show* had tumbled slightly in the ratings and was losing the brightness of its creative luster, it remained successful. Everyone on the show was shocked when ABC pulled the plug after the third year and without explanation. Duke admits to a conflicted sense of relief: "So at the same time I was feeling thrilled that the series wasn't picked up and I was free, I felt as if I no longer had an identity."[29] She slipped into a major depressive episode.

The Valley of the Dolls

Despite having three, rather than two, leads (played by three separate women), *The Valley of the Dolls* is another Duke vehicle informed by dualities over the course of its lifespan, from its initial 1967 theatrical release to its rapid mutation into a camp classic. The credit sequence opens the film with the voiceover of Anne Welles (Barbara Perkins, then a star in the popular TV version of *Peyton Place*), offering what little "moral" may exist to the upcoming tawdry tale: to experience the highs of the mountain peaks, she tells us, one must encounter the lows of the valleys. Duke's character, the singer/actor Neely O'Hara, would experience the highest and lowest of those peaks and valleys, much as Duke would offscreen. In a film stuffed with overripe performances and characters, Duke's role thus required the most performative acting of the three leads.

Jacqueline Susann's 1966 *The Valley of the Dolls* had been not only the top-selling American novel of the year but a full-blooded cultural sensation, full of juicy, risqué themes (drug and alcohol addiction, sex outside of marriage, pregnancy, abortion, and suicide) in its depiction of show business as an ugly machine that chewed women up and spat them out. The three here are talented young "innocents" who have come to New York to enter the entertainment industry—Anne as a secretary to an entertainment law firm (and later a corporate model), Neely as a singer/actress, and Jennifer (Sharon Tate) as an actor whose "talent" is said to be embedded in her physique. (In a series of depressing phone calls to her overbearing mother, Jennifer laments, "I *know* I don't have any talent, all I have is a body, and I *am* doing my bust exercises.") By the end of the two-hour film, a thoroughly jaded Anne rejects the man and the marriage proposal she has yearned for throughout the film; Jennifer, who had turned to making foreign art films ("nudies"), has killed herself after a breast cancer diagnosis that would, in disfiguring her, have ended her career and her ability to cover her institutionalized husband's care (the film's melodrama is laid on pretty thick, as is the poignancy of knowing Tate's own untimely fate). At the film's end, Duke's Neely O'Hara, with so many failures having dismantled her career, two marriages, and her sobriety, appears in a dark, deserted alley next to some ripe garbage bins, stumbling about in what seems almost bargain-basement Oscar bait, a twisted invocation of the physicality she used when performing the young Helen Keller.

Duke long referred to the film as "Valley of the Dreck."[30] She took the role of Neely to stretch her acting range; she couldn't have selected a part further from her public's view of her and she set out to dispense with her image as a clean-scrubbed teen star. But even despite the film's consistently exaggerated features, a sad pathos burnishes Neely's scenes when they mirror the life of the "real" Patty Duke that was becoming increasingly evident in the domestic and professional arenas of her life: problems with pills and alcohol, dramatic meltdowns, suicide attempts, and disruptive, abusive behavior.

Neely is quickly presented as an uber-talented young performer. Characters marvel at her singing voice (not Duke's, although she does an excellent job lip-synching and is often shown singing in close-up, in contrast to Susan Hayward's weaker lip-synching as the bitchy, more established singer, Helen Lawson, whom Susann purportedly based on Broadway legend Ethel Merman, known for her toughness). Even by the end of the film, when Neely's behavior has alienated absolutely everyone around her, they all still insist on her fundamental talent.

Valley introduces us to Neely singing in rehearsals, where the older Lawson deems the young upstart "too good" and demands that she be removed from "her" show. This happens, and Neely moves forward in her career anyway, singing on a telethon hosted by the real entertainment figure Joey

Bishop. A montage sequence follows of a spry Neely working out (shades of *Billie*), rehearsing, getting married. (Curiously, her marriage is the only montage item depicted in a black-and-white still image.) Within the montage sequence are split-screen techniques that deliberately misalign parts of Duke's body (Figure 1.8). Although such techniques were not uncommon in Swinging Sixties cinema and television (they were also used in *The Patty Duke Show*), in Duke's case, they harken back to the schism between her on and offscreen characters. The sense of splitting and duality moves full circle by movie's end, when Neely, drunk and delusional in the alley, wails loudly, on the one hand asking where everybody has gone and, on the other, screaming that she doesn't "need anybody." *Valley*'s narrative framing creates yet another duality: the innocent, kinetic intensity of Duke's early rendition of Neely morphs, by the conclusion, into such overwrought dramatic intensity that it enters the realm of camp.

Indeed, for all its performative excess (or maybe because of it), *The Valley of the Dolls* offers little emotional depth. All the suffering remains on the surface in screechy histrionics, distancing Duke's character from her audience. Her earliest scenes introduce Neely largely through the eyes of Anne Welles, who witnesses her from a distance, and then we hear her voice in the background as Anne goes to Helen's dressing room to comment on Neely's talents. Neely's offscreen singing wafts over the space, and the camera returns us to the stage, where now Neely's back is to us. Whereas *The Miracle Worker* and *The Patty Duke Show* provided a fully present Patty Duke who was upfront and close for the audience's appreciation, *The Valley of the Dolls* distances spectators from Neely from the start, an off-putting strategy that heightens

Figure 1.8 Duke Again Split in Two

the shrillness of Duke's performance and its squalid, emotional coldness. As the film trudges on, her drugged-out eyes are utterly incapable of showing her earlier twinkle.

Mark Robson's directing style did not help matters. Known for helming the film adaptation of *Peyton Place* in 1957, Robson was clinical and old-school, more concerned with camera placement than his actors, directing all of them to play each scene "to the hilt." He made things unpleasant for everyone on the set, mostly through his unabashed disrespect for his actresses, whom he tried to turn against one another. As Duke recounts, "He was someone who used humiliation for effect who wouldn't hesitate to bite your head off in front of everyone."[31] He was evidently most cruel to the young Sharon Tate, forcing her to do pointless retakes to meet his exacting demands, and to Judy Garland, whom he had initially hired to play Helen Lawson.[32]

In a highly publicized casting decision, Robson hired her precisely when Garland, beset with personal problems (including addiction) and stinging from the low box-office performances of *A Star is Born* and *I Could Go On Singing*, was desperate for a comeback. (Garland was purportedly the basis for Susann's creation of Neely.) Decades after *Valley*, Duke told a group of fans that, in an eight-to-five daytime shooting schedule, Robson arranged for Garland's scenes to be shot at four or five pm, ensuring that the star, after having been waiting around all day, would be hopelessly drunk. Eventually he fired her. Duke and others surmised that the director had cynically brought her on board solely for the publicity Garland could give *Valley* as a potential comeback. Her ignominious firing was the final straw, Duke wrote, and at this point, everyone involved had stopped caring about the production. "By the close of shooting, everybody hated everybody."[33]

At the time, Duke had no idea how campy she and the movie as a whole came off; watching it today, only Susan Hayward seems in on the joke. To Robson's great displeasure, Duke refused to do a nude scene, which she rightly called gratuitous, but was subsequently forced to do the scene stripped down to her underwear, equally gratuitously, when her character discovers her husband skinny dipping in their pool with another woman in the middle of the night. Like many of *Valley*'s melodramatic moments, the scene goes on interminably, exuding a demeaning vulgarity rather than anything at all enticing or sexually charged.

The film's many campy moments include the infamous catfight in the women's bathroom where Neely takes off Helen's wig, throws it in the john, and flings it back at her; dialogue in which Neely tells her first husband Mel (a G-rated Mark Milner) that "Ted Casablanca is *not* a fag and *I'm* the dame who can prove it!"; and Neely's walk alone through San Francisco's porno district. There, surrounded by posters advertising Jennifer's softcore "art films," Neely says out loud, "Boobies, boobies, boobies, nothing but boobies." We are worlds away from Brooklyn Heights.

Despite being a box-office smash, *Valley* has gone down in history as one of the worst films ever made. For decades, Duke refused to watch it. In initial screenings, she said that she witnessed people laughing at intense, dramatic scenes. Yet its reputation as trash has only enhanced its value as a camp artifact and polished Duke's image as a gay camp icon. In fact, not unlike Garland, another gay camp icon, Duke's beginnings as a G-rated child star and her eventual disclosure of her struggles with addiction and mental health helped her cement a fanbase as a woman who persevered through trial and tribulation. Lest there be any doubt, Duke was invited to the Castro Theatre in 2009 for a "Gala Patty Duke Appreciation Day: Sparkle, Patty, Sparkle" in San Francisco's famed queer district, where she regaled fans with stories about the *Dolls* shoot and was photographed with drag queens dressed as Neely and other characters. This is not to argue that camp is the only or even the dominant reading of Duke's persona but that it is certainly part of her image from *Valley* on. (We return to questions of camp in Chapter 4.)

Post-Valley Work

Patty Duke went on to have a decades-long career in film and television that was periodically interrupted by medical leaves and temporary droughts of acting opportunities. In addition to her Oscar for *The Miracle Worker*, Duke would win two Golden Globes and four Primetime Emmys over her career as an actor. But Duke's subsequent work in TV and film varies in quality, and her roles rarely demanded as much of her performative gifts as those earlier successes had.

This is not to say Duke didn't try. In 1969, two years after *Dolls*, she attempted to shape a serious new character for her next feature, *Me, Natalie*, about a young woman from Brooklyn on a journey of self-discovery. *Me, Natalie* seems to reference *The Patty Duke Show* not just in the Brooklyn setting but in focusing, for much of the film, on Natalie across her teen years, even though Duke was twenty-three when she made it. (Some habits never die.) Natalie almost seems to be an extension of Patty Lane as she leaves

Brooklyn to become a fun-loving, rock and roll-dancing hippie across the river in Greenwich Village, where she has her first real love affair. But whereas sheer acting ability (and minimal makeup) had triumphed over gimmickry in *The Miracle Worker* and *The Patty Duke Show*, *Me, Natalie* moves away from this baseline by presenting Duke with a prosthetic nose and a strong overbite to render her character as a stereotypically sexless ugly duckling who has to look within for strength and beauty (Figure 1.9).[34] *Me, Natalie* reminds viewers just how much "Natalie" is a facade, rather than an accomplished merging of character and actor. But our own views of the role, and of Duke's performance, were not shared by cinematic gatekeepers of the time: she would win a Golden Globe award for playing Natalie.

Appearing on an episode of *Journey to the Unknown*, a British thriller series that aired briefly on ABC around the time of *The Valley of the Dolls*, Duke is little more than adequate as Barbara, a young woman who is being terrorized in a bed-and-breakfast on the English shore. Any competent actress could take on a part like that, and Duke isn't allowed to develop the character in any meaningful way. The movie vaguely suggests that Barbara has come to

Figure 1.9 Natalie, the "Ugly Duckling"

the coast for a rest cure. There, a figure, whom she and we believe is either a weird lodger at the B&B or the estranged husband of the innkeeper terrorizes her (and us). At this point, we enter the realm of twinning or doubleness. In a twist clearly taken from Hitchcock's *Psycho*, the marauder is revealed to be the female innkeeper, who went mad after her husband drowned and has split into two identities to imagine her family is still intact.

In general, Duke's later film and television career operated across two different modes. On one hand, she becomes a queen of camp, especially in the cheesy world of overblown thrillers or monster movies with psycho killers (*You'll Like My Mother*, 1972, discussed below) or with monstrous freaks of nature (deadly bees in *The Swarm*, 1978). Yet on the other, she shows up in ambitious television fare as a woman fighting for something meaningful, be that a sense of self, or protection of her family (Duke often plays a mother or mother-to-be in some sort of predicament), or casualties of the system (as in depicting lawyers working for justice for victims of misapplied law).

Duke also starred in earnest efforts such as *My Sweet Charlie*, where she plays an unmarried pregnant teenager. The film, shot very much like a theatrical piece (it was in fact adapted from a play), feels very much of its time, 1970, when "social issue" telefilms and series were, according to conventional TV histories, entering the field. Duke plays the uneducated teenager Marleen, a "bigoted white trash girl" who, kicked out of her Texas home for her pregnancy, escapes to an abandoned house,[35] where she is soon joined by a highly educated Black lawyer, Charlie (Al Freeman Jr.) who has uprooted himself from his plush job in the north to become involved in civil rights in the south. Eventually, we learn that Charlie is on the run after accidentally killing a white man who had been beating him.[36] The two fugitives move from mutual racial hatred to an unspoken tenderness (in her autobiography, Duke refers to it as a "love story").[37] Predictably, at the end, Charlie is shot dead, after having risked his safety to seek help for Marleen when she goes into labor. The film won the NAACP's Best Film award that year, but it was not without controversy.

Another of Duke's noted movies was *You'll Like My Mother*, a gothic horror tale rife with key elements of the genre: an isolated mansion cut off from town during a days-long snowstorm, a pregnant woman forced to stay there, a cruel head of the household, a rapist/killer on the loose, howling winds, ticking grandfather clocks, squeaky floorboards, etc. It enjoyed a brief theatrical release through Universal in 1972. Here Duke portrays Francesca, a young widow compelled to spend time at the family home of her late husband, Matthew Kinsolving, whose distinctive last name hints at the stakes of finding one's place in a family. Before he was killed in Vietnam, Matthew had told Francesca that "you'll like my mother" and, for some unknown reason, Duke's (again) heavily pregnant character makes the three-day trek from Los Angeles to the Minnesota countryside to meet her.

It is immediately clear that the Kinsolving abode is not welcoming. The first words out of her mother-in-law's mouth are so malevolent as to be laughable: "You've come at a bad time, I'm afraid. It was necessary to drown some kittens, and Kathleen [her young, "feeble-minded" daughter] is quite upset about it." To keep the Kinsolving estate to herself, she tells Francesca that she will never "acknowledge [Francesca] as Matthew's wife or your child as his." Over the course of Francesca's stay, her mother-in-law drugs her, delivers her baby but spirits it away, and falsely declares the infant dead. (The young Kathleen hides the newborn in the attic, where Francesca can furtively care for her.) As the drama plays out, we learn, along with Francesca, that Matthew's mother had died soon after her son had. The woman portraying her is the late mother's sister-in-law (a double, but in the tradition of the horror genre and not of *The Patty Duke Show*), and mother to Kenny, the rapist, whom she has hidden at the bottom of the house, and the abused Kathleen, whose wild looks and rare, halting speech are reminiscent of the young Helen Keller. The false mother's "bad hearing" invokes other ghosts of *The Miracle Worker*, as does a climactic moment when Francesca (like young Helen with Annie) bites Kenny who attacks her. Ultimately, Kathleen saves Francesca by fatally stabbing her brother with a pair of scissors.

You'll Like My Mother partakes in both tracks into which we divide Duke's post-*Patty Duke Show* work, at once generic horror/thriller and the story of a vulnerable woman who needs to protect a baby. Duke's Francesca displays moments of sheer frigidity and violence in some scenes, such as those with Kenneth and his mother, along with tender, touching exchanges with Kathleen, who, not unlike Duke as a child, received no affection from her maternal figure. The film was met with mixed reviews: some praised its sense of claustrophobia, and its acting was generally well-received. Richard Thomas, "John Boy" in *The Waltons*, was cast against type as the diabolical Kenny.

Although it lacks the excesses of early Sixties horror fare such as *Whatever Happened to Baby Jane*, *You'll Like My Mother* has no shortage of fans of the genre. Most charming, perhaps, is "Eclectic Ladyland," an early 21st century blogger who references it in their endearing "Ten Things I Love About Patty Duke." In No. 5, "She Freaked Me Out!" "Eclectic Lady" writes:

As a horror fan, this is the Patty Duke I am most grateful for. . . . Duke has a presence that is at once capable and genuine and also heightens the implicit campiness of the genre. This is largely because she just does a really good job, along with the fact that she was very beautiful but with a type of beauty that seemed familiar or achievable. She lent the roles a believability that made the films all the scarier for me.[38]

Duke received an Emmy in 1970 (for *My Sweet Charlie*), but her performance at the awards ceremony arguably outstripped that of the film. Duke's acceptance at the podium gave many their first glimpse of a troubled star. Her expression was vacant, her affect robotic, and awkward pauses separated her words as she pointed into the audience, thanking her mother, who was attending an awards ceremony for the first time, and to Desi Arnaz Jr., whom Duke was dating, prior to Lucille Ball putting the kibosh on the relationship (Duke was a divorced "older woman"—twenty-three to Arnaz's seventeen).

Most thought Duke was high on drugs—she recounts that Richard Burton described her as a "dope-ridden idiot." Duke's own explanation was that she was sorely sleep-deprived and, without knowing it, on the brink of a manic episode.[39] She also claims to have been signing language for the hearing-impaired as she spoke, and that the cameras didn't catch her hands below the podium, explaining her peculiar long pauses. Whatever circumstances might have accounted for the odd behavior, Duke entered a psychiatric ward soon afterward and, with the language of twinning, described her mental health at the time as the involuntarily leave-taking of "Dr. Jekyll to become Mr. Hyde."[40]

In a somewhat gimmicky act of reverse twinning, Duke appeared in the 1979 television remake of *The Miracle Worker*, assuming the role of Annie Sullivan. Melissa Gilbert played the young Helen Keller (for some reason, NBC [National Broadcasting Company] gave Gilbert top billing). The director, Paul Aaron, was known for his work in television, particularly the long-running series *The Waltons*, in which Duke's *You'll Like My Mother* co-star, Richard Thomas, was one of the leads. Duke received another Emmy for her depiction of Sullivan. Five years later, 20th Century Fox proposed a sequel telefilm based on Keller's adult life, *Helen Keller: The Miracle Continues*. They did not ask Duke to be involved, which hurt and disappointed her.

From Actress to Advocate

Duke continued to work up until the 2010s, primarily as a lead in TV films, as a guest star, and even as a costar with Richard Crenna in ABC's *It Takes Two*, a sitcom that lasted for one season. She was also cast as the lead in *Hail to the Chief*, another ABC sitcom, in which she depicted the country's first female president (Ted Bessell, with whom she had appeared in *Billie*, portrayed her husband). That show was canceled in less than two months. Even if her acting never regained the heights of fame of her earlier work, the sheer scope of roles and genres in which the mature Duke appeared is noteworthy. Projects ranged from a Christian film called *Power of the Air*, to depicting Martha Washington in a historical drama about George Washington, to playing "Rosemary" in a TV film sequel to *Rosemary's Baby* (according to some sources, Duke had been considered for Polanski's original, in the role that ultimately went to Mia Farrow).[41]

She also appeared in a number of televised Public Service Announcements for Social Security, Medicare, and groups supporting the blind and the rights of crime victims. On some of these PSAs, she reprised her role as one or both Lane cousins along with a few other original cast members. (We discuss these quasi-reunions in the next chapter.)

In 1985, Duke was elected President of the Screen Actors' Guild (now SAG-AFTRA) and remained in place until 1988, work of which she was very proud. William Schallert (Martin Lane on the show) had served in the position earlier; Hannah Schallert recalls the appreciation that other actors had had for her grandfather as SAG President: "I remember at his [2106] memorial, some of the people who spoke were other actors who shared stories about his dedication and standing up for them."[42] One of his lasting achievements was creating a Committee for Performers with Disabilities, mirroring Duke's advocacy on behalf of people with mental disabilities, which itself bookends her career, from her start playing a woman with physical disabilities, Helen Keller. Like Schallert, who had presided over the Guild from 1979 to 1981 during a difficult and contentious strike, Duke's presidency was marred by tumult, and she was furious when Schallert offered unsolicited advice to his former TV-daughter, initiating what appears to have been their only (brief) contretemps.

But it was in her capacity as mental health advocate, especially regarding bipolar disorder, that Duke left an impactful legacy that equaled and endured beyond *The Miracle Worker* and *The Patty Duke Show*. She refers to herself, unironically and without judgment, as the "mental illness poster child."[43] For years, she served as an official spokesperson for the National Alliance on Mental Illness, touring the country, giving lectures, and doing advocacy work. In 2007 she appeared on *The Oprah Winfrey Show*, not to discuss her acting career, but to inform people what it was like to live with bipolar disorder.

Duke married her fourth and final husband, Sgt. Michael Pearce, whom she had met while working on a film in 1986. Their marriage was peaceful and rewarding, and the couple raised a son together. Duke spent the rest of her life relatively quietly with Pearce in Idaho, passing away in 2016 at the age of sixty-nine.

In 1992, not long after meeting Pearce, Duke had released *A Brilliant Madness: Living with Manic Depressive Illness*, her second autobiography. Although *Call Me Anna* had covered her diagnosis and how she managed bipolar disorder medically, *Madness*, as its subtitle implies, plumbs how the illness impacted her life and career. The memoirs overlap a fair amount. Curiously, the second invokes the specter of doubling by alternating between chapters written in the first person, ostensibly by Duke, as she recounts her life story, and chapters written by medical journalist Gloria Hochman that examine various aspects of bipolarism. (Duke's other autobiographies were also coauthored, but in the classic tradition of being ghost-written.)

Duke had come out as someone with her illness at a time when few celebrities disclosed much about any medical, and especially, psychological, conditions they had. By the time *Madness* was published, though, Duke had become a national mental health spokesperson and an admired role model. In addition to offering resources for readers, Duke writes about encounters she'd had with people she met while touring the country, and she and her coauthor are upbeat about curbing the shame attached to mental health illnesses. But as of this writing, and despite more public figures disclosing their struggles with mental illness, the stigma surrounding it still seems intractable.

Duke's desire to raise awareness about the issue crystallized her decision to adapt *Call Me Anna* into a made-for-TV film in 1990, three years after that book's publication and two years before *Madness*'s. Her goal in coproducing and starring in it was, she declared, to "use the power of television to get information through to people about mental illness."[44] As she explained, "I wanted the movie to track my illness . . . the goal was to explain a very complicated medical condition to people while they were still being entertained."[45]

The narrative arc of the telefilm literally moves from dark to light, from terror to triumph. A scream (Anna, as a child) pierces its opening shot of pitch blackness, and the film concludes with a scene of a highly poised adult Duke speaking to the US Congress, advocating for funds for mental health research. She then embraces several children and a man whom the film identifies as her husband, Sgt. Michael Pearce.

Once more, like the cousins in *The Patty Duke Show*, the character "Patty Duke" is split in this telefilm, here quite literally. One actor portrays her as a young girl; another as an older teen; and Duke depicts herself as an adult, starting with her marriage to her third husband, John Astin, the actor known for his role as Gomez in *The Addams Family*.[46] A young Matthew Perry, later of *Friends* renown, appears briefly as Desi Arnaz Jr.

Scored almost like a horror film, *Call Me Anna* doesn't shrink from depicting Duke's frequent, often violent outbursts and their impact on those closest to her. At times the movie feels sensationalistic, particularly when one forgets that these events stemmed from actual occurrences. Ethel Ross's over-the-top wickedness toward Anna's mother seems especially cruel, though it must be said that the adaptation largely hews to Duke's written account.

Duke had doubts about working on the project and, during production, left the set whenever one of the younger "Pattys" was enacting her troubled earlier years. The physicality of the screaming scenes, she later reflected, recalled *The Miracle Worker*: "Helen was trapped physically, I was trapped emotionally."[47] Duke worried about the impact that the film might have on her relationships with her children and with Astin. Indeed, their thirteen-year marriage coincided with what were probably the worst years of her then-undiagnosed disorder. To his great credit, Astin put Duke in touch with his therapist, Dr. Harlan Arlen, the physician who diagnosed her and later helped Duke's mother manage her own lifelong depression. Arlen served as a medical consultant for the TV movie, and was portrayed by Karl Malden, the only established name on the project other than Duke. His depiction is that of another kind of "miracle worker" for having cured Duke and her mother.

In episodic fashion, *Call Me Anna* hits the most dramatic milestones Duke had recounted in her book, beginning with the TV quiz show scandal, her training for *The Miracle Worker*, and the evil of Ethel Ross (who, after obstreperously disinviting Patty's mother from the Oscars, is shown attending the ceremony with her pet chihuahua in her lap) and John Ross (creeping into bed with Patty, who screams NOOO! in a mercifully darkened image). It covers her life with Falk and her fleeting second marriage to her subletter,

Michael Tell, who fathered her first child, future actor Sean Astin. Astin's name, of course, was given to him by Duke's next husband, who adopted the child, although Sean's paternity was not discussed publicly.[48] Decades later, a DNA test would confirm that Tell was in fact Sean Astin's biological father, something the movie understandably omits since Duke was still denying it.

Call Me Anna resonates thematically with some of Duke's previous performances, especially in the sense of detaching from a stable, singular identity. In the first five minutes, the young Anna mouths off (unrealistically) to John and Ethel Ross, who are attempting to convince her that being prepped for the TV quiz show is the thing to do, telling the pair, "I'm not playing a part, *it's me in the booth*," as if preternaturally aware that her identity was distinct from the roles she would play, including the domestic ones assigned to her by the Rosses. Later in the film, Dr. Arlen (Malden), addressing Patty as Anna, asks, "Do you always be what other people expect?" to which she combatively responds, "Always . . . for years I've been pretending to be Patty Duke." (Duke always told interviewers how painful it was for her to "play herself" in this film.)

Truth be told, the filmed adaptation of *Call Me Anna* is not very good. Like many telefilms of the time, its production values are less than stellar. But it took courage on Duke's part to put her story out there, and the movie shows every indication that her goals for it were ingenuous. For, despite its histrionics, *Call Me Anna* genuinely seems to want to shun pretense, and presents the same idiosyncratic straightforwardness that characterizes some of Duke's other adult appearances, where she appears accessible, unscripted, and quite human for an actor of her acclaim. And that image coincided with the way colleagues perceived her. Paul O'Keefe said that Duke never acted "the star"; Schallert made much the same comment, appreciating the sheer talent of his down-to-earth costar. To be sure, Duke's episodes of manic and destructive behavior, often interpreted as signs of drug or alcohol use, alienated more than a few friends and colleagues along the way. But, although it gets us no closer to a real "Patty" or "Anna," her adult acting style suggests a lack of pretense in "Patty Duke" distinct from the radically new identities she had assayed decades earlier in *The Miracle Worker* and *The Patty Duke Show*.

Figure 2.1 Comedy's Iconic Mirror Stage, Patty Duke style

2

The Patty Duke Show

Production History

Pre-Production: William Asher and Sidney Sheldon

The Patty Duke Show's cocreators were William Asher and Sidney Sheldon. Established in film and television, Asher had been the chief director of the *Our Miss Brooks* series and, more recently, of 110 episodes of *I Love Lucy*. He helmed the episode in which Lucy and Harpo Marx twin each other at an imaginary mirror, restaging the classic scene from *Duck Soup* with Harpo and Groucho, which *The Patty Duke Show* would in turn revive in its opening credits with the twin cousins (see Figure 2.1). A handful of Asher's films were "beach party movies," which participated in a youthful obsession with surfing and beach culture of the time and, in similar fashion, during the run of *The Patty Duke Show*, he worked on the initial episodes of *Gidget*, the Sally Field vehicle that was ABC's other Wednesday girl show that also capitalized on the beach culture fad. According to Ralph Rosenblum, the editor of *The Patty Duke Show*, Asher was extremely unpleasant and early on was pushed away from the series.[1] Asher did direct most of the series' first episodes. Contracted for ten, he periodically returned to the shoot, but effectively left the show early on to develop *Bewitched* (1964–72) with his wife Elizabeth Montgomery, its lead. Asher was replaced by Stanley Prager, a colleague Duke enjoyed for his great sense of humor. Soon, though, the Rosses, resentful of the pair's good working relationship, not only had Prager fired but made Duke do it. "It's among the ugliest things I've ever done," she later recounted.[2]

Although Asher had initial responsibility for developing the show, Sidney Sheldon was the primary mover and shaker in refining the premise of *The Patty Duke Show*. He was not, however, particularly attached to the series, regarding it in his later, self-serving memoirs as little more than one chapter in a packed and peripatetic career in entertainment. Most people know Sheldon for his hefty popular potboiler novels (*The Other Side of Midnight* his splashiest), which he claimed to prefer to television.[3] From the late Fifties

The Patty Duke Show *and the American Sixties*. Caryl Flinn and Dana Polan, Oxford University Press.
© Oxford University Press 2026. DOI: 10.1093/oso/9780197667439.003.0003

into the Sixties, movie opportunities had been drying up for Sheldon, who realized television might offer new potential for scriptwriting. For him initially, TV was a quick cash cow, turning to it only after losing the mortgage on his house. He was, in fact, concerned that TV work might damage his screenwriting reputation.

Production/distribution company United Artists (UA-ZIV) had approved Asher to develop a new series and had selected Patty Duke as its star, but he notes that after the sophisticated drama of The Miracle Worker, it had been difficult to determine the right sort of show for her talents and "hard to find a character for her."[4] Sheldon, for his part, had been impressed by Duke's performance in The Miracle Worker but claimed that he initially resisted Asher's recruitment as series writer to a medium he considered too lowbrow for both the star and himself. He then relented and met with Duke at Hollywood's Brown Derby restaurant, an iconic spot for Hollywood dealmaking, and found himself entranced by her vitality and vulnerability. As he started to warm to the idea of the series, he went so far as to invite the young star to spend a few days in his home with his wife ("she was kind of our daughter").[5] Convinced now that Duke was so talented that she could play identical twins, he agreed to come on board. He also claims that Asher came up with the more absurd premise of them being identical cousins (Asher claims not to remember who came up with either premise).[6]

Sheldon managed to write enough episodes for The Patty Duke Show to create a backlog of scripts. Yet no sooner had he started, he had one foot out the door, spending more time on the West Coast to work on I Dream of Jeannie. With his immodest drive, Sheldon asked producer UA-ZIV if he might write all the scripts for The Patty Duke Show, something rather unheard of in TV scriptwriting. Despite being overburdened, Sheldon's output for the series is astonishing. An undated folder in his archives contains a wide range of story ideas and plot premises he'd crafted.[7] Some eventually became episodes, and several have a handwritten "OK" next to them, confirming that Sheldon had shared them with others. Many of his suggestions were taken up but there were also intriguing, unused premises. For instance, he writes that there could be "Wild money–raising schemes" and offers one plot in which Patty "Writes to Harvard–offering to sell her brain." In one uncanny idea for an episode, Sheldon suggests that, "Patty Duke, the movie star, comes to town. Patty Lane is mistaken for her. The complications ensue from there."

When The Patty Duke Show moved production to Los Angeles in its third season, Sheldon, already working there, was pursuing other projects, such as *I Dream of Jeannie*, and a proposed series for NBC, *The Paul Lynde Show* with the eponymous comedian, who had made the entertaining cameo early in *The Patty Duke Show*. Sheldon was clearly eager for success in Hollywood; he'd won an Oscar for writing *The Bachelor and the Bobbysoxer* (1947) whose premise and scattered bits of dialogue reappeared in *The Patty Duke Show* two decades later. His move to Los Angeles suited him, although UA-ZIV, back in New York, found it problematic.

In a letter to his lawyer to counter a claim by UA that he was spending too much time on other projects and was away too often during the show's first two seasons, Sheldon asserted that he was on top of things and spells out, usefully, his tasks for the series:

> I would like to clarify for you what my function as Script Supervisor consists of: The Producer and I discuss story ideas and we mutually agree on which ideas shall be turned into scripts. If they are my ideas, I write the script, go over the first draft with him, polish it and send it to mimeo. . . If it is the idea of another writer, I meet with the writer, discuss the idea and have him do an outline. I then go over the outline with him and suggest whatever changes I feel are necessary. He then writes a first draft script. The Producer and I go over the first draft script with him, make any further changes that are needed, and he makes his revisions. At that point, I do a final polish on his script, sometimes a minor one, sometimes a total rewrite.

Neither Duke, William Schallert, nor Paul O'Keefe recall Sheldon being present very much on set, and once the first season was over, it seems he was largely a structuring absence on the show. It was soon clear that Sheldon had taken on too much and, by Season 2, for regular script input, he helped bring a second writer on board, Arnold Horwitt, who had worked on *Dobie Gillis* and, later, would write for *That Girl*. Wanting to cultivate synergy between the series and the recording industry, Sheldon encouraged Horwitt to write episodes about pop music featuring cameos of singers. In a December 2, 1964 letter, Sheldon reminds series producer Stanley Prager, "I discussed with you an idea where Patty gets involved in the record business. I think it's a good idea and gives us a legitimate chance for music," noting that Horwitt had come up with an idea for a "Swingy Zook" (whatever that is). Horwitt would in fact be responsible for several episodes centered around the music business, such as one in which Patty tries to build publicity for a singing duo, played by pop performers Chad and Jeremy, and another, featuring

Sammy Davis Jr. in what might be the series' strongest episode, discussed in Chapter 5.

The Companies Behind the Sitcom

UA-ZIV, the production/distribution company behind *The Patty Duke Show*, had acquired its hyphenate name in 1959, when United Artists purchased ZIV, a recording company (named after its founder, Frederick Ziv) with a side interest in television (it had made the successful series *Men in Space*). UA, a relative latecomer to the television scene, hoped by the purchase to gain an in-house TV production and distribution arm.

From 1960 to 1963, UA-ZIV had come up with twelve series that it tried to sell to CBS (Columbia Broadcasting System), but the network picked up none of them. Its first breakthrough came when it sold an hour-long Western, *Stoney Burke*, to ABC in the 1962–63 season. The following year, UA-ZIV found even greater success with the network, selling hour-long dramatic shows like *The Outer Limits* and *The Fugitive* and half-hour comedies like *The Patty Duke Show*. *Gilligan's Island* joined the ABC lineup in 1964. Around 1964–65 (i.e., when *The Patty Duke Show* was between Seasons 1 and 2), UA exited from TV production, deciding henceforth to treat TV as a venue to which they could sell feature films.[8]

Chrislaw

UA-ZIV subcontracted the actual work of producing *The Patty Duke Show* to Chrislaw, a company owned by actor Peter Lawford (Chris was his son's name, Law a diminutive of Lawford). Chrislaw had been the production firm for *The Dick Van Dyke Show*, and Lawford's father-in-law, mogul Joseph P. Kennedy, paid for that series' pilot. Few archival traces of Chrislaw remain, but it seems that it worked with the talent and arranged the hands-on aspects of production, while UA-ZIV paid the bills and communicated with ABC.

As with his other efforts in the entertainment world, the notoriously lackadaisical Lawford appears not to have had much direct involvement in Chrislaw and likely regarded it as a cash cow. He did, however, make a brief cameo in a *Patty Duke Show* episode as himself, and may have helped land

Figure 2.2 Peter Lawford and Patty Duke

fellow Rat Packer Sammy Davis Jr. for a fuller star turn in the same episode. Paul O'Keefe, however, does not recall Lawford ever having been present during the making of *The Patty Duke Show* (Figure 2.2).

For all his lack of involvement in it, Lawford clearly appreciated the success of the show. At the end of the first season, he sent a telegram to Sidney Sheldon: "Dear Sidney: It would take more space than this telegram allows to express my complete incredulity about the monumental job you have done so well in such a short period of time...."[9]

The Cast

William Schallert

William Schallert, who played Martin Lane, was a versatile actor whose six-decade acting career spanned television, voice work, film, and the stage

Figure 2.3 William Schallert as Martin Lane

(Figure 2.3). Born and raised in Los Angeles, he initially aspired to a career in music, studying under no less than composer Arnold Schoenberg at UCLA, but during and after college quickly drifted toward the stage. After returning from WWII, where he fought as a pilot, Schallert landed a few small roles in films "that convinced me I could make a living as an actor."[10] He even portrayed an assistant director in the Hollywood classic, *Singin' in the Rain*, although his scenes ended up on the cutting room floor.

Schallert is one of those omnipresent TV and film actors who was more than a background character but never quite a leading figure. As his granddaughter Hanna Schallert fondly recounts:

> A common experience . . . was people coming up to Grandpa and recognizing him. Sometimes they knew him from "Patty Duke," . . . but people weren't always sure where they knew him from. To me this seems related to his ability to be 'the average guy', 'the steady authority figure/father', [adding],[11] "If they didn't know where they recognized him from, my dad says people would ask if he'd sold them a car or grown up together."[12]

Schallert got the part of Martin Lane after Mark Miller, who had depicted Martin in the pilot, declined to continue the role (why is unclear). Comparing the two reveals strikingly conflicting versions of early Sixties suburban fatherhood: Miller had a physical, almost rugged solidity, and classic square-jawed good looks that might have given him the appearance of a stronger family patriarch, whereas Schallert had a lankiness that could tip his performance into a slouching awkwardness more timorous than forceful, a physical skill he brought to bear in other roles. In Edgar Ulmer's 1951 *The Man from Planet X*, Schallert played an evil scientist who spent much of his time lurking in shadows, as if avoiding confrontation even as a bad guy. His most conspicuous use of body was when he played his favorite role as a guest character on *Get Smart*, the Admiral, an aged commander working for CONTROL who always seemed ready to fall over at the slightest touch. Schallert deployed a physical, almost slapstick, comedic aspect to his performance that was never exhibited on Duke's show. It might seem an odd choice for Schallert to single out "The Admiral" so favorably, but his family underscores the extent to which he "was a total ham ... always joking around testing out voices, characters ... pratfalls etc." His wife Leah [spelled Lia by family members] was only able to shut him up in public by declaiming "I married Jerry Lewis."[13] Duke recalled her younger self being annoyed by Schallert's insatiable appetite for pulling pranks between takes, especially when he bounced around, pretending to be a large ape.

Before *The Patty Duke Show*, Schallert appeared in all sorts of television Westerns, sitcoms, and variety and anthology shows in the Fifties. It wasn't until *The Many Loves of Dobie Gillis* that Schallert became a recurrent sitcom character. He played a high-school teacher, Mr. Pomfritt—"Mr. Fried Potatoes," as the crew nicknamed him. When that series wrapped in 1963, he shot a pilot for a show that would combine live action with animation, *Philbert*, centered around a bachelor animator (Schallert), who lived with his cartoon character, Philbert. The series was never picked up, in large part because of its price tag of $75,000 per episode, when most sitcoms of the time rarely exceeded $50,000 per installment.

Despite playing a seemingly infinite number of good guys, bad guys, and "fathers, mayors, etc" over his long career,[14] Schallert is best known for his role as Martin Lane, and headlines in his obituaries in 2016 routinely singled it out. His image as Patty's "nice father," as he called it, remains seared into the minds of baby boomers and later audiences who discovered the show in syndication.

Duke recalled Schallert with deep affection, appreciating his "calm, fatherly presence. But also funny. Hard-working and made it look easy."[15] As Joseph and Brendan state, their father had become a sort of surrogate father for Duke, who "would call him later on in life when she needed someone to talk to. He was very understanding and patient and knew her well." Adds Hannah, "this showed they were really friends, that Grandpa had meant something to her, as a child actor. She felt she could reach someone who had been her father, from the past."[16]

After the series was canceled, Schallert did extensive voice work and worked steadily across screen and stage almost up to his death at ninety-three. His diverse roles spanned from an appearance in an Elvis Presley film (Presley called him "sir"); a 1967 episode of *Star Trek* that remains a fan favorite ("The Trouble with Tribbles"); the sensationalist reality show *Desperate Housewives*; and a theatrical production of *Candide*, of which the actor was especially proud.

Jean Byron

Born in Paducah, Kentucky, Jean Byron (Natalie Lane) began her entertainment career as a singer, working with the Tommy Dorsey Band for several years (Figure 2.4). She got her start in Hollywood playing in the kind of B monster movies that Patty Lane was always watching, such as *The Magnetic Monster* (1953) and *Voodoo Tiger* (1952), where she costarred with a chimpanzee and Johnny Weissmuller of *Tarzan* fame. During the Fifties, Byron's spots on television were largely guest appearances until, like Schallert, she landed a semi-regular role as one of Dobie's teachers in *Dobie Gillis*. In the first season, she played a high-school math teacher and later, in Seasons 3 and 4, a college professor, Dr. Imogene Burkhart—Byron's birth name. Byron portrayed the mother of Dobie's girlfriend in the pilot for a spinoff series that was never picked up. In 1961, she played yet another sitcom mom in the pilot for *Daddy-O*, a Don DeFore vehicle about a reluctant TV actor—and another feckless father—that was also not picked up. *Although Daddy-O displays every sign of being a silly show*, filled with pratfalls and clichéd characters, Byron's performance is imbued with the same subtle grace she would bring to *The Patty Duke Show*.

Still, *The Patty Duke Show* never gave Byron's Natalie Lane much to work with. Her character seldom departs from the family home, and the reasons

Figure 2.4 Jean Byron as Natalie Lane

for those rare sorties are hardly rousing: she goes to a cake-baking contest, visits a fortune teller, spends an evening at an espresso bar, and has dinner (or maybe just tea—it's unclear) with a vaguely delineated friend from whom she needs advice. One of the rare times she initiates an evening out with her husband, it's simply because the kids have commandeered the kitchen, and she sighs upon their return, as if the two have simply gotten a marital duty out of the way. Throughout, Byron brings a refreshing solidity and calmness to the tired housewife image, although things, as we shall see, changed in Season 3.

Byron's three-year role as Patty's mother was the steadiest of her career. After the show wrapped, she would appear in small supporting and guest spots in film and TV, including the cartoonish, campy *Batman*. Unlike Schallert, her work on screens large and small fell off by the early Seventies, after which she continued to appear in regional theater, often in musicals. Byron reprises her part of Natalie Lane in the 1999 TV reunion movie *The Patty Duke Show: Still Rockin' in Brooklyn Heights*, making clumsy jokes about Viagra with Schallert in the writers' awkward efforts to have the old series appear more with the times than fans might have been willing to allow. In 2006, Byron died at the age of eighty, the first of its central cast to pass away.

All the other "Lanes" loved working with Byron. Paul O'Keefe recalls the small, motherly ways she took care of him, straightening out his collar that was overlooked by production assistants, and noting the close relationship she shared with Duke. Duke herself acknowledged, appreciably, that Byron "took [her] under her wing."[17] When Patty Duke and Harry Falk Jr. married, Byron hosted their wedding reception at her home in Los Angeles at a time when everyone else was wagging their tongues in disapproval.

Duke described Byron as "a real grande dame, bawdy, outrageous, [who] swore like a trooper, really my first experience with a woman who is able to maintain her grace and dignity and still be one of the guys."[18] She also proffered advice about working in show business and confided details about her personal life and relationships with men: Byron was in a long-term relationship with a married man and strongly counseled her young costar against doing the same. In the mid-Fifties, Byron had briefly been married to Michael Ansara, the Lebanese-American actor best known for his role as Cochise in the TV show *Broken Arrow* and, later, for marrying Barbara Eden of *I Dream of Jeannie*, where he occasionally guest starred as a male genie. "When Jean mentioned him," Duke recalled, "she would always talk about his beauty, as he was an extremely handsome man. I just wish that she had found a person she could love later in life, instead of turning to alcohol for happiness."[19]

A 1964 *TV Guide* cover article, "Patty Duke's 'Parents,'" jauntily displays the schism between Byron's and Schallert's personalities when the unidentified interviewer visits the set for the filming of "Pen Pal," an episode where Patty and Richard, unbeknownst to each other, exchange romantic missives under the pseudonyms Lancelot and Guinevere (Camelot!). For Schallert, the moral of the episode was that "you can't judge people by their surface. I always viewed Richard as a distinct jerk. Just shows. Romantic idealism may lurk deep in the heart of the lowliest clod."[20] After Schallert freely admits to his own idealist demands, especially in his "intense" and "violent" attachments during his own Lancelot-like youth, the interviewer asks Byron about any "Guinevere-like" features of her own youth, to which she mockingly responds: "I was *the most* romantic creature that ever walked on shoes." Their contrasting attitudes—Schallert's deep sincerity, Byron's mildly sardonic detachment—seep into their characterizations of Natalie and Martin Lane on screen. After Schallert takes leave of this interview, Byron, in a wry, observational mode that is not without affection, remarks to the interviewer, "He's very vulnerable, isn't he?," echoing Natalie Lane's mention at one point to Patty that what first attracted her to Martin was "his helplessness."[21]

Paul O'Keefe

Paul O'Keefe was already an established child actor in New York when producers started looking to cast Ross for the series (Figure 2.5). Born in Boston, O'Keefe had moved to New York, where his career had an auspicious start when he was picked as the first replacement of Winthrop in the original Broadway run of *The Music Man* with Robert Preston. When O'Keefe started work on *The Patty Duke Show*, he had moved on to the Broadway musical production *Oliver!*

O'Keefe did not play Ross for *The Patty Duke Show* pilot, but when series production moved to New York, he was cast without even having to try out for the part. He told us that a recorded audition he had done for a Mel Brooks project called "Inside Danny Baker" (never picked up) was screened

Figure 2.5 Paul O'Keefe as Ross Lane

for a *Patty Duke Show* producer, who selected O'Keefe based on it. O'Keefe recalls that the show's producers were especially happy about his ability to deliver "zingers," a prerequisite for any actor playing a wisecracking little brother.

O'Keefe's "Lane family" colleagues remember how hard the young boy worked, and, like other cast members, O'Keefe has fond memories of working on the show, telling us in a 2023 interview that "It was *fun* to do." He appreciated Duke's talents, got along with everyone, and retrospectively (and perhaps even back then) understood how fortunate he was to have had such positive experiences as a child actor.

After the series wrapped, he remained in Los Angeles for a year before moving back to New York, where he appeared in the soap opera *As the World Turns*, and then enrolled at Columbia University, where he received a BA in economics. Since then, O'Keefe has continued his work as an actor on screen and in commercials, and as an actor and musician in national and international stage productions, including the long-running musical *Rent*. Early, in the Eighties, he made a surprise appearance when Patty Duke was on *The Sally Jessy Raphael Show* promoting her memoir *Call Me Anna* and also took part in the series' 1999 reunion film, in which the writers transformed the grown-up Ross into a Broadway producer. While this lined up somewhat with O'Keefe's own biography, the actor said he always thought that Ross would grow up to work at NASA.

Eddie Applegate

In *Call Me Anna*, Patty Duke claims she wanted Tommy Rettig, who had played Jeff Miller on the *Lassie* show, to be cast as her boyfriend Richard Harrison because she thought he was "cute." Eddie Applegate, by contrast, who played Richard in the pilot, was rather generic-looking and, significantly, was a full twelve years older than Duke and married at the time the show started (Figure 2.6). All accounts attest that Applegate was easy to get along with. Yet, while not prone to complaining, he let loose a bit in a 1965 *TV Guide* interview, voicing frustration about playing a boy of seventeen as he neared thirty. He also lamented that everybody assumed that he was actually "Patty Duke's boyfriend,"[22] which caused problems when he went out with his wife, whom he'd married at twenty-three (eventually, Applegate took to carrying their marriage license to ward off the doubting

Figure 2.6 Eddie Applegate as Richard Harrison

tongue-waggers). For their part, ABC permitted him to tell people he was married, but insisted that he claim he was only twenty-four, and kept up appearances by confining any "adult activity" such as smoking or drinking to his home. "This he's-only-17-tag they've hung on me robs me of my identification as an actor," he said. "That hurts. No one's to blame, but it hurts. You'd be surprised how deep the impression's gone, too" (13–14). Indeed, this very article conflated Applegate with his role as Richard by introducing him as "one of the more tolerable 17-year-olds currently running loose on television screens" (12). Applegate happily, but incorrectly, told his interviewer that in the show's upcoming (third) season, the writers were planning to have his character marry Patty Lane, and he was looking forward "to talk[ing] as an adult in—you know, like, interviews." He was also upbeat about *The Patty Duke Show*'s imminent move to Los Angeles, where he could seek out other acting jobs in his spare time. "Who knows," he said, "maybe I can turn up a baby-faced killer there and *blam*—there goes the image!" (15).

Duke remembers Applegate as a low-drama person who "never had an unkind word to say about anyone";[23] adding that his depiction of the "goofy" Richard was convincing but nothing at all like him in real life.[24] After the series was canceled, Applegate took a recurring role as Bob Mooney on *The Lucy Show*, but as time wore on, his film and television work became sporadic and he became a serious amateur painter for much of his life. Applegate passed away in 2016, the same year as Duke and Schallert.

Early Announcements in Trade Journals (Correct and Incorrect)

A few 1962 notices and brief articles offer partial glimpses into the show's inception and start of production, but there are enough gaps, contradictory details, and outright inaccuracies to derail the historical record, or even a clear understanding of what happened when.

Many of the extant announcements come from *The Hollywood Reporter*, but in the form of tiny, hidden paragraphs that were often vague and incorrect, or, more reasonably, relaying the fluctuating decisions involved in any show in development. For instance, early on, the *Reporter* announced that the role of Mrs. Lane had been offered to acclaimed actress Patricia Neal, who had appeared in the stage version of *The Miracle Worker*.[25] Published tidbits announced various actors who had "accepted" Duke-adjacent roles; that Duke would only play a single role (!); that Cathy "instead of being Scottish, will now be an American girl educated and well-traveled in the capitals of Europe." The "purpose of the switch," it noted, "is to give writers more leeway on plots."[26] Perhaps the silliest item came from Asher himself, who told an interviewer that Patty would be six months older than her European "twin"![27]

Up to then, most articles about Duke had concentrated on her post-*Miracle Worker* acting ventures. In an episode of *Ben Casey*, she guest-starred as a young woman going blind after surgery, leading the *Hollywood Reporter* writer to compare it unfavorably to her depiction of Helen Keller. Another *Reporter* piece discussed her appearance in a new Broadway show, *Isle of Children*, and then speculated that she might return on the boards as June Havoc in a follow-up to *Gypsy*, retold from daughter Havoc's perspective (never happened). On July 23, 1962, trade journals finally, and accurately, proclaimed that ABC had won the bidding war over *The Patty Duke Show*.

Dated July 2, 1962, ABC's contract with UA-ZIV (and by extension, Chrislaw) for Patty Duke's series is at once generic and strange. While the document required that Duke, like the other principal performers, be made available for promotional commercials (although at twice those actors' scale), a detail not unheard of at the time stipulated that she could not "do commercials for depilatories, underarm deodorants, feminine hygiene and similar products" or "any commercials which are in bad taste or inappropriate for a minor."[28]

The contract also spells out the conditions for a pilot for the show that, if picked up by ABC, would lead to the series airing by October 1963 (the actual premiere would be a month earlier, on September 18). The first season was to include a minimum twenty-six episodes (there were thirty-five), with subsequent years consisting of at least thirty-two (actually ending up at thirty-six and thirty-three, in Seasons 2 and 3, respectively). And although the contract speaks of five seasons, ABC, as we know, canceled after three. Had the black and white show switched to color, ABC also pledged to assume any additional costs. (However, Duke would later claim in her memoirs and in interviews that it was the very expense of production in color which led the network to cancel the show just at a moment where color programming was becoming the norm.)

Early on, TV critics were starting to weigh in on the show's prospects. In August 1963, for example, the *Gallagher Report*, a publication "designed to aid advertising, broadcasting, and newspaper executives," released its predictions for the "top 20" of the upcoming television season. *The Patty Duke Show* was listed among them, but only *My Favorite Martian* was expected to be a "shoo-in."[29]

Asher actively promoted the series in the months leading up to its premiere, lavishing as much attention on Duke's casting as to the show itself. In a lengthy *Baltimore Sun* piece by Donald Kirkley (August 4, 1963), Asher took credit for the show's twinning premise: "I wanted to do a series about two 18-year-old girls living with a widowed father [n.b.], who had a hard time coping with them," and claimed later to have realized that Duke had the talent to play both. A few months after the show had begun to air, critic Kirkley judged it "still in the yes-and-no category," and that he was waiting for it to get better. The twinning gimmick, he maintained, was robbing the series of the necessary time and energy to create better, more novel scripts. For him, "The main gimmick . . . loses its value after one demonstration," maintaining that it did the talented Duke no favors either, as she was "forever stealing scenes from herself."[30]

That difficult duality was reflected in the rather gimmicky production set-up. Duke was obliged to use two separate dressing rooms, each filled with wigs, costumes, and other items evoking each cousin's personality, and she ran back and forth as shooting required. The crew was instructed to call her "Patty" or "Cathy," depending on the identity she was inhabiting at the moment—a detail not that far removed from the Rosses punishing her for breaking her assigned role of the day.

In another, even more unsavory detail that echoes her treatment by the Rosses, Asher boasted that, "In the studio during the day we have completely eliminated Patty Duke as a person." He recalls that he once told the young actress that Cathy was stealing Patty's scenes (as that reviewer had noted), adding, "It's beginning to be a little schizo." When Patty Duke herself entered that on-set reportage and was queried by Asher, "'Do you know who you are right now?' . . . She laughed, shrugged and, with little choice but to play along, answered, 'I'll just go home and figure it out.'"[31]

How They Did It

If Asher's memory later in life was fuzzy about whether he or Sheldon had come up with the idea of identical cousins, he recalled vividly that "playing two characters took a lot of time [and expense]."[32] That "how did they do it" question was not only key to the show's fundamental gimmick, but generated enough curiosity and interest in *The Patty Duke Show* so as to perhaps rival even its catchy theme song in terms of audience interest.

How in fact *did* they do it? Scenes had to be shot at least twice to get footage for Duke to appear as two characters in the same shot. To do this, the camera—a single one, as O'Keefe confirmed—had to remain in a precisely fixed position, and nothing on set could be altered between takes.[33] In the first, Duke would perform the scene on one side of an inviolate dividing line (with the film stock matted over so that the other half wouldn't be exposed) and then repeat the scene on the other side of the line, changing outfits in between, for a new strip of film matted to block out the first space. The director and camera operator had to meticulously time and choreograph Duke's body placements and movements and her facial cues to maintain screen direction and reaction shots. After shooting, the two filmstrips were fed into an optical printer and rephotographed.[34]

The results were highly successful—only a few episodes reveal the join line. (For less complicated over-the-shoulder shots in scenes with both twins, the show used a double [Patricia Landy] who was shot from behind.

Figure 2.7 A Rare Sighting of the Optical Line

On this front, though, it doesn't take much work to notice that Duke's stand-in doesn't quite match up; Landy is slightly thinner and taller than Duke.)[35] In a few scenes—notably, one in the pilot—where Patty and Cathy circle one another and the viewer can well see the dividing line, the "how they did it" question emerges just a bit more (Figure 2.7). Later, Duke recalled how proud she was of a system she claimed to have devised during filming to ensure that the two takes with herself lined up. She recorded her own dialogue during the first take as one cousin and played it back as she depicted the other in the second take. Most actors would have used a script reader.

The Pilot

Produced and directed by William Asher, the unaired pilot of *The Patty Duke Show* presents the show's main characters, its twinning premise, and themes that will run throughout the series, although some establishing details would morph. It begins with the Lane family preparing for Cathy's imminent arrival from Scotland to their residence in San Francisco (not Brooklyn Heights). The Lane home is more upscale than it would be in the actual series: a brief exterior shot reveals that the Lanes' "middle-class" home is actually a mansion, and inside there is a maid, rooms filled with chandeliers and cut flowers, and a far more elaborate staircase. Interiors were shot at Goldwyn Studios in Los Angeles, and little use was made of the San Francisco location where a second unit had been dispatched for exteriors; a few shots place the newly arrived Cathy within the city, but most used generic cutaways to present the sights she was taking in.

The initial glimpse of the home's exterior is superimposed with a close-up of Patty, and then her boyfriend Richard as he drives over. He strides to the door and announces to her that he's decided to "pin" her over Sue-Ellen, the girl who will be Patty's rival throughout the series. Patty kisses him, to her younger brother's disgust (here, Ross is played by Fifties/Sixties child actor Charles Herbert).[36]

Martin (again, Mark Miller) works as the managing editor at the *San Francisco Express*. He is introduced in a heated phone argument with his boss, J. R. (played with gusto by character actor John McIver, who continued the role in the series), after the latter has made changes to one of Martin's editorials. Martin angrily threatens to "take a plane to Tahiti and never come back," exuding far more bravado than Schallert likely would have. Taking the threat literally, J. R. blasts his secretary, "The only one who is irreplaceable at the paper is me! Lane can be replaced!"

The next scene is brief. Cathy is seated in a plane flying to San Francisco from Scotland. Initially filmed from behind while she looks out the window, Cathy turns to face the camera and gives audiences the reveal of a second Patty Duke. Her backstory unfolds in conversation with a stewardess; Cathy, born in Boston, has spent most of her life with her widowed father in Scotland, a fact that immediately instills her with a cosmopolitanism that will run throughout the show. But her father's busy travel schedule has convinced him to move her to his twin brother's home in the United States to attend high school there.

Cathy bears little trace of a Scottish brogue in the pilot. In Duke's account, one confirmed by *TV Guide* in advance of the show, she had perfected it too strongly, and producers "got nervous that the viewers wouldn't like or understand it so they decided on a general European nothing accent, a kind of 'anyplace but America' speech."[37] The softness with which the character speaks is its most pronounced feature. To hint at her discarded Scottishness, the pilot has Cathy wear a tartan beret and play traditional Scottish tunes on the bagpipes.

The pilot's farcical elements begin once the Lanes pack themselves into a car to pick Cathy up at the airport. The traffic scarcely moves, and they miss her flight. Cathy, who has already disembarked, first calls their home (where the maid, vacuuming with the television on, cannot hear the ringing phone) and then decides to go to Martin's newspaper office in San Francisco to look for him there. At the office, J. R.'s secretary confuses Cathy for Patty (mistaken identities being as key to farce as missed rendezvous) and, after asking where her father is (by which she means Martin), the secretary relays the teenager's response, "Glasgow." Infuriated, J. R. blasts a perplexed Cathy: "I hope he enjoys living in Scotland!"

Cathy arrives at the Lane household before the family returns and is greeted by the maid, who, taking her for Patty, orders her to clean up her room. Richard returns to the front door and, mistaking the cousin for the newly pinned Patty, kisses her twice, and is slapped twice in return. He runs off, presumably to pin Sue-Ellen. When the family finally returns from their botched trip to the airport, it takes them a while to realize that Cathy is already there, while the television audience gets the more privileged point of view through a well-timed sequence of near-visual misses: in one, Cathy crosses the front of the set with a pile of laundry mere seconds before Martin, Natalie, Patty, and Ross enter the home in back; moments later, she closes her cousin Patty in a hall closet, assuming the door is simply ajar.

Patty and Cathy finally meet almost a minute and a half into the sequence and, when they do, they circle each other via optical effect. Patty goes, "Holy moly—it's me!" Adds Ross: "I don't know if I can stand two of them!" (Tiger, the family's Old English sheepdog, who appears in the series only occasionally and without fanfare, does a couple of doubletakes as well, a bit of footage later re-used in the opening credits when the series was picked up.) Natalie greets Cathy warmly, telling her niece, "You're the most exciting thing that's happened to this family in years!," an odd remark given that the show used the reserved cousin as the quiet, calming counterpoint to Patty's zany American teenager.

The next scene, and the show's most well known, replays the Marx Brothers' "mirror sequence" from Duck Soup. The identical cousins mimic each other's expressions and gestures as they face one another in a nonexistent mirror. It's a clever gag for showcasing both Duke's abilities as a performer and the special effects that made the scene possible. The sequence was cut in subsequently as a flashback in an episode that aired at the end of Season 1 in which Cathy and Patty were reminiscing about Cathy's arrival, and it also closes the opening credit sequence in every episode of the show's first two seasons.

Three main sequences follow the mirroring scene. In the first, Patty and Cathy get to know one another in their soon-to-be shared bedroom by contrasting Paul Anka to opera; or Patty's slang ("goof," "rocking the mashed potato") to, of all things, Cathy's ability to spout phrases in Latin. Both agree that Cathy seems to be "from another planet." But Patty immediately sees potential in her being there: "what a weapon we have on our hands! Separately, we're two girls who have a few talents, just like anybody else. Your brain— I like sports; you like opera—I like to dance. But together, we're really on the beam. . . . we can be in two different places at the same time." (Ever the schemer, Patty immediately thinks of Cathy attending her Latin class for her.)

The second sequence has the two of them plotting to play a trick on the family (in the series itself, Cathy rarely initiates the hijinks). Patty goes downstairs in the guise of Cathy and hears a mouthful of critical comments about her (Patty) from her parents and brother as they try to welcome the girl whom they have mistaken as Cathy into the household: Patty, they declare, needs a "steady influence"; she is "less mature," "flighty" and "sometimes a little selfish." Patty returns upstairs in tears, angry at her cousin to whom she has just been so quickly and unfavorably compared. Seeing this, Cathy goes downstairs as Patty and gets the gist of the previous conversation, saying under her breath "I have to prove to her that I'm on her side." Cathy redeems herself by answering the doorbell and, seeing Richard again, kisses him quickly. When he asks her to explain why she "clobbered" him earlier, Cathy instructs him to "Yell 'Patty.'" Though confused, he complies, and after an excited Patty zooms down the staircase and Richard sees the cousins side by side, says "Holy cow, I've got a harem!" Richard and Patty are re-pinned.

The final sequence resecures Martin's job at the paper. He is clearly not comfortable staying at home and fumes when he reads what he calls the "flat" editorial of that day's paper. We cut to J. R. in the newspaper office and having the same reaction. When the two talk on the phone, J. R., still believing that his employee is in Scotland, employs the loud voice sometimes required by long distance calls of the time. When Martin finally realizes that J. R. thinks he is in Scotland, he whispers it to the family, and Cathy picks up her bagpipes to fabricate a sense of location. Afterward, Martin coos that it is "all because of Cathy" that J. R. agreed to stop interfering with Martin's editorials and, in a line of twinning dialogue, tells Cathy "You're the most exciting thing that's happened to this family in years." The pilot closes with the family singing along to Cathy's bagpipes. Instead of "The End" appearing over its closing image, there is a hopeful "The beginning . . . of the Patty Duke Show."

Evident is the absence of Sid Ramin's clever theme (obviously, there can be no mention yet of "Brooklyn Heights" here), and arranger/composer Sonny Burke, known for his work in the Big Band era, receives music credit. Burke's involvement probably explains the difference between the pilot's background music and the actual show's, which revealed a greater jazz influence in its final year. Svengali John Ross is credited as associate producer.

Overall, the pilot was a solid effort that productively established the show's premise and themes and gave a tantalizing glimpse into its comedic potential. We can only conjecture why ABC never aired it. At over twenty-nine minutes, it might have been too long to be broadcast with commercial breaks, or it might have seemed slightly obsolete when production moved to New York. Still, the last episode of Season 1 uses portions of it as flashbacks, and several clips from it appear in the series' opening credits, including the mirror scene, Patty racing down the stairs, and the family dog Tiger.[38]

Behind the Scenes of the Pilot

Several drafts for the pilot exist in the Sidney Sheldon papers at USC and reveal paths untaken. "Patty" initially is named "Nancy" (boyfriend Richard is "Tommy" and Martin's twin brother is "Greg," not Kenneth), but "Nancy" drops out as the drafts are refined, with a crossing out by hand and "Patty" written above the effaced "Nancy," suggesting a late but definitive alteration. All drafts for the show's pilot are set in San Francisco, with one early exception that has the family living in Sausalito; that locale is crossed out on the draft and "Palo Alto" is penciled in its place.

Quite strikingly for a series that would turn out to be fairly unadventurous in visual style, one draft for the pilot contains a fantasy montage in which Patty, immediately aware of the "weapon" she has in having a twin, makes use of Cathy to pass a Latin test, beat Richard at swimming, and take over her piano practice so she can sneak out with Richard. ("We are projecting Patty's fantasy. . . " the draft states simply.) But a revised script eliminates the montage, replacing it with what would be used in the actual pilot: Patty simply listing vocally the crafty things she can do with a double in her life, including succeeding in her Latin class.

The successive drafts contain a weird, sustained subplot that disappears from the actual pilot. In these variants, only Martin heads to meet Cathy's plane—Natalie stays home to prepare the house for Cathy's arrival, and Ross and Patty are at school. In a bizarre plot twist, Martin accosts Cathy at the airport, thinking it's Patty who's skipped school to greet her cousin (no one in the Lane family seems to know about the twinning). When Cathy screams to be saved from this seeming stranger, airport security takes notice. At the police station, after Martin explains that Patty skipped school to be at the airport, the police call Patty's school and learn she's been there all day. When they finally release the *paterfamilias*, he goes home where an alarmed Cathy, who has by now arrived at the Lanes, identifies him as the masher from the airport. Eventually, when the cousins manage to be in the same room, everything is set right. Martin says to Cathy, "At the airport—I must have scared you out of your wits."

Perhaps Sheldon, or others, perceived the masher subplot to be too far-fetched to include in the final script—if Cathy knows that her dad and Martin are twins, why wouldn't she recognize Martin at the airport? Or perhaps the idea of a man accosting a young woman seemed too indecorous for TV comedy. Yet it's worth noting that the same year that the *Patty Duke* pilot scripts were being fashioned, ad campaigns for Stanley Kubrick's adaptation of Nabokov's *Lolita* flooded American media, insisting on the scandalous nature of the story's pedophilia by asking, "How did they ever make a movie of *Lolita*?" Film could exploit topics that TV predictably wouldn't go near.

The Show's Premiere and Initial Reception

The Patty Duke Show premiered on Wednesday, September 18, 1963, in ABC's evening lineup. Initially airing at 7 p.m., between *Ozzie and Harriet* and *The Price Is Right*, it was soon moved to the more desirable 8 p.m. slot, where it stayed through most of its run. In its 1964–65 season, ABC followed *The Patty Duke Show* with teen-targeted music show *Shindig*, and in 1965–66, it led into *Gidget*, solidifying the network's commitment to tween and teen girls. It's possible that ABC, consistently ranked at the bottom of the broadcast networks, was more willing to take risks, such as handing its Wednesday lineup over to a relatively untried young, female audience.[39]

Despite the fact that Westerns were highest in ratings, *The Patty Duke Show* did quite well. At its debut, Nielsen ratings showed that while it didn't beat NBC's *The Virginian*, the popular Western programmed against it, it outperformed CBS's public affairs offerings like *The Chronicle* and *CBS Reports*. Articles frequently mentioned the "millions" of viewers tuning in, and Moya Luckett notes, "*Patty Duke* was the unexpected big hit of the 1963–64 season, its first episode rated number two overall and number one amongst new shows, with a 'whopping 48 share.'"[40] For even the fraught week after the Kennedy assassination, Nielsen ranked the show sixteen out of the top twenty shows (*The Beverly Hillbillies* was number one and would remain so for a long time).

While existing paper trails are thin, girls and other young viewers clearly took to *The Patty Duke Show*. *Calling All Girls*, a monthly magazine dedicated to younger girls and tweens, ran a cover story on the star (its title, of course, emphasized the show's doubling, "The Two Faces of Patty Duke: TV's Top Teenager") in which Duke jokingly, and heartbreakingly, says, "Sometimes I think I'm becoming a split personality."[41] *Good Housekeeping* was among countless others with similar titles; its "The Double Life of Patty Duke," of course, had no idea about the double life the star was actually leading, although it included lines such as "offscreen as well as on, television's big little star has two roles, two families—and twice as much talent as any teenager around."[42]

In a promotional piece published by *Variety* several months after the show appeared, series personnel reflected back on the origins of the show, publicly musing, as Asher and Sheldon had in private conversations, on the original challenge of finding a project for the multitalented Duke. "How could you take advantage of her tremendous ability when most teenage roles had become stereotyped long ago? The answer was to *un*stereotype her role. Instead of giving Patty only one part, give her *two* parts—identical cousins with diametrically opposed personalities." The article goes on to boast that by January 1964, "Over 12,700,000 homes tune in every week. Patty's devoted followers include over 15,500,000 grownups, many of them young adults with children of their own."[43]

By the end of its first season, the show had been picked up by countries as widespread as Nigeria, England, Mexico, Finland, Peru, Serbia, Australia, Thailand, Argentina, Brazil, and Spain. (Distributors worked assiduously to get their shows licensed in other regions, but that didn't guarantee that they were aired there.) In an undated letter to Sheldon, Duke speaks glowingly of the series' success while on a promotional tour of Japan, and her delight at meeting the *two* young women who did the dubbing for Patty and Cathy (splitting the work that Duke did single-handedly for her US viewers).

Though in its first season, it made the top twenty, in the next, it fell to twenty-eight, and, for Schallert at least, the "handwriting was on the wall." What accounted for the decline? For Schallert, "no one watched" *CBS Reports*, a news program that ran against his series, until one of its episodes featured the Kennedys, after which, he claims, "our ratings were in the toilet." At that point, he noted, the viewing audience, which *The Patty Duke Show* had hitherto essentially shared only with NBC, was split among the three top networks. In its third and final year, *The Patty Duke Show* was pitted against the new *Lost in Space*, another family sitcom, though with more dramatic and science fiction elements, which featured tween girl (Angela Cartwright) and younger brother (Bill Mumy). At that point, Schallert opined, our "ratings tanked."[44]

The Show Unfolds

The inaugural episode of *The Patty Duke Show*, "The French Teacher," guest stars Jean-Pierre Aumont and features a surprisingly generic plotline that makes little use of the show's premise of twinning. It opens with Patty receiving failing grades on her report card, and, since her parents have to sign off on it, she tries to pass Cathy's card off as her own, a substitution that has little to do with their being twins.

Patty develops a crush on her French teacher and mistakes his interest in her schoolwork for romantic reciprocity. Suddenly, Patty throws herself into studying French (the subject she received her lowest grades in), wearing her hair up in a bun, baking brioche, and pretentiously dropping phrases in French. When Martin meets the teacher (not knowing that Patty has a crush on him), he congratulates him for inspiring Patty to improve her grades, referring to the instructor in a self-conscious detail as a "miracle worker." But when the teacher tells him that Patty is infatuated with him ("I think she wants to marry me"), the concerned and angry father retorts, "It would serve you right." Meanwhile, the rejected Richard, seeking attention, threatens to drop out of school and join the merchant marines. He falters at school and is kicked off the football team. For whatever reason, this news brings Patty back to her senses. She "breaks up" with the French teacher, who, though empathically relieved, goes on to enact stereotypes of Frenchness, reputing the preposterous idea that he had been romantically rejected, and so on.

There had been plenty of buzz for the show before it aired, thanks primarily to the excitement of Duke's move to television and its strange premise. But reviews written after that first episode were mixed. "The TV Scout," a syndicated column that assessed the potential of new shows, hailed Duke as a "brilliant young actress," but noted the premiere's storyline was "hardly a new idea or an auspicious beginning for the series." This column added though that the second episode, "improves considerably over its debut."[45] The *Los Angeles Times* lauded the cast's acting chops but found the writing lacking, entitling its initial review "Patty's Show Triumphs over a Weak Script" but went on to say that "it still had the makings of a cute series." Notably, the reviewer attributed *Patty Duke*'s potential as "family" fare *not* to its novel teen-girl-oriented perspective but to its compatibility with older, domestic sitcoms stuffed with intergenerational comedic conflict told from the perspective of the parents. "With better material," he writes, "this cast could produce award-winning family-series in the *Father Knows Best* or *Donna Reed* vein."[46]

The first episode, in addition to initiating the trope of Patty developing crushes on older, often professional men, sets other recurring themes into motion. Most salient is how Patty flirts with a rose-colored, clichéd view of a world beyond Brooklyn Heights. As in several other episodes, she embraces a romanticized French culture just as quickly as she arbitrarily dismisses it. Normalcy is restored when Patty returns to being an average teen, as enacted through her relationship with Richard, her poor grades, and her boisterous, unpretentious Americanness.

Again, little in the inaugural episode involves confusing the twins. Indeed, it fails to energize, or scarcely even to activate, the series' premise— Cathy isn't even in the French class where Patty falls for the dreamy teacher. In a very real sense, the episode is a harbinger of what's to come. This was noted in another initial review: "The purpose of having the star play two parts . . . wasn't quite spelled out in the series' opener, 'The French Teacher.' "[47] Indeed, the two of us were both surprised that *The Patty Duke Show* as a whole didn't make more use of twinning as a resource for flipped identities and the farce and chaos that would then ensue, as the pilot had so effectively done.

Selling "Patty Duke"

Under the watchful eyes of Ethel and John Ross, the series' creators assumed that Patty Duke's status as a teen star could be exploited across other media and commodity platforms catering to middlebrow teens and preteens. Duke was compelled to advertise various products on television, record those pop records, give interviews to adult and girls' magazines, and lend her image or name (as Patty Duke, not Lane) to an extensive array of ancillary products, including novels, board games, paper dolls, puzzles, even jewelry kits, and geisha robes. In *Call Me Anna*, Duke states that she never saw "a dime" for her clothing line and other tie-ins but noticed that the Rosses' vacations were suddenly becoming quite lavish.[48]

Although the era's girl fans were likely to skew slightly younger and less in charge of their wallets than their male counterparts, they were not so young that they couldn't pester their parents to buy items for them. Breck shampoo was included in the show's credits (and Duke did ads for them as well), and a line of clothing was sold under Duke's name—ironic for Duke, who disliked Patty's and Cathy's outfits, finding them of tune with the times. The Patty Duke fashion line was produced by the Juniorite clothing firm, which also designed Duke's outfits for the series and, at the end of 1963, started offering a line of Patty Duke casual clothing—dresses, culottes, bathing suits—in petite sizes 3–13. An outrageously creepy 1964 ad in *Women's Wear Daily* features a businessman's piercing eyes at the top of the page, under which a question appears in large type: "Are you taking advantage of all the juniors 5'1" and under?" "We do!" and clarifies, channeling Humbert Humbert, "We love every one of them . . . they represent a billion dollar sportswear market." The ad's crude implications were underscored by a smaller-sized graphic of a beaming Patty Duke inside a circle that looked like a bull's eye (Figure 2.8).[49]

From documents in the Sidney Sheldon archives we learn that, in its first year, the series grossed over two and a half million dollars, including syndication and foreign sales. Merchandise licensing brought in another eighty-five thousand, of which UA-ZIV claimed thirty-four thousand as a "handling" fee; twenty-one thousand (25 percent) went to "Patty Duke," that is, the Rosses.

A budget, also found in the archives, spells out that all licensing, foreign sales, and syndication incomes would be measured against the show's outlay of expenses, which included $2,000 per episode as a "production fee" to UA-TV; payments to backup writers, including for unused scripts (total: $9,500);

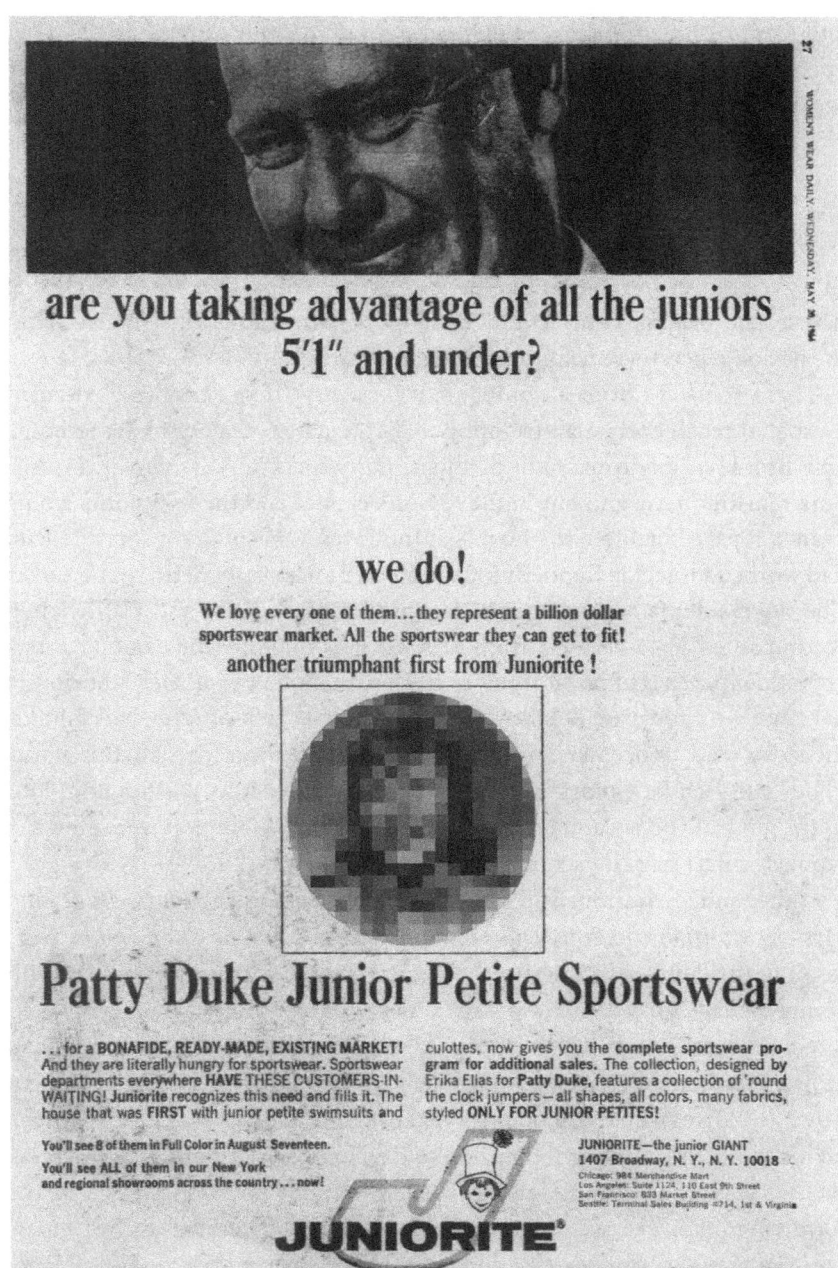

and fees to William Asher ($1,000 per episode), Stanley Prager ($1,500 per episode as producer, $1,750 as director), assistant director Harry Falk Jr. (around $12,000 total), and talent and crew, and others.

To the Teens: Beyond *The Patty Duke Show*

In its references to the eventual tie-ins, sponsorships, and other marketing devices, the original contract for Duke's work in the show is instructive about the period's lucrative, commodified teen culture.

Three spin-off novels accompanied *The Patty Duke Show* and extended its spatial reach and narrative options by traveling outside the Lane home and Brooklyn environs. One of them, *Patty Goes to Washington* (1964), puts Martin on assignment in the nation's capital and the kids come along. Frances Spatz Leighton, the novel's author, was a Washington socialite who had worked for Jackie Kennedy and published an account of that experience. The novel adopts an anodyne pedagogical tone as Patty and Cathy, often accompanied by cute guys from around Washington (for example, congressional pages and naval trainees from Annapolis), visit sites laboriously narrated with touristic detail. With its noticeable lack of screwball hijinks, the story reads more like a project of Americanization than anything else. (The "Patty Duke Coloring Book" also entails a visit to Washington, DC. In the glow of JFK's Camelot, real-life voyages to Washington were almost a requisite pilgrimage for schoolchildren on field trips.)[50]

Quite unlike the touristic *Patty Goes to Washington*, *Patty Duke and Mystery Mansion* and *Patty Duke and the Adventure of the Chinese Junk* were resolute thrillers, and closer to the *Nancy Drew* franchise so popular with young teenage girls.[51] As they track quickly into suspense, their plots venture far from the everyday life in the Lane household that TV audiences had grown accustomed to seeing. In *Mystery Mansion*, Patty and Cathy help an elderly widower whose distant relatives are trying to drive mad in order to sell off his sepulchral Brooklyn mansion to developers. Along the way, the book accrues ghostly sightings (actually gaslighting schemes orchestrated by the conniving relatives), secret passageways, and frantic car chases. In *Chinese Junk*, Patty and Cathy, vacationing with their family in the woods, foil a nefarious plot against a grizzled but friendly sea captain. This novel piles on scene after scene of boat chases, fisticuffs (Richard, more macho than in the TV series, saves the day), further ghostly visitations, secret compartments filled with riches, menacing strangers, and even a wildcat that causes a frightened Patty to fall into a ravine and be knocked unconscious (fortunately, an aspiring folk singer passes by and pulls Patty out with her banjo!). Credibility is nowhere in sight. Ridiculous as these tales of mystery and adventure may seem, they nonetheless give young readers octane-fueled fantasies of self-empowerment in the absence of adults—and, more specifically, of girls operating largely independently of boys and men (see Figure 2.9).

Like the series itself, the tie-in adventure novels always return to the Lane home in the end, reaffirming the initiatory assumptions of domesticity. Nothing, in other words, happens in these novels to change or challenge the sitcom's premise and promise of life back home.

Unlike these adventure/thriller novels, *The Patty Duke Show* itself was firmly rooted in an ostensibly everyday, contemporary vision of all-American reality. At the same time, there were constant temptations for Sixties sitcoms like *The Patty Duke Show* to dip into more fantastic realms of derring-do and exotic exploits, and plenty of episodes, especially in the last season, took that up, coming to resemble the tie-in novels in that way.

Whereas the Patty Duke novels and coloring book tell stories that remove us from the anodyne reality of Brooklyn life only to return to it, the Milton-Bradley board game for the series (1964) surrenders storytelling altogether. Players have to match (twin) cards that show the kind of activities that middle-class teen girls were expected to indulge in: "playing records," "dancing," "watching TV," "water skiing," "babysitting," "shopping," "going to movies," "sipping soda," "telephoning," and, of course, "talking." None of the activities hint at a plotline or eventual vocation for the girls. Even the "Studying" card pictures Patty fiddling with a radio instead of hitting the books, which, of course, Cathy is shown doing (Figure 2.10).

End of the Line: Season 3

Taken as a whole, the episodes of the third year of *The Patty Duke Show* suggest that the series' best ideas had run their course. To be sure, the season included several standout episodes, such as "Fiancée for a Day," but most brought little new to the series and instead disclosed its showmakers' straying attention. Cheap gags suffused the episodes, abetted by a more pronounced laugh track and sillier, generic plot lines: the Lanes adopt kittens, Patty wants to be a spy, Patty ties up the family's telephone line, and so on.

Figure 2.9 *Mystery Mansion*: Richard Does a Double Take. Illustration by Wilbur A. Howe, from *Patty Duke and Mystery Mansion* by Doris Schroeder, Whitman Publishing Company, 1964

Figure 2.10 Playing the Patty Duke Game Across Generations. Photograph Courtesy of Andrew Shappard

The opening credits, including "Cousins," were given acoustic and visual facelifts that year (for further discussion, see "Coda"), now ending on a freeze frame of Patty, pensively walking down a sidewalk, a twin notably alone. Palm trees are plainly visible behind her (how is this still Brooklyn Heights?) in marked contrast to the opening credit's iconic sequence of the first two years, which concluded with the cousins at the mirror, mimicking one another and cracking up in laughter. Now, Cathy is nowhere to be found, much less showcased, and the absence of the mirror sequence confirms the last season's movement away from twinning, doubling, and, as we will see, Cathy's relevance to the show altogether.

Unsurprisingly, given the move to Los Angeles, more of the series was now shot outdoors. From a production standpoint, exterior shots were of course more economical, reducing costs associated with lighting, set design, and so forth. There are views of tree-lined streets with sidewalks and free-standing homes (not row-houses) that look like nothing of Brooklyn Heights of the time. The Lane homestead now is architecturally more at one with SoCal than it ever would have been in New York. It is conspicuously larger and has a sizable front lawn, unlike before, where the front door opened onto a

Figure 2.11 A Tent Grows in Brooklyn: Fake Camping on a Fake Set in a Real Borough

few parking spaces. The Lanes were now also given a backyard, though one clearly shot on set, given its artificial look (Figure 2.11). (O'Keefe recalls that the show was primarily shot on a satellite lot of Paramount.)[52]

The last season also upped the formal gimmicks of the series. Along with the more conspicuous laugh track, frequent iris-ins and -outs connect scenes, and are almost always accompanied by the obvious sound of a studio clapboard. These stylistic flourishes gave the show a low-cost means of appearing to be modernized or updated—and such inexpensiveness mattered. The easily deployed effects may well have compensated for the costlier (and far more time-consuming) technique of split-screen filming, which itself was newly minimized by Cathy's increased absence.[53] Along with ABC's stubborn refusal to film in color, such modest and compensatory formal devices reveal a literally diminished investment in *The Patty Duke Show* on the part of its producers.

Just as *The Patty Duke Show* appeared to be flirting with a hipper, more modern (or at least "West Coast") look and sound in the opening sequence, depictions of the Lane characters and their interrelationships, by contrast, took a decidedly backward turn. Suddenly, Natalie hangs around in the kitchen, sporting a more constrained hairstyle (pulled back) and a white apron while performing household tasks. The signs of her shift to full-time housewife are purely visual, unremarked upon in dialogue or plotlines, drawing our attention away from the regressive, lazy turns of the series. Precisely when the country's sociopolitical realities were moving away from such clichés around women, *The Patty Duke Show* became even more out of touch. Third-season Natalie and other characters are straight out of central casting of the late Fifties, whose well-worn images of domesticity subordinate the wives into the role of housebound partners of authoritative male lords of the manor.

To be sure, this did not happen all at once in Season 3. Plenty of silly episodes aired before then and, as early as Season 2, directors had Jean Byron and others mugging it up in reactive close-ups. But Season 3 raised the ante considerably. In "Our Daughter the Artist" (S3E5), Natalie reacts to Patty's earnest attempts at abstract modernist painting with exaggerated facial contortions, complete with bug eyes, which the camera captures in a freeze frame and encircled by an iris, to end the show's pre-credit sequence (Figure 2.12).

Figure 2.12 Bug-Eyed Mom

Martin is similarly transformed into a retro cliché. By 1966, the white sitcom-dad-as-problem-solver was unquestionably past its expiry date. But that's what producers and writers resurrected, creating Martin as a less tolerant, less bemused observer of Patty's escapades, cloaking him in the fraying clichés of white male moral authority from the fathers of instructive sitcoms such as *Father Knows Best, Leave It to Beaver*, and *My Three Sons*. Suddenly, Martin is golfing and hunting with male buddies and a newfound masculinization anchors episodes such as "Poppo's Birthday," in which Martin covets a Swiss Army knife advertised in a hunting magazine (when the kids find the clipping, they think their dad wants the far pricier rifle pictured on the reverse side).

The season also has Martin orating unending lessons to his daughter, which has the effect of both forcing the assistance of an older generation to help the teen resolve her escapades and of wrapping up individual installments, giving him more narrative power. In "Too Young and Foolish to Go Steady" (S03E23), he scolds Patty for inventing a new boyfriend to inflame Richard's jealousy, and in "Don't Bank on It" (S3E28), he sends Patty to the bank to make a deposit on his behalf and, when she misses the bank's closing hours, remains bizarrely punitive and cantankerous for the rest of the episode. The rebooted Martin is emphatically on view in the aforementioned "Do You Trust Your Daughter?" (S3E25), when Martin believes that Patty, out on a date with a slightly older man, has ignored her midnight curfew (she hasn't, and the misunderstanding structures the episode's thin plotline). His anger, which swells with each ticking minute, is difficult to align with the mild-mannered Martin we'd come to appreciate.

The transformation of Mr. and Mrs. Lane redirected the series' focus, placing far more weight on intergenerational relationships, particularly the father–daughter one. (How many sitcoms featured mother–daughter relationships at the time?) It was an odd pivot for a series that had initially, and appreciably, constructed Martin as a benign, reactive figure to Patty and her various exploits. Patty in turn becomes slightly more obsequious. Rather than pursuing her own adventures to widen her sense of self, she turns to Daddy worship. In "The Greatest Speaker in the Whole Wide World" (S3E20), she finds herself on her eternal quest of landing a guest for a school function, here for her creative writing class. She selects Martin, comparing him to LBJ in terms of the men's import and rhetorical skills.

Like us, Moya Luckett has noted that, in reducing Cathy's influence and presence, Patty's role was remodeled. Instead of being a cousin or a teen hell-raiser, now she is first and foremost a daughter, a cog within the predetermined confines of a heteronormative white family. In short, this last season transforms the series into a conventional, parent-oriented domestic sitcom, zeroing in on Patty' relationship with her parents over the one she has with Richard and, more importantly, with Cathy, who had been her partner in so many escapades and fantasies.[54]

In an essay on mid-Sixties spy shows and their parodies, Tricia Jenkins argues that commercial TV at the time was losing a sense of freshness and originality. Things seem to reach a low point when in 1965 no Peabodys—the prestigious award for excellence in television—were awarded. She observes that the TV industry was turning massively to what she terms "retreads" — new iterations of formulaic genre work (such as the 1966-67 one-seasoner *The Girl from U.N.C.L.E.*) as a cheap, easy way to maintain the popularity of the medium, eager to grow, but saddled with new expenses such as filming in color. Jenkins's argument seems to intimate that in the mid-Sixties, many sitcoms had reached their peak and were now beginning a decline in quality of humor as they found little to do but fall back on parody or pratfall comedy.[55]

Indeed, as the storylines of *The Patty Duke Show* got sillier, slapstick and parody started trumping originality. More than one installment has Patty going on bird-brained spy capers that fit Jenkins's notion of the uninventive retread. In one especially inane one, Patty cons Cathy and Ross into joining her as she trails a visiting British friend of Cathy's father whom Patty believes to be a secret agent who is up to no good. Donning the fraying tropes of trench coats and sunglasses, Patty and company skulk across cafes, movie theaters, and other locations that lead to a big narrative nowhere. This episode was entitled "The Girl from N.E.P.H.E.W." after the popular series *The Man From U.N.C.L.E.* (1964–68) and its spin-off, *The Girl from U.N.C.L.E.*, manifesting *The Patty Duke Show*'s desire for contemporary currency and tongue-in-cheek parody, even as the results ultimately read as uninspired.

Truth be told, the fatigue was everywhere evident and not just in the easy knockoff installments. Whereas the comedy had previously derived from Patty's can-do American energy and experimentation with social roles, the series now devolved into quick, reactive gags. In an episode in which she flails against her camping tent, fast-motion filming (something the series had never employed before) renders its ballooning even more ridiculous. In "A Very Phon-y Situation" (S3E16), when Patty demonstrates a weight-reduction belt to her family and guests, the contraption predictably overheats and singes her in a slapstick sequence more typical of Lucy Ricardo than Patty Lane.

Some of the last season's episodes doubled back on other ones, in another kind of twinning or self-cannibalizing retreading. There are two spy caper episodes and two involving fortune tellers: in Season 1, Patty had convinced herself she was psychic and set up shop at home. But by Season 3, after staking out a "phony" fortune teller, she helps the police arrest the woman, transforming her character from a teen with entrepreneurial gumption to one who submits to the gatekeepers of law and order. "Operation Tonsils" (S3E2), in which Patty develops a crush on her surgeon (Troy Donahue), recycles "The French Teacher" and "Don't Monkey With Mendel" (S2E26, featuring science teacher Robert Goulet and discussed later).

Like Duke, critics took note of what would be the series' final season. *Variety* noted, "In its third season *The Patty Duke Show* looks a little stale. The adventures of the typical teenage girl appear to lack the fresh spark that ignited the half-hour series the previous season.... [The script of 'Operation Tonsils'] had many twists and turns but failed to strike fresh chords." One of the faults, the writer conjectured, was that that episode explored a "theme long associated with teenage fiction, that of puppy love, and while the half-hour was diverting, it also had a stale quality...."[56]

Cancellation

It's not without irony that *The Patty Duke Show*'s growing embrace of stock depictions of the family and outmoded gender and generational functions occurred just as it was becoming clear, even for the mainstream of middle-class Americans, that the United States was moving into a period of open unrest. While conservatives retained power in juridical and governmental institutions, youthful and minoritarian populations were openly questioning and rebelling against that political authority. Such pronounced shifts were yet another way of rendering *The Patty Duke Show* even more out of touch than it had always been.

Even in the limited space of its three-year run, many early young fans of the series were turning to ostensibly more rebellious forms of older teen culture (recall Douglas's "hinge years" or Schallert's comment that the series ran during "an odd time" in history). As Schallert put it, "we were on the cusp" and "got *some* things right in terms of the "coming-of-age-teenager" with guest stars like Chad and Jeremy, but "in a way, that dated us—we weren't part of the rock and roll generation."[57] (Male heartthrobs whose photos graced Patty's bedroom walls included Ricky Nelson, Vince Edwards, and Jimmy Dean, clean-cut singers who were not exactly rock-adjacent. And although these short-haired idols were not without teen popularity at the time—especially Nelson—it's more likely that fifteen-year-old girls would be hanging pictures of more recent cuties, such as The Beatles, a group to which the show makes periodic references.)

The show may have also been aging in another way. By the time of the third season, eighteen-year-old Duke was no longer a tween or even a "poor little in-between" like Billie, but a young woman, something that several episodes seem to acknowledge. In "Operation Tonsils"—in which Troy Donahue played the physician the cousins call "Dr. Dreamy"—Patty, learning that she'll have to have her tonsils out, responds to his disinterested, professional request for her age that, "I'm older than I look." It is far easier to read that remark as coming from Patty Duke than from Patty Lane. (Curiously, even though he's not credited with writing this episode, the line is verbatim with one Sidney Sheldon penned decades earlier in *The Bachelor and the Bobbysoxer*, also delivered by a teenage girl [Shirley Temple] to a handsome older man [Cary Grant].)

Again, surviving documents fail to indicate definitively why the series was canceled but plausible conjectures exist. For Schallert, it was declining ratings. Along with Duke, Paul O'Keefe maintains that the network balked at the higher cost of filming in color (ABC tended to restrict its use for specials.) Producers were also growing impatient with Duke's increasingly mercurial behavior. In our interview with him, O'Keefe speculated that the cancellation of the series might also have been connected to syndication, which generates profits without the need to generate new content. When the show ran, O'Keefe explained, all that was needed to go into syndication were three seasons worth of episodes. Given ABC's extensive cost-cutting on the show (it even reduced the number of guest stars), this hypothesis seems highly plausible.[58]

A brief notice from a January 26, 1966 issue of *Variety* hints at another possible factor. ABC was concerned about finding the right slot for its popular new youth-oriented show, *Batman*, which had premiered in 1965; for some reason, the series did best when it aired on a different night than *The Patty Duke Show*. Were Duke's declining ratings impacting tune-ins to *Batman*? ABC, the piece claimed, was taking a "wait-and-see" attitude to Duke's show and even considered suspending production of its last four planned episodes—and indeed, Season 3 ran four episodes shorter than the other two.[59] The cancellation may also have been connected to United Artist's decision to get out of television production, which would have left ABC to find a new producer had the network wanted to continue broadcasting the series. Whatever the reason, the decision to cancel was made abruptly once the third season wrapped. The last installments of *The Patty Duke Show* were light as air, unaware of any pressure to tie up loose ends, and as unimaginative and ridiculous as most of the year's output.

The Reunion TV Movie and PSAs

Thirty-three years after *The Patty Duke Show* ended, the cast reunited for a television movie, which aired on CBS in 1999. *The Patty Duke Show Reunion: Still Rockin' in Brooklyn Heights* centers around Patty and Cathy's old school, Brooklyn Heights High, which, if corrupt and snobby real-estate agent Sue-Ellen (Cindy Williams of *Laverne and Shirley*) gets her way, is about to be replaced by a shopping mall. Patty, now a longtime drama teacher at the school, helps lead a drive to match city funding to save it. The rest of her family shows up during Alumni Week in anticipation of Patty receiving (unbeknownst to her) a teaching award. The adult Ross (a barely recognizable Paul O'Keefe) is a Broadway producer; Richard (Eddie Applegate, who seems out of breath through much of the ninety minutes) owns a construction company. He and Patty are now divorced after twenty-seven years of marriage, having wed "too young," although he still pines for her, which Martin notices. (Just like the show, there seems to be an injunction against depicting the pair as a married couple.) Martin and Natalie (Schallert and Byron) arrive from out of state, and Cathy, a widow, flies in from Edinburgh with her son Liam, who is keen on attempting American accents. This resonates with the series' initial theme of performing identities, passing the baton to a newer generation.

Family and family loyalty give the movie its thematic foundation. Everyone plays a role in helping Patty save her high school, be it Natalie and Ross needling Sue-Ellen; Richard getting a second building inspector to look at the school after Sue-Ellen has sabotaged its pipes; Patty's granddaughter working with Liam to find a location for the celebrity party after the auditorium is temporarily condemned; or Martin, ever the newspaperman, doing some "deep digging" that reveals Sue-Ellen's criminal record as a realtor.

Unlike the series, which never operated in a perfect moral universe, the reunion contrasts good and bad agents in glaringly obvious strokes: bassoons and discordant music accompany Sue-Ellen, whose gestures are blunt and her speech snooty (she is outfitted in a leopard coat and owns a "Jag," no less.) In the end, she gets a custard pie thrown in her face, as does the accomplice-assistant she has been bossing around. All of this adds up to a character drawn as little more than a dastardly cartoon and leads to a happy ending with victory for the "good guys." Brooklyn Heights High will be saved; Martin has dug up enough dirt on Sue-Ellen's shady dealings to have the mayor's office investigate her, assuring that her evil deeds will not continue; Cathy decides to stay in the United States for a while and agrees to date an impossibly handsome, persistent local admirer named Rock. Richard and Patty agree to "start over," and seal the deal with a kiss, minutes after having sworn to each other that they'd given up on the opposite sex.

With its values of firm resolution over bad guys, the reunion movie seems very much in the mold of an after-school film, with corresponding low production values. In his late-life interview with the Television Academy, Schallert called it "an ill-considered redo."[60] A sample review didn't contest the point: "Was 'The Patty Duke Show' always this lame, or has it just become that way over the intervening generation or so? . . . What was once fresh and perky has grown stale and frightening. . . . So what new does 'Still Rockin in Brooklyn Heights' bring to the table. . . . Nothing. Nada. Zip."[61] Natalie Lane's public reference to Viagra arguably stands as its low point. There had been talk of getting Sidney Sheldon on board, but the show was ultimately written by a somewhat run-of-the-mill TV and film director Neal Israel ("based on characters created by Sidney Sheldon") and directed by Christopher Leitch (from unmemorable tele-films), neither of whom had anything to do with the original series. Duke executive produced.

To recount the trials and tribulations of the older Patty Lane's fundraising efforts, the reunion movie borrows from the plotlines of several *Patty Duke Show* episodes, most notably the iconic mirroring scene (Figure 2.13). In the new version, Patty discovers that Cathy has arrived at Brooklyn Heights High as each stares at her reflection on two sides of a glass door and they wonder if they're seeing something other than themselves. (Cathy had just

Figure 2.13 The Mirror Scene Mirrored

stumbled upon a school meeting to condemn Sue-Ellen's plans and steps up to impersonate an absent Patty.) After this, Cathy remarks in uninspired dialogue, "It's like old times, people mixing us up," a confusion that, as we've already noted and will discuss further in Chapter 4, scarcely existed on the original show.

The ever-villainous Sue-Ellen arranges and pays the two student leads of a school play of *Romeo and Juliet* (directed by drama teacher Patty) to disrupt the production by staging a squabble, and Patty and Richard are forced to step in for them at the last minute. Patty freezes in fear. At this moment, footage appears from the old series' episode in which Cathy and Richard discuss Patty's stage fright, which might have made sense in high school but seems incongruous now, given her career as a drama teacher. Once again, Cathy serves as a secondary lead to Patty as the narrative's gravitational center. In another allusion to the show, the older Patty is having trouble securing a star to lead her celebrity dance—she wants to recruit a singing actor named "Stone" Adams, a former drama student of hers (why are all the good-looking men stones or rocks?)—aping numerous episodes in which the young Patty is charged with landing talent for her high school dances. Even the telefilm's credit sequence is folded into the original show's, with updated color images of the lead characters cut in just after their younger, black-and-white counterparts appear.

By incorporating black-and-white footage from the original series, the telefilm amply reminded its audience of the passage of time, augmenting the nostalgia it relied on viewers having for the show and reminding them how young the now much-older actors had once been. Yet as much as the reunion movie banked on audience nostalgia, it featured a few departures as well. For example, many of its indoor scenes look as if they take place in actual buildings, especially Patty's home, rather than fabricated sets. (*Still Rockin'* was shot in Montreal as a budget-saving measure, due to tax incentives at the time.) A use of voiceovers (by Patty) to externalize the character's thoughts also distinguishes it from the series—and indicates its less than optimal writing and budget.

Like *The Patty Duke Show*, the reunion film is careful not to lay on the twinning premise too thickly but rather plops it into the plot occasionally. There is the scene at the high school where Patty's colleagues mistake Cathy for their fearless leader; the restaged mirror scene; the *Romeo and Juliet* play where Cathy tries to sub for panicked Patty; and a scene where Cathy distracts a security guard by disguising herself as Patty so that Patty can sneak onto a film set and invite Stone Adams to the high school event. Generally, though, the sense of performance that Duke had exuded while performing two twins is now displaced onto Cathy's son Liam, whose skills with accents is showcased when he impersonates the local city mayor on the phone.

The telefilm does its best to give Patty Lane the same high-voltage energy of her Sixties predecessor: the character is constantly on the move, dashing between appointments, leaving or entering rooms, devising schemes. Its opening scene tries to establish this frenetic, interruptive energy as Patty disrupts her granddaughter, who is trying to practice the piano, by playing rock music while exercising on another floor. "Our Patty likes to rock 'n roll": point made. But Patty (Lane or Duke) is no longer flippant or young, and details like this feel forced. More important is the fact that Duke, like her character who is intent on preserving her old high school, is trying to preserve her old television show by keeping it alive in cultural memory, something she had been unwilling to do earlier. By 1999 with *Still Rockin' in Brooklyn Heights*, Duke knew that the series, however hokey it might have been, had meant a great deal to fans across the world, and she was intent on honoring that.

Other Afterlives

The reunion special was the last time that the main actors from the original series performed together, and all reported that they enjoyed the experience. During the Eighties and Nineties, Patty Duke returned to small screens in what might be called light extensions of the sitcom. Even before the reunion film, Duke and Schallert had a reunion of sorts when both appeared in a short-lived Disney sitcom, *The Torkelsons* (1991–92), in which Schallert played Wesley Hodges, a boarder at the Oklahoma home of the financially struggling divorcee, Millicent Torkelson (Connie Ray). Duke guest-starred in one installment as Hodges's estranged daughter-in-law, reconciled with Wesley in the episode's finale. With an emotional leave-taking scene, the episode could well lead the viewer to wonder if Duke and Schallert might have thought this was the last time they'd be working together.

Earlier partial reunions of cast members, most of them involving Duke and Schallert, also occurred in their appearances in PSAs (Public Service Announcements) for Medicare and Social Security. O'Keefe and Applegate appeared on several. Close to ten of the Social Security/Medicare ads are available on the sitcom's DVD boxset and several have been posted to YouTube. (References to one for the postal service exist but we have not found evidence of the PSA itself.)

Whereas Richard and Patty are divorced in the reunion special, at least one PSA has them married. All of these post-series texts seem to explore possible futures rather than trying to stand as definitive extensions of the series, a move that honors the original show's investment in fantasies and opportunities over iron-clad conclusions. Some of the PSAs awkwardly move the Lanes' fictional world into contemporary times. In one, Patty—sitting next to Richard, her presumed husband—declares that being able to sign up for Social Security or Medicare online is the "best invention since the jukebox." The PSA with perhaps the most complex story-line has Cathy, Ross, and Martin worrying that Patty and Richard will arrive late for Thanksgiving at the Lane family homestead, delayed by interminable bureaucracy as they try to sign Richard up for Medicare. Cathy assures them that since Richard is doing the application online, it will be quick. Sure enough, Richard and Cathy show up just as the turkey emerges from the oven (Figure 2.14). This one-minute PSA opens in newly shot black-and-white footage under the original *Patty Duke Show* theme song, and other echoes follow: Patty rushes downstairs and shakes her hands frenetically,

Figure 2.14 The Lanes Reconvene for Thanksgiving

as if channeling her Sixties self. She claims that signing up online is easier than "relearning the Watusi," which may have been what younger Patty was dancing in the show's original credits. In other reflexive moves, another PSA uses split screen to show Patty and Cathy side-by-side as Patty explains that filing online is "groovier than a Brooklyn hot dog," and Cathy adds "or a crêpe suzette," and in one moment Patty tells Cathy she's a "miracle worker" (!) for knowing how to file online.

Reminders of, and references to, the show paired Patty Duke with actors outside of her TV family. In yet another Medicare/Social Security PSA, Duke was partnered with George Takei (of *Star Trek* fame) about boomers "boldly going" into retirement, nicking the key phrase from the intergalactic cult show, which began airing the year *The Patty Duke Show* finished its run. Both wear Starship Enterprise blue uniforms as they chat on the ship's bridge, with Takei assuming his iconic role of Sulu. Takei/Sulu is skeptical of signing up online for Medicare/Social Security but Duke conspiratorially convinces him that it's so easy "even Kirk could do it." Coupling a *Star Trek* actor with the star of *The Patty Duke Show* long after the their shows had ended offers a double dose of nostalgia and reflexivity, this one circling not back to just one show but to an era at large—that of the mid and late Sixties—that was also being revisited by nostalgia cable channels that replayed these series, one after the other, for veteran TV viewers as well as for first-time and younger ones.[62]

In spite of the show's endurance in popular culture and in these PSAs, its continuing absence in so many accounts of television history is puzzling. Its position as a sitcom specifically directed to young female consumers within a gimmick-driven decade might account for some of the airs of superiority which obscure it from view, an issue to which we now turn.

3

Sixties Sitcoms

Trends and Forms

Just as social historians tend to split the American Sixties into distinct phases, scholars of American broadcast television typically divide the sitcom into three discrete phases that the writers match to individual decades. The phases are assumed to have clear, homogenous contours that have become so axiomatic as to be nearly automatic, especially among early television scholars. Gerald Jones's *Honey, I'm Home!* and David Marc's *Comic Visions: Television Comedy and American Culture* serve as foundational texts here. In their Introduction to *The Sitcom Reader*, editors Mary M. Dalton and Laura R. Linder start off with a long excerpt from Marc, and the anthology's contributors adhere to the standard story he elaborates. Similarly, Joanne Morreale's anthology *Critiquing the Sitcom* organizes its entries in chronological sections that follow these phases, with section prefaces by Morreale that take that standard account as a given.[1]

As this common historiography tells it, television's early, live "Golden Era" sitcoms and other comedy shows featured colorful characters, with often ribald couples and families. Many carried over from successful radio shows, some of which, inflected by a vaudevillian ethos, employed established comics who maintained stand-up qualities even in narrative situations. Series and variety shows gave off a sense of performative, self-conscious spontaneity (especially variety shows), often relying on jokes based on class, gender, and generational differences and on ethnic and racial humor that might be of dubious taste today.

Ethnic sitcoms often centered on urban and working-class communities, such as *Mama* (1949–57), whose Norwegian immigrant family strove to fit into an established white-American community, and the Jewish urban New Yorkers in *The Goldbergs* (also 1949–57). *The Honeymooners* (1955–56, developed out of skits from *The Jackie Gleason Show*) focused on working-class, white city-dwellers, also in New York—where most early TV shows

The Patty Duke Show *and the American Sixties*. Caryl Flinn and Dana Polan, Oxford University Press.
© Oxford University Press 2026. DOI: 10.1093/oso/9780197667439.003.0004

were filmed. Shows tended to avoid or downplay people of color. In one exception, *Bachelor Father* (1957-62), the sitcom family's Asian American servant (comedian Sammee Tong) was a featured character alongside that of the white patriarch and series star, John Forsythe. The controversial *Amos 'n' Andy* (1951–53) was a more widely noted exception to the white ethnic and working-class sitcom. In the long radio run that preceded it, the two lead characters had been performed by white actors using blackvoice; the TV series used Black actors, but instructed them never to mention race, and to maintain the vocal styles of their predecessors. Due largely to objections raised by the NAACP, the show was soon dropped from the airwaves. Until the mid to late Sixties, nationally broadcast television shows, unlike local radio station fare, offered few opportunities to people of color, who were frequently hired below the line as uncredited laborers or, on screen, as minor (often uncredited) household workers or as entertainers appealing to crossover audiences.

Scholars conducting the standard history inevitably single out *I Love Lucy* (1951–56) as the key transitional series from the earlier ethnic comedies into a phase of domestic sitcoms dominated by white middle-class characters. Against the relative roughness of its predecessors, *I Love Lucy* enjoyed high-end visual quality, including a (hitherto unused) three-camera set up and a lighting strategy developed by emigré Karl Freund, whose reputation as a cinematographer in the German Expressionist film movement added to the show's sense of overall "quality." Here, though, Freund eschewed expressive cinematography, uniformly lighting the set in relative brightness, which reduced the time needed to change lighting setups between shots and confirmed moving image comedy's long-running association with even lighting.[2] Although filmed in front of a studio audience, *I Love Lucy* was not broadcast live. By using film stock over video, Desilu (the production company run by Desi Arnaz and Lucille Ball) was able to generate a reserve of episodes for reruns and syndication.

Lucy also marked the American sitcom's shift away from working-class "white ethnics" to white Anglo middle-class leads. Despite featuring an interethnic couple, Lucille Ball's antics were firmly at the helm, and her megawatt star status laid to rest network and advertisers' concerns regarding the depiction of such a couple. In fact, producers were far more unsettled when Ball became pregnant, a fact that was written (under the watchful eye of religious leaders and censors) into the series. Scholars have also lauded *I Love Lucy* for its reflexive dimension, not merely for depicting Ball's pregnancy, but for being set in the world of showbiz—in Ricky's club and the real-life celebrities he frequently brought home.

Without wanting to minimize the accomplishments of *Lucy* or its innovative place in television's history, that status has practically transformed it into a museum piece, "the" artifact that single-handedly enabled the TV sitcom to move forward. To the extent that domestication was Lucy's fate (however much the homemaker railed against it), *I Love Lucy* overlaps ideologically with the suburban, white domestic sitcoms that followed in its wake, imprinting comedy onto the norm of the newly normalized nuclear family.

Domestic sitcoms were an effective mass venue for replacing idealized wartime images, such as the "Rosie the Riveters" on whom the country relied for factory work, with new postwar role models: unpaid homemakers in households ruled by the male breadwinners who had reclaimed the jobs women had held, temporarily, during the war.

To be sure, even the privileged few who might be able to identify with TV's new ideals were buying into highly manufactured images. The Fifties were not just an era of conformity and peacetime prosperity; they also saw the decline of local "mom and pop" businesses as alienating, corporate workplaces (the nascent stages of multinational conglomerates) emerged, creating employment circumstances in which individuals, including those moms and pops, exerted little control over their work conditions. This did not go unnoticed; consider the heavily cited sociological study of the time *The Lonely Crowd* (Riesman et al., 1950), the film *The Man in the Grey Flannel Suit* (Johnson 1956), and Arthur Miller's play *The Death of a Salesman*, which opened in 1949.

Mainstream media, including journalism, worked in tandem with entertainment businesses to create norms of white economic stability and prosperity, overlooking more contentious movements in civil rights and union rights that ripped through the country. The sitcom genre created a fantasy of domestic harmony, a sort of peacetime media project of re-Americanizing and smoothing out the rough edges of actual domestic and working life. The problems of these TV families could be reduced to such trivialities as the entire plot of a December 1957 episode of *Ozzie and Harriet* devoted to a quest for tutti-frutti ice cream.

Thus, from the late Fifties into the Sixties, as the story goes, American sitcoms helped perpetuate dominant norms and fictions of a stable, white middle class. Many domestic sitcoms posited the family and family home as safe harbors of comfort, support, and intimacy; even the more stylized and unreal comedies promoted images of family togetherness—the Addamses or the Clampetts against their uncomprehending neighborhoods. Sitcoms' relative lack of interest in stylization and performative acting styles made them appear, even unconsciously, to represent as reality the fantasies of postwar prosperity in which everyone could buy a house, new appliances (again, to entice women to retreat back into the home), and big new cars. For John Caldwell, the sparseness of televisual style helped elevate a new medium seeking a foothold in respectability: "critics and learned viewers now could celebrate the birth of a TV art that was defined structurally by its sparseness and intellectual seriousness, not by messier formal excesses, kitsch, or camp."[3]

Typically, these sitcoms would place their fantasy families in homes that closed in on themselves, abandoning the tightly knit, broader communities of earlier series like *The Goldbergs*. The maneuver wasn't always successful: when CBS moved the Goldbergs into the suburbs, ratings abruptly tanked and the show was canceled. (In fact, in Fifties America, Jews, along with people of color and unmarried women, were frequently forbidden to buy homes in white suburbia, especially in upscale developments.) For much of the public, these suburban TV offerings, however unrealistic, have come to metonymically sum up the American domestic sitcom, whose sometimes quaint, but often unsettling, norms continue to be ridiculed into the twenty-first century.

Enter the second phase of standard sitcom history, which both included and extended the domestic subgenre. The early to mid-Sixties was an era seemingly overrun with implausible sitcoms with gimmicky premises. Take just those beginning with M: *Mister Ed* (a talking horse), *My Favorite Martian* (a live-in male Martian), *My Living Doll* (a live-in female android), *The Munsters* (a family of green monsters), *My Mother the Car* (a deceased parent who speaks to her son through a 1928 automobile). With their (to many of us, enjoyably) ridiculous premises, most of these shows met with journalists' and critics' dismissal or disdain, although their theme songs tend to be the ones people remember with fondness.

Although earlier, established domestic sitcoms, such as the long-running *My Three Sons,* continued to air in the Sixties, much of that subgenre's territory was ceded to such "silly sitcoms." Those with more exaggerated themes and styles are readily divided into subgenres, such as the "rural rube" category, which, like *The Andy Griffith Show* before it (and continuing its run alongside it), depicted life in an imaginary community of rural folks with loads of free time and cornpone humor. Lynn Spigel shrewdly identifies a subset of Sixties sitcoms that captured the decade's obsession with space exploration and helped American audiences make light of ongoing Cold War anxieties by featuring unthreatening aliens of silly varieties: actual outer space aliens and robots (*Lost in Space*, *My Favorite Martian*), and "ghoulish" families (*The Munsters*, *The Addams Family*) who were outsiders in their white communities (the Munsters even had green skin).[4]

Whereas any anti-war commentary in the Sixties' military sitcoms was, as we mentioned in our Introduction, blunted, criticism and jokes directed against action in the then-current conflict in Vietnam were more prominent in comedy clubs of the time, especially in the work of controversial stand-ups like Lenny Bruce, George Carlin, and Dick Gregory. The military sitcoms broadcast on television, by contrast, usually featured one or more inept, unthreatening goofballs (*McHale's Navy*, *Gomer Pyle*) or, occasionally, a battalion full of them (*F Troop*), and the rank and file would continually outwit or outmaneuver their hapless, softheaded commanding officers. Generously read, such details hint that the shows might be harbingers of a rising "antiestablishment" sentiment while also maintaining the tradition of American pop culture's long-running championship of the underdog.

Gimmick sitcoms also parodied popular culture of the moment. Mel Brooks's clever spoof of James Bond's slick and sexy spy phenomenon, *Get Smart,* exemplifies this subgenre, but *The Addams Family*'s and *The Munsters*'s reworking of the monsters that ran rampant across Thirties and Fifties horror films could also be considered parodies. After all, both featured reincarnated Frankenstein monsters, with Herman Munster's "creature gone good" unaware of his scary looks, and Lurch simply too haughty to assimilate. Like the Aurora monster model kits so popular at the time, the monster sitcoms seemed to domesticate horror for the consumption and amusement of children.

By the late Sixties, as TV historian Aniko Bodroghkozy notes, TV series began to edge away from weirdly exotic or space-age fantasies and broach more grounded issues of the time. Typically, this occurred outside the parameters of the sitcom, in crime dramas such as *The Mod Squad* or comedy-heavy variety shows like *The Smothers Brothers Comedy Hour* or *Laugh In*.[5] For an example of the socially committed sitcom of the late Sixties, Bodroghkozy attends to *Julia*, a domestic sitcom (what would be termed a dramedy today) that began airing in 1968. It featured a Black nurse (Diahann Carroll) who was shown both at work and at home, where she was raising a son after her husband had been killed in Vietnam—a strategic move to endow a character whose race might have otherwise ruffled fragile white sensibilities (namely, those of advertisers) with patriotic sacrifice. Bodroghkozy positions *Julia* as a significant transitional text that combined traits of the "incomplete family" sitcom of the earlier part of the decade (a widowed mom, in this case) with aspects of the social relevance trend that historians argue would dominate sitcoms in the third phase in the next decade.[6]

By the Seventies, second-wave feminism joined anti-war and civil rights activism in becoming broadly acknowledged by and represented in journalistic and fictional media alike. It seemed only reasonable, then, for critics advancing the standard account of television history to maintain that the outlandish gags and premises of mid-Sixties shows gave way to proto-feminist tales of unmarried working women (*The Mary Tyler Moore Show*), anti-war messaging (*M*A*S*H*), or families enmeshed in exaggeratedly controversial social and political discussions (*All in The Family*).

By the end of the Sixties, networks had started phasing out their silly sitcoms to make room for ostensibly less gimmicky fare. In 1971, CBS abruptly canceled all its rural sitcoms, despite their ongoing popularity, especially in Southern and rural America: *The Beverly Hillbillies*, *Green Acres*, *The New Andy Griffith Show*, *Mayberry RFD*, *Petticoat Junction*, and *Gomer Pyle*. Even *Lassie* was deemed "too regional." Historians refer to this as CBS's "rural purge" and Pat Buttram, a secondary star of *Green Acres*, called 1971 the year when "CBS killed everything with a tree in it." That murder was attributed to Fred Silverman, the newly arrived executive at CBS, who openly sought more upscale "relevance."[7]

In a common move, David Marc asserts that the ostensible banality of Sixties domestic sitcoms (including, presumably, *The Patty Duke Show*, though he doesn't mention it) "developed in a relatively monolithic fashion," effectively transforming the decade's output into a cultural desert wedged between the Fifties' "Golden Era" and the esteemed "relevant" sitcoms of the Seventies.[8] Gerald Jones likewise sandwiches the Sixties between two superior decades, describing it within a "shift away from scattershot innovation and toward the refinement of proven products."[9] For Marc, "The [Sixties] sitcom, which for many people had epitomized all that was distasteful and moronic in television—and in mass culture in general—had achieved a kind of maturity in the early and middle 1970s." Invoking what has become an enshrined triumvirate of quality shows, he argues that *M*A*S*H*, *Mary Tyler Moore*, and *All in the Family* "drove the sitcom to the brink of respectability," bracketing out all the Seventies sitcoms that don't fit into the model of quality and discerning taste (*Highcliff Manor*, anyone?)[10]

Critics always cite the increased production values of these Seventies sitcoms (bigger budgets, better writers, directors, and set designers) over those of the sitcoms so rapidly "churned out" in the Sixties (note the insinuations of accomplished Art trumping the sameness of generic mass reproduction, even as it is also mass-produced). Marc goes so far as to intimate that the more mature content of the new shows outstripped the sitcom form itself, as new, relevant subject matter awakened a moribund genre: "Playing against the sitcom's historical barrenness, they [again, the holy triumvirate of Seventies series] proved that content—in the form of broad brushstroke writing—could energize even the most banal of forms."[11] This is not to say that domestic sitcoms disappeared in Seventies television, but some of their details started shape-shifting. Rather than atomized suburban homes, lead characters were often situated in communities forged through the workplace and other non-domestic spheres, places that were—occasionally and tentatively—less white and male-exclusive. This was not altogether novel: some domestic sitcoms had eschewed the family-based formula in the Fifties; *Our Miss Brooks*, for example, placed its eponymous lead at school where she taught, and its plots often dealt with exchanges with her colleagues. *Miss Brooks*'s descendants such as *Taxi* (1978–82) were similarly set outside the home; the Black-led show *Sanford and Son* (1972–77) cast the peerless comedian Red Foxx as a junk dealer (as a single father, he still had to be a widower and not a divorced man). For her show, Mary Tyler Moore advocated for her character, Mary Richards, to be a divorcee but the network found the idea too risky; it was enough just to feature an unmarried woman.

Theme songs were not immune to these kinds of changes. Taking the perspective that singles out Seventies shows for their emergent quality, Amy Argetsinger unpacks the song that cold-opened *All in the Family*, "Those Were the Days." Its lyrics, she rightly notes, quickly establish the bigotry of Archie Bunker, who sings it with his wife at his living room piano, a setting that overall "inject[ed] a bit of kitchen-sink realism into the opening credits of a sitcom." As people claim for the series itself, she argues that the song initiated another new complexity and maturity into sitcom theme songs: "'Those Were the Days' offered multilayered poetry at a time when most TV themes were lush instrumentals or manic overexplaining expositions ('Meet Cathy who's lived most everywhere . . . ')." The premise of "Those Were the Days," she writes, "resided . . . in its nuanced character, not some antic storyline." Following the evolutionary model of sitcom history, and its belief in the superiority of the Seventies over the Sixties, Argetsinger asserts that, after "Those Were the Days" in 1971, it would be impossible for songs to return to "'Here's the story of a lovely lady' [*The Brady Bunch*] or a 'three-hour tour' [*Gilligan's Island*]."[12]

In general, TV historians maintain that the aesthetic value of Seventies shows continued into the Eighties, often considering the latter as another somewhat refined era of broadcast television. Dramatic hits such as *Hill St Blues* (1981–87) are often cited, and critics praise a number of popular sitcoms of the Eighties and Nineties, such as *Diff'rent Strokes, The Cosby Show*, and *Roseanne*, for their innovations on Black and working-class characters. By late century, cable TV was overtaking broadcast series. Unregulated by the FCC, cable did not have to abide by its censorship rules, and thus took advantage of what was advertised as "adult" content, riskier and, again, more sophisticated, storytelling representations, as in runaway hits as *The Sopranos* and *Game of Thrones*. Sitcoms were rarely at the top of those lists, although exceptions such as *The Larry Sanders Show* and later, *Curb Your Enthusiasm*, were well received and lauded.

By not attending to the particularities of series that fail to fit the periodizing model, this three-phased standard history casts more than a handful of shows to the side, where they remain underappreciated and underexamined—the usual fate of *The Patty Duke Show*. Curiously, that oversight includes some sitcoms that challenged representations of race, gender, and class, deprioritizing those features by focusing on prestige over questions of representation and politics. Popular sitcoms like *Sanford and Son, Grace under Fire, Diff'rent Strokes*, and *The Jeffersons* didn't revolve around middle-class whiteness, for instance, and are seldom listed alongside their "quality" brethren. (One later exception is *The Cosby Show*.)

While this historical account of broadcast-era sitcoms is not erroneous per se, it presents the transitions between phases as both logical and inexorable. And as we argue, that standard history, usually matched to decades, downplays the contradictions, counterexamples, and nuances that inform every phase within sociocultural slices of time that are themselves smoothed out and homogenized.

Sitcom Structure: "Formula"

The most damning charge made against the Sixties domestic sitcom was its supposed formulaic nature, a condemnation that some critics often extended to the sitcom at large, or even to the medium of television per se. Gerald Jones identifies what he calls the all-consuming structure of family sitcoms at large as one in which a misguided initiative of one of the kids fails and the child receives corrective advice from the family patriarch. This "little drama," as he calls it, has "played hundreds, thousands of times" with different characters and different pretexts. All threats to domestic harmony are ultimately dispatched in a manner that leaves everyone, "including the dissenter, . . . happier than at the outset." (Jones elaborates on the formula's end-goal: "discussions; quiet resolutions: the surrender of disruptive urges; consensus for everyone's own good.")[13]

When applied to sitcoms, "formula" can hold two overlapping but distinct meanings that scholars tend to blend more than they perhaps should: the formulae of individual sitcoms (such as trying to get off of an island but never making it), and the larger formula or common narrative structure to which sitcoms typically adhere as an aggregate. "Formula" becomes an inexorable logic, nearly mathematical in its fixity and omnipresent in all sitcoms. Early mass media and cultural commentators, in conservative and left-wing circles alike, dismissed the medium of television as formulaic, brainless, and monolithic. For instance, Theodor Adorno, in his "How to Look at Television," critiques all the medium's subgenres as nothing but pseudo-individualized cases of a singular form run through with undifferentiated inanity.[14]

Commentators attribute a fixed, tripartite structure to TV sitcoms of stasis, disruption, and renewed stasis that repeats across weekly episodes. Jones avers that the "different characters and different pretexts" of individual sitcoms matter less to sitcom narrative than the overall drama being told again and again.[15] From this it follows that the overriding structure determines meaning, and that the content specific to any given sitcom doesn't have much to do with what it ultimately "is about." At some level, though, scholars know that content *does* matter: take, for example, the recurrent discussion of the racialized dimensions of *The Cosby Show* before and after its star's downfall; many wondered whether that show actually revised the sitcom form by focusing on an African American family, and in particular, an upper middle-class one headed by a crossover star who exerted considerable control over its production.

We emphatically resist that claim that the form came of age, aesthetically and socially, after the Sixties. For David Marc, sitcoms of the early Seventies such as *All in the Family*, *M*A*S*H*, and *The Mary Tyler Moore Show* manifest what he approvingly terms "a literate strain"; they were more complex, adult, and socially relevant than the white bread domestic sitcoms of the previous decade. (Even the industry called the era one of "Quality TV.") Marc characterizes television of the Sixties as market-driven, formulaic, conservative, conformist, reassuring fluff and "relatively monolithic."[16] In contrast to the dismissive tradition that Marc exemplifies, we also wish to challenge the idea of monolithic television types or periods.

Although there is some truth to the three-phase structure given to sitcom history, plenty of shows depart from it, including much of *The Patty Duke Show*. Acknowledging the sheer proliferation of genres upsets the notion that sitcoms of the Sixties belong to one emphatic sort. And stressing the multiplicities of sitcom types provides a fruitful starting point to engage with the complexities and contradictions within what is often simplified under the moniker "Sixties sitcom"—silly or otherwise. We bring this closer to home, first by examining the variants of the domestic sitcom and, second, by showing how *The Patty Duke Show* in particular offers narrative and thematic possibilities all its own.

The Domestic Sitcom: Characters and Characteristics

What Gerald Jones calls the instructional sitcom comes immediately to mind when most people think about domestic sitcoms of the period. Because breadwinning fathers were typically absent by day, each episode was impelled to focus on the daytime domestic sphere and *not* the workplace, which usually went unpictured or was afforded only brief screentime. Dad returned in the evening to eat dinner and resolve the crisis du jour by imparting Solomon-esque lectures to the children who had provided the best laughs of the show. Rarely funny, TV dads tried to whip the antics of the domestic space into line with a seriousness of purpose; their housewives, on the other hand, typically had little to do but say "wait until your father gets home." Impeccably dressed as they were while supervising children and doing chores, the mothers, their writers made sure, were deprived of the knowledge or authority to dispense the moral guidance that would resolve the crises of the day/episode. Even *The Donna Reed Show*, with Reed a more established star than her physician husband (Carl Betz), is depicted as just another TV homemaker. For decades, Americans considered June Cleaver, "Beaver's mom," as the embodiment of the acquiescent sitcom housewife, although ultimately so clichéd—vacuuming in dresses, heels, and pearls—as to become camp. Gone were the feistier female characters audiences had seen in *Our Miss Brooks, Mrs. Goldberg,* or *I Love Lucy.*[17]

After years of husbands such as Ricky Ricardo, Jake Goldberg or George Burns playing the straight man in the face of their wives' attention-grabbing exploits, it is easy to wonder if, by the late Fifties and Sixties, the idea of male familial authority needed reinforcement. Certainly, TV produced a sense of overcorrection. In the words of one critic, *My Three Sons,* which featured a superficially mild-mannered father who was actually quite stubborn, "dug in its heels against the liberalization of America."[18]

In some shows, women were so unimportant as to be absented altogether, as in the strangely common "widowed male parent" sitcom: *Father Knows Best, My Three Sons, Bachelor Father, The Andy Griffith Show, Family Affair,* and *The Courtship of Eddie's Father.* Even as this subgenre encouraged audiences to prioritize and sympathize with men (in and out of the domestic sphere), it reinforced the norm of an intact heterosexual family by having woman function as a structuring absence—an absence that, as producers and writers were well aware, generated situations for the widowers to engage with potential romantic partners (but usually just for one episode). Explanations for the emergence of this subgenre may be found on the one hand, in the smothering American mothers that in the Fifties Philip Wylie invented and vilified in *A Generation of Vipers,* and, on the other, the fact of the frustration housewives were starting to express about their domestic responsibilities, as revealed in books like *The Feminine Mystique.*

Minimizing mothers helped keep the threat of (reproductive) heterosexuality at some remove and thereby maintained a domestic core of a single dad and children that resisted change and held at bay topics risky for family viewing such as sexuality and procreation. Wifely duties were often performed by servants played by actors of color, as TV scholar Melissa Phruksachart trenchantly shows for the case of *Bachelor Father.* As part of the cultural and political project of the United States after WWII and Korea, this substitution, she maintains, forced actors of color into a historically and ideologically determined holding space, rendering them "harmless" and subservient to white, masculine American authority.[19]

Yet not all writers at the time were uncritical of the ideals peddled by television. In her two-part *TV Guide* essay, Betty Friedan writes, "Television's image of the American woman, 1964, is a stupid, unattractive, insecure little household drudge who spends her martyred, mindless, boring days dreaming of love—and plotting nasty revenge against her husband."[20] For Friedan, the "bachelor father" sitcom variant cashed in on the desires of married women without threatening the status quo: they could fantasize about lives or affairs with the dashing single men or solo fathers, along with the sparkling homes maintained by someone other than themselves. These series acknowledged the drudgery of women's marriages and domestic lives by *not* representing it, putting in its stead fantasies of camera-ready bachelors or widowers in immaculate homes free of financial woes. What's more, those shows with housewives, Friedan notes, seldom gave credence to women's skills and expertise, even in the domestic realms that they supposedly ruled.

By the Sixties, the domestic sitcom also intensified its emphasis on children. If Lucy Ricardo's pregnancy had become a key plot point, little Ricky scarcely mattered once he arrived. Yet soon after that, sitcoms pivoted and made kids a key focus and concern; some shows were even named after them. In contrast to titles like *Life with Father, Father Knows Best*, and even *My Three Sons* that announced a paternal perspective, shows like *Dennis the Menace, The Many Loves of Dobie Gillis, Gidget*, and *Leave it to Beaver* placed children front and center and seemed to take kids' affective needs more seriously as plotlines moved into the Sixties. This shift subtly illustrates the increased importance of children as consumers and of the TV industry's desire to expand audience demographics; early postwar baby boomers were growing up at this time, and, as Susan Douglas has stressed in her work, American media culture happily adapted its products to this expanding population—and to their parents' wallets. Even ads for tinfoil-covered TV dinners (convenient for busy housewives) featured children and parents watching television together. Contemporary television-oriented print media occasionally offered consumer guides separating "adult" from "family" series, with Duke's show inevitably listed in the latter. One critic, writing for an adult homemaking magazine, described *The Patty Duke Show* as "Situation Comedy with good values in characters and motivations" opposing it to series like *The Addams Family*, whose humor was strangely "too sophisticated"; *Get Smart* was "suitable for adults only"; as was, for more obvious reasons, *My Living Doll*.[21]

In conjunction with the established convention of the advice-dispensing patriarch, the newfound emphasis on children meant that some sitcoms began to posit family dynamics as multidirectional rather than top-down. The cliché of the solid, stolid father may have stood for a wisdom of the ages, but the kids modernized and softened his perspective, helping him adjust to contemporary youngsters and lifestyles. In widower sitcoms, offspring often wondered and worried about their fathers' need to find love again. The relationship between Gidget and her father in the eponymous series has a not-really hidden two-way charge in which each cares for the other and advises them on their love life. Their mutual dependency is so intense, in fact, as to be borderline incestuous: the show's credit sequence unfolds as a series of still shots of the two of them, ending with a kiss (the song—sung from the father's perspective—closes on the lyrics, "Gidget is mine!"), and its plotlines eternally return Gidget into the arms and approval of her father (Figure 3.1). (As scholar Ilana Nash notes, the name Gidget—a combination of 'midget' and 'girl'—also suggests, 'gadget', a girl object that was made "young enough to be innocent but old enough to be sexualized.")[22]

Figure 3.1 *Gidget*'s Creepy Credits

Children Fixing Families

In contrast, *The Patty Duke Show* perpetually seeded the (usually nonfamilial) dreams of a young, middle-class girl by breaking from the model of two-way dependency and focusing instead on the teen world of Patty, and sometimes Cathy. Patty is more devoted to her own schemes and ideals than to meeting the needs of her parents, particularly in the first two years of the series. The show's lack of a two-way orientation was evident in its focus on teen life—the constant allusions to dates and proms, references to popular rock bands, and the steady stream of heartthrob male guest stars to swoon over—along with its depiction of Richard, who extended to girl viewers the reassuring image of a realistic, unthreatening boyfriend who was a fantasy of stability rather than a charismatic beau. In fact, *The Patty Duke Show* pushes that teen world toward new areas of concern. The girls frequently get involved in civic realms and pointedly, do so with little immediate help or advice from the parents, who often learn of the younger generation's public engagement after the fact.

In this way, the dreams of young girls and teens involved more than attracting boys or assuming a heterosexuality that isn't fully intact in some of these shows. They also involved imaginary worlds free of domestic discord, divorce, poverty, racism, school bullying, and so on. *The Patty Duke Show* was exemplary in showing the force of that dreamworld. Actors Duke and O'Keefe have both stated publicly that the fictional Lanes—enacted by generous, down-to-earth adult actors—"felt like a family," a remark made more poignant knowing what Duke's domestic life was actually like at the time. (Like her other costars, O'Keefe had no idea what she was experiencing at the Rosses.)[23]

That familial image of *The Patty Duke Show* comforted not only its young participants but its viewers. As an adult, Duke claimed that kids "loved the love. This was a healthy family. . . . there was consistency, which a lot of kids who watched it didn't have."[24] Thus, however ideologically prescriptive idealized TV families like the Lanes were, they offered solace to children in families who struggled. For Paul O'Keefe, the show displayed a "larger than life version of family people" and depicted the family in "heightened reality."[25]

Narratives in other popular media of the early to mid-Sixties catered to childhood fantasies of reworking the family. Several prominent films tasked kids (sometimes with the help of a sympathetic woman) with correcting the fathers, making them less remote, more present and emotionally involved

(*Mary Poppins, The Sound of Music, The Parent Trap*). By seeming to repair the nuclear family, whether by engaging those distant dads or cheering on single parents' remarriage potential, these child-driven narratives indicate very real concerns about the family's stability and sanctity at the time. Yet, there was never much to "fix" in the Lane household.

In his study of the Fifties sitcom *Mama*, George Lipsitz underscores the fondness with which adults who grew up watching such domestic shows recall them. This affection, he argues, is borne not just of retroactive nostalgia, but what he labels "mediated false memories." These series endure precisely because this fantasy of loving, intact families not only provided a salve to viewers when they were children, but comforted them as adults, creating an impression of past security that they have sustained throughout their lives, however marred by false memory and ideologically mediated ideals. These loving, middle-class television families probably never lined up with anyone's actual lives, but the comforting feelings they provided turned into a widely experienced fantasy.[26]

No Room for Patty

Clearly, *The Patty Duke Show* could easily be situated within the gimmick sitcom subgenre, and a few critics do just that (Douglas, Jones, and Luckett). But it's far more common for scholars not to mention the show at all, effectively damning it as unworthy of discussion within an already undistinguished monolith of "silly" series. Its exclusion is almost universal in the archly agreed-upon trajectory of "the" American sitcom. David Marc, for instance, writes that "The popularity of *Father Knows Best* (1954–60), *Leave It To Beaver* (1957–63), *The Donna Reed Show* (1958–66) and other nuclear family sitcoms produced during this suburban ecstasy period has endured," thereby consigning an awful lot of series ("*other* nuclear family sitcoms") to critical and scholarly oblivion.[27]

There are several possible explanations for *The Patty Duke Show*'s omission from these standard accounts. First is its "hinge" existence within mid-Sixties mass culture, neither a Fifties holdover that capitulated to the instructional paternalistic sitcom, nor a rebellious, countercultural series that funneled the agitated zeitgeist of the Sixties. Commentators may have considered it to be so formulaic and indistinct from like-minded series as to render mentioning it unnecessary (but since it is rarely cited in any manner, this is merely a guess), or that it is so aesthetically inferior—a "turkey classic" per Douglas—that it is unworthy of citation in the first place.[28] (But would anyone really want to make the case for the creative superiority of *The Donna Reed Show*?)

Another possibility, which we uphold, is that *The Patty Duke Show* offers qualities that don't conform to the common conceptions and conventions of domestic sitcoms, silly or not, and therefore make it hard to fit into the standard story. (Here, we must acknowledge that Jones, for all his adherence to the standard story, does devote a few paragraphs to the series and argues that it was "the only show that made a point of examining the mechanics of a teenager learning to make sensible life decisions."[29])

As puzzling as the absence of *The Patty Duke Show* in Sixties TV sitcom histories might be, we wonder if it's because the series does not concern itself with what those other shows were doing. *The Patty Duke Show* was not terribly compliant, for instance, with domestic comedy's rendition of the nuclear family across gender and generational lines. Young Patty's ventures usually leave Martin and Natalie absent, oblivious, and in the dust. Moreover, the inevitable clean-up of her antics at the end of each episode rarely results from a moral lesson given by an instructional father. This strikes us as important, unexplored territory, even if the results don't add up to a single, unified understanding of the show. How could they, in a series based on twinning and multiple identities?

The narratives of *The Patty Duke Show* are irreducible to a formula shared by all sitcoms. It matters, for instance, that the series deals centrally with teenage girls (more than one, of course) and it matters that it articulates its plots around the challenges and opportunities they seek out. It matters that this occurs in the Sixties, allowing the show to spill beyond a relatively fixed generic structure and formula and speak to its moment.

Consider "The Elopement" (S1E3), in which Martin thinks Patty and Richard are eloping because he mistakes their application for a fishing license for him as a marriage license for the two of them. While adhering superficially to the stasis-disruption-stasis formal structure, this culturally resonant episode can't work without understanding that "the real world" of the Sixties entailed similar challenges to family stability and parental authority. In other words, its meaning comes not just from its formal structure but from specific, real threats to domesticity—namely, premarital and/or teenage sexuality and elopement—that, thanks to broader, more far-reaching representations in mass media had recently become more visible and publicly discussed (in

1967, The Beatles would release "She's Leaving Home," a poignant ballad about a girl running away from her family). The episode is also framed as a lesson on the real-life topic of the runaway: it begins with Martin writing an editorial decrying what he sees as a worrisome trend of teen girls running off with beatniks. Mid-episode, Martin laments to boss J. R. "How can Patty get married? She's still trying to figure out roller skates."; J. R. replies wryly that maybe Richard and Patty "aren't planning to do much roller-skating," eliciting a look of horror from Martin that might articulate a "structure of feeling" held by some parents of the time.

That *The Patty Duke Show* debuted three years after the US Food and Drug Administration (FDA) had approved the Pill raised a twofold response to the prospect of women having control over their sexuality. Whether it was thrilling or chilling depended on one's religious beliefs, age, gender, generation, income, among other factors. "The Elopement" evokes unease. Its subject matter was definitely risky for a sitcom of that era, as it raises not only the topic of "runaway teens" but the far more frightening idea of Patty Lane having sex. To be sure, *The Patty Duke Show*'s generic contours assure us that the end of the episode will return to the sitcom status quo, but only after exploring these seismic issues.

Paradoxically, *Bewitched*, the contemporary sitcom that insists on Samantha's desire for the stability of the heterosexual domesticity of a non-supernatural, human realm, has received feminist attention from scholars such as Douglas and Bodroghkozy. While *Bewitched*'s other witches, Samantha's mother most of all, evince disdain for human life, and Darren in particular, and urge Samantha to employ her talents in the service of supernatural adventure, Samantha usually deploys them when she needs to solve some problem in the human sphere and restore normalcy to it. It is very much a series about resecuring homey values. In contrast, Patty sets out on schemes that will take her beyond domestic surrender—and that often change domestic life into something extraordinary, for instance, when she transforms the Lane household into a business venue, which she hopes will expand into something even greater. Patty may fail at her ventures, but the show consistently stresses that they are deeply important to the young girl as she aspires to be an adult. This seems quite different from the case of Samantha who repeatedly accepts that any pursuits beyond the human realities of the household must be curbed to maintain her anodyne marriage. The pattern of renewed stasis in *Bewitched*'s plotlines leaves Samantha in the same place as at the outset, whereas in *The Patty Duke Show* it often points to possibilities outside of Patty Lane's domestic life. This is not to argue that *The Patty Duke Show* is feminist, or any more feminist than *Bewitched*, but to suggest that its structure is more pliable, offering social models for girls and young women to experiment with versions of adulthood, even if their presentation, like Samantha's, are often hare-brained.

A typical episode of *The Patty Duke Show* is driven by a sweeping scheme or initiative Patty devises and attempts to put into practice. This often begins before the credit sequence, with the proverbial light bulb going off in Patty's head, revealed by that sly twinkle in her eyes, before the episode dashes into the theme song and credits. Patty may face failure by the narrative's end (she gives up tuba-playing, shuts down her babysitting business, returns to Richard) but the sitcom's recursive structure means that she will relaunch another venture with fresh enthusiasm once the next episode gets underway.

Critically, Patty's enterprises migrate beyond family relations. For instance, "Can-do Patty" (S2E14), begins with Natalie and Martin calling their daughter lazy, unambitious, and unable to accept responsibility, preferring to goof off with Richard. Taking umbrage, Patty decides to prove herself as a person of "can-do" commitment (one of the series's defining phrase). In a blink-and-you'll-miss-it gesture that reiterates the series' investment in performance, Patty declares her newly found enthusiasm by gliding her hand across her face, altering her expression to reflect her change of attitude. As she volunteers for every job at home, school, and in the community, Patty tries to act as if she were fully in command of her excessive initiative, unlike episodes, discussed below, such as "The Tycoons" (S1E18) or "This Little Patty Went to Market" (S2E12), where capitalist ventures take out-of-control command of her. But here, as in her entrepreneurial endeavors where she can't keep up with the speed of enterprise, she quickly becomes stretched too thin and starts dumping her responsibilities onto others, especially Cathy, the "assistant" (cheap foreign labor?).

Such episodes move Patty from inside to outside, and plotlines usually return her home only after her ventures have gone awry in a too-big world. In a dressmaking episode (discussed in more detail later), the Lane residence is transformed into a factory of sorts, with Patty making products intended to be distributed to teenware stores, even abroad. Another episode inverts this focus on initiatives beyond the home with the children, led by an overzealous Patty, unionizing against their parents who respond by negotiating endless chores within the home in exchange for "worker" benefits. This episode softly yet significantly imports the politics of the outside world into the home.

The differences with other sitcoms are instructive here. Lucy Ricardo, for instance, is an adult, and any real-world counterpart would likely know better than to persist at clawing her way into an entertainment business with shut doors. Yet she keeps trying. Like Samantha Stevens, whose goal is to maintain her marriage, Lucy repeats an obsessive quest: to get out of the home, frequently to get into Ricky's nightclub act. She soldiers on with zeal, innocence, and the drifting focus of an immature adult immersed in a project. As Patricia Mellencamp puts it, "Weekly for six years, she accepted domesticity, only to try to escape the next week."[30] Patty Lane pursues a wider array of goals in a series itself based on the idea of multiple identities. As an adolescent without the maturity to know that her enthusiasms will bump up against the established limits of adulthood, Patty is not simply trying to get out from under a familial iron hand, not trying to "escape" that domestic world so much as widen it and its options. As we'll see in our chapter on twinning, the diversity of Patty and Cathy's schemes has a cultural resonance that, for girls and women at the time, mattered a great deal. As Moya Luckett states, "*The Patty Duke Show* ... center[ed] the narrative around a doubling, a disruption of identity, thus representing the difficulty, unpredictability, and protean nature of teenage behavior. Using the same actress to play both Patty and Cathy implied the extreme mutability of the teenage girl's identity."[31] Still, Luckett goes on to maintain that, at heart, Patty and Cathy did represent a duality of extremes, neither of which, she says, "could be fully assimilated within mainstream adult society."[32] For us, the "extremes" were situated primarily in the efforts made by the two cousins individually in any given episode, not within the twins that Luckett positions against each other.

Even if Patty's dreams aren't fully actualized in the show's plotlines, they are never fully abandoned, suggesting that girls' fantasies of adult possibilities end up deferred rather than dismissed. Patty's precocious quests to engage in grown-up ventures might explain why *The Patty Duke Show* had greater resonance with younger teens than mid-teens (like Cathy or Patty) or older ones during its run. Older teens were further down the road to adulthood and guided by a different cluster of opportunities and fantasies that might have seemed more closely in reach, be it the hip looks of Swinging London, rock groups, "the sexual revolution," various countercultures, or the worlds of political and social justice,

Just like the magazine *Seventeen*, which, since its inception, had always been geared toward girls *under* seventeen, it's unlikely that many girls over fifteen watched *The Patty Duke Show* regularly. (Pamela Wojcik makes much the same claim about the consumers of *Gidget*: its biggest fans were younger than the main characters of that franchise.) The trend was hardly new or unique to the time. As Kelly Schrum notes in her work on youth-oriented film series from the late Thirties and Forties, the Andy Hardy movies were more popular with girls 14 and under; high schoolers tended to be more interested in adult fare, and/or adult male stars.[33]

The decades-long book series of "girl detective" *Nancy Drew* (which preceded both *The Patty Duke Show* and *Gidget*) initially had a sixteen-year-old heroine but aged her at eighteen in later novels, perhaps to adjust to her aging readers or, more likely, to the swift maturation of teens in the postwar decades. By contrast, ABC, as we've noted, locked Patty and Cathy Lane's age at fifteen for the three years of the show. Moreover, its many tie-ins offer material proof of the young audience to which the series was pitched: paper dolls, board games, even "petite" girl clothing lines, not the commodities that older teenage girls typically swoon over. This is not to say that actual viewers of the show were mainly or exclusively young female teens; plenty of boys enjoyed the show and recall it fondly to this day.

The dressmaking episode, "The Tycoons," exemplifies both young persons' ambition and their ability to easily get in over their heads. Opening on a rainy day that keeps the twins inside, Cathy calmly sews a design onto a dress while Patty is just busting to get outdoors. She proposes going to the movies, but Cathy is too caught up in her sewing. At first, Patty dismisses her cousin's DIY cat-motif as woefully uncool, but when Cathy wears it to school the next day, the girls all flock around, asking Cathy to make one for them, and Patty's light bulb goes off. She starts taking orders for a dressmaking business that she imagines will garner a fortune, despite Cathy's protestations that they're taking on too much and she (Cathy) won't be able to keep up. After enlisting Richard as a business advisor, along with another boy, Craig, Patty takes Cathy to consult with a famous designer (played by TV and radio comedian and game show star Robert Q. Lewis) and then to the buyer for a department store chain. Their support allows Patty to lease sewing machines, buy fabric, and enlist classmates as dressmakers as she envisions an ever-broadening enterprise; even Natalie gets swept up into the fervor—it seems a capitalism of contagion (Figure 3.2). Martin returns from work to find the dressmaking operation has completely overtaken the house and insists that you can't

Figure 3.2 Entrepreneurialism Gone Amuck

succeed in business from scratch. But when Patty's business seems to be on the path to profitability, he converts to the cause.

A first setback occurs when a government official shows up and cuts into the venture's profits after delineating legal requirements like insurance and benefits for workers, a business license, tax payments, and rezoning a residence as a commercial venture. Patty would never have guessed that the explosive seriality of unfettered capitalism had to submit to the banal restrictions of state bureaucracy. And entrepreneurial episodes such as this seem as much as about capitalism run amuck as they are about Patty getting in over her head.

Luckily, Martin is good with paperwork and straightens out the government exigencies. But setback number two lies in wait. Initially, the girls at school seemed to have had nothing but cat designs on their minds (and bodies), but when a classmate launches a line of competing dresses (customized with a photo of their boyfriend!), Patty and Cathy's cat dress instantly becomes obsolete. Unsold outfits pour into the Lane household, and Patty's debt mounts until Martin steps in, offering an advance against their allowances to pay off their financial obligations as long as the girls give their remaining stock to charity. Thus, Martin cleans up Patty's mess, one that he himself readily was willing to let balloon out of control when he saw the profits pouring in. The coda, enforcing the theme of doubling, mirrors its opening, placing the cousins once more in the living room on a rainy day, Cathy sewing once again. Patty calls the hat that her cousin's working on "cute" and the same entrepreneurial flash goes off. Reading the signs, Cathy rips up her project and suggests going to the movies.

"The Tycoons" is part of a subset of episodes in which Patty attempts to put business-oriented skills into play. In "This Little Patty Went to Market," for instance, Patty forms Patty Lane, Inc. This installment elaborates a somewhat different relation to business than "The Tycoons," focusing here on producing and selling jam. It starts with Patty learning that some stock Martin had bought her to teach her how investments operate is doing quite well. Freshly inspired to exploit the market, she does some research on modern industry, incorporates herself, and seeks out a product for which she can sell stock. Luckily, Cathy has an old-world jam recipe; Patty enlists her in production and Richard and Ross in marketing, while classmates buy up stock and market the product to local stores. Inevitably, it all comes crashing down—literally, in a scene where the Lane kitchen becomes the site of overflowing jam and broken jars.

In their concern with teen entrepreneurialism, specifically a female teen overseeing a capitalist project, these mass-production episodes foreground not just Patty's failure to succeed, but the ease with which an out-of-control capitalist process can go off the rails. The lesson is not that capitalism doesn't work, but that it works too well. It carries on, leaving individual entrepreneurs like Patty and the workers she enlists out in the lurch. Nearly every entrepreneurial episode fails due to production going haywire, and the show represents this through slapstick humor, as if capitalism can be equated with the causation of mayhem, not unlike Lucy and Ethel's chaotic assembly-line work at the chocolate factory. (Yet it matters that Lucy and Ethel are mere employees of a system that they can't keep up with while young Patty tries to be boss, though also to no avail.)[34]

Consumption

In an early episode of the series, "The Slumber Party" (S1E6), Patty organizes a girls' sleepover and the kids hold a conversation about teen girls in their common role of consumption. Yet Patty's mind never strays from the topic of *production*. When one of the girls states, "Whoever thought of boys must have made a million dollars," Patty rejoins, "Then somebody came along and thought of girls, think of the money there must have been in that." Although this detail appears to play into stereotypes of girl consumption as somewhat out of control, the series overall tends to avoid condemning "female" consumerism and in fact complicates the standard gendering of consumption and production. For one, Patty doesn't always target teenage girls in her business ventures: she sets up a babysitting enterprise geared to adult couples and sells products door-to-door (a vacuum cleaner, a waist-thinning machine) to adult consumers.

This flies in the face of numerous analysts of mass culture who imagined "consuming" as emotional, unimportant, and conclusively *feminine*, but aligning "production" as a nobler masculine venture requiring knowledge and skills. The pliable "masses" that so many sci-fi and horror films depicted in the Fifties were, by the Sixties, less often aliens or pod people, but what journalists and news reporters considered the equally frightening, alien power of young girl consumers en masse. Whether chronicling a Beatles gig or a feminist rally, the media made much of the hordes of young women who suddenly seemed too numerous, too visible, and way too full of sexualized energy.

Teen show producers were certainly aware of the buying power of television's youth audiences, much as the recording industry had been of teens in the Fifties, when the emergence of 45 rpm records coincided with the explosion of rock and roll. Original cast recordings and soundtracks of theatrical musicals and films also soared during the decade among all generations. Most scholars situate the initial rumblings of a mass American girl culture in the Forties, when magazines such as *Calling All Girls* and *Seventeen* debuted. *Seventeen* is typically heralded as an early (1944) example of mass media that acknowledged teenage girls' spending power. Girl culture blossomed during the postwar era, a time of relative prosperity and leisure time for many Americans, as industry and media stepped up active, augmented commodity production of items like cameras, cars, refrigerators, and pop and rock recordings.

Such expressions of "structures of feelings" fed on tweens' and younger girls' aspirations for the life-phases that would soon be thrust upon them—full adolescence, young adulthood, working, marriage, and child-rearing. Dolls and trolls could be mothered or strolled around in carriages, hard-plastic Barbies allowed kids to enact adult jobs, and pint-child-sized fishnet stockings and go-go boots let girls feel like they looked just like the models in *Seventeen*.

As we saw in the previous chapter, the tie-in products that swirled around *The Patty Duke Show* reveal the extent to which industry figures behind the show were eager to capitalize on a demographic of teenage girls they defined first and foremost by their consumerism. Of course, *The Patty Duke Show*, as a text of girl culture, was scarcely unique in that way. Barbie had lunch boxes and plenty of accessories, the Gidget franchise involved a universe of tie-ins and media extensions, and on and on. In 1963, *Seventeen* magazine released a short marketing documentary for potential advertisers that was called *The Age of Curiosity*. It began by stressing the newly active role in society that the teenage girl enjoyed, and concluded by giving statistics about the spending power of said teenager, referring to her as "a big, big buyer now and for a long, long time to come. Remember, it's easier to start a habit than to stop one … with your brand! Seventeen!" (One of the average teen consumers the film focused on is played by a young, almost unrecognizable, Mia Farrow.)

Certainly, as an industrial product, *The Patty Duke Show*—along with its merchandise—was built upon, and sustained by, the expectation of an eagerly consumerist female base. Yet the thematics of the show itself tilted away from that. *The Patty Duke Show*—especially in entrepreneurial episodes like "The Tycoons"—clears space for a material notion of production that teenage girls could activate, or take part in, over mere consumption.

Moreover, episodes of the series are surprisingly devoid of stereotypical assumptions of Cathy and Patty as mindless purchasers driven by desires for mindless products/objects. Patty's impulses, thought out as complex schemes, are to acquire new skills, do new things, assume new roles, not to acquire goods. For instance, in S2E2 ("Practice Makes Perfect") she wants to learn how to *play* the tuba, not to buy one, and becomes emotionally and intellectually invested in trying to succeed at the task. Even seemingly frivolous episodes including ones in which Patty sets out to prove she has talents in the cultural arena (as a novelist, songwriter, or a modernist painter) show how Patty strives with commitment to create things, not purchase them. In "Author, Author" (S1E19), when Patty devours a novel by French author Françoise du Play (clearly modeled after teen success Françoise Sagan), she doesn't stop with the act of mere consumption but becomes inspired to assume an important cultural role as America's answer to the French chronicler of modern teen life. Patty carefully plots out how to turn the Lane home attic into a garret for writing and dons the garb of a hip writer. "Author, Author" is a rare episode in not disabusing Patty of her dream: when Martin discovers that a publisher who contracted Patty's book (which Martin reads in draft and finds terrible) actually runs a vanity press, Martin essentially threatens him with legal action for contracting with a minor and gets the publisher to print a limited run of the book. Martin and the rest of the family never reveal to Patty what happened, and she remains in clueless delight over her status as a productive, published author. At episode's end, she even has a next novel ready for publication.[35]

As we've noted, whether focusing on the teen sitcom per se or on girl teen culture overall, scholarly study can't always find an effective place for Patty Duke's series within the cultural landscape. The scholars of girl culture who have attended to teen girl series have for the most part produced work that largely reinforces the presumption of a feminized culture of *consumerism*. For instance, Bill Osgerby uses the parallel rise of postwar girl consumerism and of the genre of "teen TV" to assimilate various teen sitcoms around what he terms a narrative "relish for autonomous active fun" (71) as if that is the only way to define the concerns of diverse series. Yet, "fun," we maintain, is only a sideline in *The Patty Duke Show* to Patty's expansive ambition to make a mark in the world. The series is not centrally about a "commodity desiring" teen girl or, put slightly differently, a "fun through commodity desiring" teen girl subject (although the show's tie-ins do nuance that more than a bit). The series is driven by the girls' desires for new skills and experiences rather than consumer goods. Contra Osgerby, *The Patty Duke Show* isn't really defined by, in his words, "a kind of 'consumerist hedonism,' young women using the products and resources of commercial youth culture to carve out a space for self-expression and personal pleasure that was independent of parental (and often masculine) authority" (82). At the very least, Duke's sitcom implies a potential fissure between 'self-expression' and 'personal pleasure,' to cite two concepts Osgerby conflates. (Earlier [72], he speaks "an ethos of dynamic self-expression and autonomous pleasure.")[36]

Scholars of commodity society sometimes employ the notion of "consumer-citizen," and the term can seem tempting as a way to model behavior within girls' culture in particular. For example, influential girl studies scholar Mary Celeste Kearney takes up the phrase to describe the massive marketing of products to girls in the long postwar period and their generally wholehearted embrace of that marketing, culminating in consumerist teen girl TV. No doubt, as the historians of girl culture are wont to reiterate, there was indeed a conjoining of several developments that brought girls and consumer goods together: an increasing availability of disposable income for teens (such as the widespread practice of babysitting by middle-class white teenagers); the canny recognition by manufacturers that teen girls represented an important new market for goods; and, quite often, an affirmative response by the girls to that marketing through widespread acquiescence and endless acquisition.

Yet to define modern citizenship as primarily or solely consumerist as the term "citizen-consumer" implies risks oversimplification. At the very least, it downplays the salient ways that citizenship is defined through activities other than consumption: thus, while in a recent volume, *The Age of Choice,* the intellectual historian Sophia Rosenfeld does accept that a consumer revolution from the 18th century on gave women a field of purchasing choice around goods destined for, and targeted to, them, she also analyzes the historically parallel activism by women (around the vote, for instance) that provided them realms of choice that don't fit easily under concepts of women as mindlessly, frivolously, wanting goods only.[37] To speak of modern social subjects, women especially, as "citizen-consumers" is to elide how women of different eras can find modes of citizenship apart from consumption, such as in the political realm.

Within the consumerist understanding of girl culture, the gaining of the disposable income that seemingly enables girls to purchase goods is taken itself to be little more than a path to consumption, rather than productive activity in its own right. In this respect, it is revealing that both *The Patty Duke Show* and one antecedent sitcom cited by Kearney, *Meet Corliss Archer*, have episodes that focus on the activity of babysitting and emphasize the hard work that it entails. True, each show's babysitting episode has the girl protagonist engaging in labor for a vain purpose: both girls want to buy a dress they can wear to a party with their respective boyfriends. But the last scene in each—wherein the girls come downstairs to show off their dresses and get approval from their family—almost seem an afterthought and have a perfunctory quality to them. In contrast to the quick endings, both episodes show the babysitting activity in detail, and depict it is as ambitious and ever increasing in scope. Both girls realize that the more babies they tend to, the more money they can make, so they organize rationalized procedures for taking on many babies at once, including enlisting their boyfriends in the cause, in what then becomes a veritable mimicry of capitalist enterprise rather than a quaint habit of a single girl charged with caring for a single child.

It is striking how often episodes depict Patty as a doer, rather than a consumer pure and simple. She is a songwriter as well as a singer, a gossip columnist as well as a clairvoyant, an actor, a writer, a tutor, and on and on. Often, as with "The Babysitters," what is given the most narrative attention is the labor, not its fruits. That she has predictable difficulties in following through on many of her ambitions doesn't alter the emphasis on the teenage girl as a figure of initiative and plucky ambition. (And many people we spoke to pointed to this "pluck" and drive as qualities they loved about *The Patty Duke Show* and what distinguished Patty Duke from other young stars.)

The historical fact of disposable income for teen girls doesn't predict what is done with that income: coming from a perspective indebted to political economy, girl-studies scholars like Kearney assume that girls readily devoured the goods mass-marketed to them and in fixed, predicted fashion. On the one hand, such a determinism can add a pessimism to girl culture studies: girls *had* to be frivolous and mindless because the culture industry made them so. In *American Sweethearts*, for example, Ilana Nash stops her history of what she terms "Teenage Girls in Twentieth-Century Popular Culture" in 1965, when she argues that top-down mass culture had become so entrenched and solidified that nothing more was needed to advance its negative and repressive ideology around girlhood. Other scholars view that system of control as fully pervasive but allow that challenges to it were enabled but only under *later*, different conditions. In an oft-cited essay, "Productive Spaces," Kearney argues, as her subtitle has it, for the idea of "Bedrooms as Sites of Cultural Production" for teen girls. But this, she argues, was made possible only through developments, *beyond the Sixties,* in electronic and digital cultures which allowed teens to use those private, domestic spaces as public-facing venues for blogging, filmmaking, music-making, and so on. Kearney thus shares Nash's historical pessimism about mass culture but differs in positing that later breakthroughs in cultural production enabled girls to offer glimpses of change and challenge.

That one purchases a narrative in an industrial form (including the mediated purchase of a television show through the advertising that sells additional things to the viewer) does not at all mean that the content of the narrative is necessarily consumerist or that one engages with the many moves of the narrative in simple fashion. Although *The Patty Duke Show* merchandise like coloring books or cut-out paper dolls requires that the commodity be consumed in the act of playing with them, it is not inevitably the case that episode storylines celebrate commodity culture or invite mindless consumption. (Theorists of narrative do well to argue that following a story involves retrospective and anticipatory productive activities, imagining options, envisaging alternatives. As we have seen with *The Patty Duke Show*, narratives can be sites for reflection, even when formulaic.) Certainly, the tie-ins and the show are industrial objects proffered to girls, yet the narratives the series offers are not necessarily bulwarks of consumerism.

The series, moreover, seldom shows Patty spending money. Although she has a few LPs scattered around her bedroom, we never see her buying any. In an insightful nod to the many kids who had to wear hand-me-downs, "High Society" (S2E15) displays Patty panicking at the prospect of Sue-Ellen wearing to a dance a dress that she (Patty) can't possibly match or afford. The episode highlights that anxiety when Patty, looking for a bargain in a second-hand shop, inadvertently purchases a fancy dress that Sue-Ellen had once worn. After being humiliated at the dance when Patty and several others learn that the dress used to be her rival's (there is even a framed painting of Sue-Ellen wearing it), a wealthy relative of Sue-Ellen, seeing her distress, saves the day by saying "Patty, what a lovely dress. It's all the thing these days. I see that Sue-Ellen had one for a while. I have three nieces who all have the same gown—it's what well-dressed young women all have," a simple line that reverses the criticism the show might have been making of teenagers' need to conform, such as in slavishly purchasing Cathy's "mass-produced" cat dress. It also redeems the attempt at thriftiness over lavish expenditure.

The Patty Duke Show pushes the idea of a gendered mass consumerism into unexpected directions, emphasizing *masculine* consumption. Few men are shown producing: most of Martin's work occurs off camera and out of sight; his boss is presented as a buffoon; and no male teens launch the kind of "start-ups" that occupy Patty's time so often. Whereas Patty is constantly on the prowl for work (babysitting, door to door sales, soda jerking), there is but one episode which finds Richard eager to land a job (to help his father's construction company), and his father ends up dissuading him.

More often than not, *The Patty Duke Show* assigns male characters the ostensibly feminine features of consumerism. In "The Tycoons," Natalie informs a skeptical Martin she's having fun helping out in the dressmaking and tells her husband not to be "a big-business pooper." After seeing all the customer orders, he starts changing course, but this is when the government agent shows up and takes all the profits away by licenses, permits, zoning, etc. and Martin mutters under his breath, "big-business pooper." Thus, early on, it is Natalie who joins the girls in exuberant embrace of the production enterprise, and tells her husband how much fun she's having, a sitcom mom who recognizes the value—monetary as well as for one's pleasures in life—of productive labor.

The series reserves its most elaborate masculinization of consumption for Richard, a guy constantly on the prowl for food. When he visits the Lane house, the boy's motivations are often as much about eating as they are of seeing Patty. A fleeting moment in "The Songwriters" says it all: Richard shows up at Patty's house and at first hesitates to enter, but Patty announces that her father is out and the coast is clear. Richard rushes in, not to cuddle with Patty but to energetically suggest, "Why don't we have a sandwich?" In another episode, Richard moves into the Lane home while his parents are out of town and he ravages the family's foodstock; other episodes show him gleefully stuffing burgers and sandwiches into his mouth or talking with a mouthful of food (Figure 3.3).

Figure 3.3 Richard Stuffing His Face

Going Intragenerational

Unlike most domestic comedies of the time, *The Patty Duke Show* downplayed intergenerational conflict (*Dennis the Menace*, for instance, was constantly misbehaving and anguishing his parents and their neighbor). Patty was too busy with her self-concerned schemes and fantasies, and Natalie and Martin rarely scolded or lectured their kids for being bad. Indeed, the show's lack of generational misunderstanding, cross-purposes, and tension marks a critical difference from canonical domestic sitcoms, particularly the instructional ones.

Different generations cannot be in conflict if one side or the other isn't there in any potent tension between them. As we've noted, Natalie and Martin's presence carries relatively little weight, and the series displaces generational skirmish into a division within one generation—that of teenagers, particularly teenage girls, sometimes Patty and Cathy, but also Patty's rivals at school, like the girl who comes up with the idea for sweaters with boyfriend photos on them. This displacement makes the series stand out in the Sixties, especially given the rapidity (and mediatized notoriety) with which "the generation gap" moved across American screens and protests in the street.

To be sure, there is plenty of intergenerational interaction in the show, as when the children try to unionize against their parents, but overall it is seldom fraught, redirecting the viewer's focus to what Cathy and Patty, as stand-ins for their generation, are up to. Martin's and, to a lesser extent, Natalie's interactions with Patty, Cathy, and Ross are warm and affirming, but they are somewhat detached as TV families go—less unconcerned than simply unaware. (Byron's and Schallert's unassuming acting styles are also a factor.) Quite often, Patty hatches her schemes without her folks knowing anything at the outset, or even after things have gotten well underway. Reviewer Cleveland Amory went so far as to write "... the adults on this show are strictly new-fashioned types—to be, when the kids are around, seen but not heard."[38]

The absence of parental interference detaches the adults from their children's world. It gives Natalie's character several interesting features, including a degree of autonomy enjoyed by few TV homemakers—there is no "wait until your father gets home," and, as we've noted, she is rarely shown performing household chores. Although this changes in the third season, when the series drops her into domestic cliché, Natalie is overall awarded a degree of dignity, especially when contrasted with the show's depiction of hapless fatherhood. But one can't run too far with this: her character's advice is rarely solicited, and the series only vaguely intimates how she spends her days. Actor Jean Byron wasn't even listed in the opening credits until Season 2.

Feckless Dads and Boring Beaux

The Patty Duke Show joins a continuum of other contemporary sitcoms whose patriarchs were neither imperial nor imposing. At one end of the spectrum was the relatively retiring Ozzie in *Ozzie and Harriet* (1952–66); at the other, the over-the-top performances of a bawdy masculinity in perpetual crisis, exemplified by Ralph Cramden and Ed Norton on *The Honeymooners*. Martin Lane's incompetence appears so clearly that, in one episode, he is not even able to help his son put a model airplane together. And the man is perpetually late to the game. In "The Working Girl" (S1E35), where Patty takes on a job as a soda jerk at the shake shop and is driven into the ground with overwork, all of the Lane family knows how much she is suffering except for Martin, who keeps proclaiming how great it is that Patty has such stick-to-it-ness. When she has a chance to quit, which she desperately wants to do, her clueless father resecures the job for her behind her back, and the show ends there, a rare instance in which Martin determines the finale to Patty's exploits.

Martin's clueless belatedness shows the loosening of the TV patriarch's grip over his family and helps explain a significant narrative motif: Patty may be in a liminal state as she tries to move beyond domestic teendom, but her father lives in a liminality of his own, returning home at the end of the day to what was supposed to be a smooth-running haven but is anything but. Echoing the meager control he exerts over his workplace, Martin Lane's home is not his domain, let alone his castle; there is almost a placelessness to him, a wandering, misplaced masculine authority. When he does spout the moral homilies of the instructional sitcom dad, it is with little force or verve. And even more importantly, that paternal advice in fact is seldom sought out, particularly in the first two years of the series. Television scholar Lynn Spigel observes the trend revving up even earlier, noting how critics in television's early years were already disgruntled over the unmasculine appearance of fathers in domestic sitcoms.[39]

It is perhaps no coincidence that as the fiction of white patriarchal authority was losing its televisual grasp in the Sixties, sitcoms were introducing what we term the "woeful boyfriend" in series like *That Girl* and *The Patty Duke Show*. For sitcom girls like Patty, Cathy, and *That Girl*'s Ann Marie, their boyfriends suggest not only the dullness of monogamy but of the future they portend as the next generation of beside-the-point fathers.

Viewers have endlessly wondered what Patty sees in Richard. His fundamental ineptitude renders his rare moments of virility to be a sham: his remark in the pilot that he now has a "harem" is more awkward than funny or erotically energized—Richard just isn't playboy material. In one episode, when all the high school girls suddenly find him hunky, it's played for a joke, one that lasts just a single episode, feeding off of the short-term memory required of the sitcom form. Richard's dullness only deepens when contrasted against Patty's spunky energy, and Applegate truly excelled at performing that dorkiness with unthreatening charm.

Richard, in short, is simply around. Beginning with the pilot, he's nothing more than Patty's steady, and the show evinces little interest in developing or deepening their relationship. Unlike romantic comedy, where couples must fight for their love by surmounting obstacles, *The Patty Duke Show* offers no such tilting at windmills. For David Grote, one of the first scholars to write at length on TV sitcoms, such lack of fighting for love means that the sitcom as a form of television comedy betrays the dominant tradition of romantic comedy as a genre, which focuses on the progress of a couple over the resistance of an authority figure, such as a parent who is opposed to unions based on love and not economic benefit.[40] On sitcoms, only deromanticized situations endure, leaving little to be fought over. Sometimes Richard will break up with Patty for another girl, or vice versa, but they always return to one another, like default settings. What is more, the breakups typically dramatize Patty's rivalry with another girl, usually arch-enemy Sue-Ellen, in plots that result in confirming Richard's quite relative significance for Patty, not as a romantic preference but as a means of preventing her rival from getting him. In one especially silly episode, Patty thinks the mob may be after her for witnessing a crime. She implores Cathy to marry Richard but only, she clarifies, because she doesn't want Sue-Ellen to get him if she is rubbed out.

The series eradicates nearly any intimation of sexual impulses or impropriety. When Richard temporarily moves into the Lane household (as will a young beatnik and a good-looking high-school basketball player in other episodes), no one bats an eye. This contrasts sharply with the utter horror

Martin exhibits whenever Patty and Richard seem to be moving forward in their relationship: going steady or, worst of all, getting that marriage license. So, Martin and Natalie allow for boys to be close at hand, sometimes as close as an extra bed down the hall, but the moment the prospect of marriage comes up, chaos and moral panic take over.

The Patty Duke Show seems unconcerned about premarital possibilities, which it simply ignores. Worry is reserved for marriage, which the show resoundingly characterizes as stultifying and unsatisfying. Even monogamy is taken off the table. Cathy, for instance, is not tied to one steady, as is Patty, and while she has a few crushes and dates across the series, they are seldom emphasized, and the characters remain undeveloped. The closest Cathy comes to expressing romance occurs in an episode where she overcomes conflicting dating advice from each member of the Lane family and declares her attraction to a boy, who reciprocates and is never heard from again. Cathy may be more serial than Patty, but, like her cousin, her relationships are chaste to the core.

As sitcoms moved into the late Sixties and Seventies, not only were instructional dads fewer and far between, but husbands and boyfriends became similarly less crucial: Shirley Jones ran the busload of singers in *The Partridge Family* as a single mom; Julia raised her child without a male partner; and Mary Tyler Moore, Phyllis, Grace (of *Grace Under Fire*), and all the *Golden Girls* were single, without steady men in their lives. This was not simply a reversal of the single father sitcoms of the Fifties and Sixties, but a firm reworking of them: these women were fully unmotivated by ideas of marriage or the quest for permanent romance. Since then, instructional sitcoms—and the stiff white, male authorities they supposedly command—have become out-of-date jokes.

Defanged Erotics

Abetted by William Schallert's sympathetic performance, the relationship Martin has with Natalie is rendered nearly as chaste. Though a mature, married, and affectionate couple, the pair reflects the same anemic degree of sex and romance as the adolescents Patty and Richard. It's strange, given their relative obliviousness to their children, that Natalie and Martin didn't direct more attention to each other, as couples did in childless sitcoms of the early to mid-Sixties such as *I Dream of Jeannie* and *My Living Doll*, series that exploited a carefully managed salaciousness through their fantasy-based premises. Procreation was also excised from the realm of numerous TV family sitcoms at the time. Some began with an already established number of offspring, as if all were over and done with. *The Brady Bunch*, which started its run slightly later, famously merged two widowed parents with three children each into one sitcom family of six that was never to expand. 1965's *The Sound of Music* did much the same thing for the movies, overlooking the historical fact that Maria and Georg von Trapp produced three more children after they married–Maria in fact was pregnant when the family arrived at Ellis Island.

As Melissa Phruksachart has asserted, the single-dad sitcoms offered powerful examples of an "immaculate family romance," a form of colonialist and patrilineal succession in which white American dads expanded their families either by adopting (often war orphans) or hiring people of color who would function as new, added members of the family. In *Bachelor Father*, the orphan is a white American child (the title character's niece), and fatherly wisdom is transferred onto the Asian "house boy" Peter who offers sage "Oriental" advice to his white employer/family patriarch. *The Patty Duke Show* had its own adoption episode, but it's Patty who accidentally adopts a Korean war orphan, momentarily extending the family by the means of that immaculate family romance. A symbolic mother for twenty-six minutes, Patty operates without any involvement of physical, sexualized maternity (we return to this adoption episode later). In its own way, Cathy's arrival into the Lane household "immaculately" extends the family, too, though without the racialized terms so crucial to Phruksachart's analysis.[41]

Revising Sex and Love in the Sixties

In several episodes, a desultory Patty strays from Richard and pursues another beau. It might be a new boy at school, the older brother of one of Ross's friends, an out-of-town visitor, a physician, or a visiting teacher, but they are always one-offs, sometimes played in cameo appearances by recognizable entertainment stars of the era such as Troy Donahue, Jean-Pierre Aumont, Sal Mineo, and Robert Goulet. Typical here is "Don't Monkey with Mendel" (S2E26) in which Patty falls for her science teacher (Goulet). It begins with Cathy explaining to her cousin the concept of genetic transmission after newborn guinea pigs arrive with fur colors that had been predicted in science class. Patty whips into high gear, convinced that she can biologically engineer superior offspring for herself, whether superior in brain or brawn or, optimally, both. She surveys the male stock around her, ultimately determining that the dishy science teacher has both, and tries to court him. Aware of the inappropriateness of such a relationship, Goulet's character labors to keep her at bay and, when another guinea pig's offspring fail to fulfill Patty's genetic predictions, he informs her about recessive genes and the unpredictability of genetic transmission. Resigned, Patty goes back to Richard and restores their sexless status quo.

For a show airing in the mid-Sixties, it's significant that "Don't Monkey with Mendel" even raises biology as a factor in approaching the matter of future generations. While the series obviously can't talk about sex per se, it seems to recognize the mandate that procreation should be an inevitable aspect of reproductive heterosexual development, and that women are expected to have kids and therefore need to engage in procreation—so they might want to selective in choosing their male partners. Whereas some romantic comedies will bracket out sexual desire or pit sex against love, "Don't Monkey with Mendel" acknowledges sexual activity while also disconnecting it from amorousness. After all, most of the men that Patty considers for a procreative mate only represent a biological opportunity and have nothing to do with libidinal desire on her part.

Conversely, in Season 3's opening episode, "A Foggy Day in Brooklyn Heights," in which Frankie Avalon guest stars as himself, the possibility of romantic desire beyond the norm of family-building presents itself. Avalon enters the Lane family after knocking at their door for help for his car, which had broken down nearby on the way to the airport. Patty and Cathy are both stunned. (Cathy has become Americanized enough not just to recognize him, but to have fantasized about him in a previous episode, "How to Be Popular.") Once Avalon's car is repaired, the teen idol heads out, but not before giving Patty a kiss on the cheek, which she asserts she'll never wash off. Later that night, Richard comes over to propose a movie, and Patty suggests they listen to records and dance instead. Richard: "Ok. The Stones? The Animals? The Beasts?" "No," Patty replies, "Frankie Avalon." After Richard puts one of his records on, there's a close-up of Patty as a man's hand enters the frame to hold her. A reverse angle reveals Avalon singing to her as the two sway together, and when the song concludes, he kisses her deeply and a close-up shows Patty swooning. But the next reverse shot reveals Richard standing in Avalon's place, who says "Boy, you never kissed me like that before, Patty," to which Patty smiles wanly as the episode wraps. The intrusion of this dream moment that concludes the episode provides a vague glimpse of possibility. Can romantic desire be admitted if it appears onscreen only in the form of a character's dream?

Marriage-Phobia to the Fore

While dreamboats can, as their name implies, be dreamt about, dreaming here can be done only furtively. What the young men offer Patty will not extend beyond fantasy. Thus, while *The Patty Duke Show* flirts with the imagination of romance, it grants it no solidity, especially the solidity that might accompany a socially sanctioned couple of husband and wife. In this way, the series unrepentantly resists the marital destiny that Paul Goodman and others assumed was young women's defining fate in the Sixties. Indeed, marriage-phobia, or at least, marriage-evasion, might be embedded in the underlying structure of the sitcom, in which marriage would disrupt the premise, character functions and narrative directions of a show.

In "Every Girl Should Get Married" (S2E17), guest star Frank Sinatra Jr. (whom Duke dated, platonically, and to whom she refers as her "first romance"[42]) plays David, the marriage-shy betrothed of Natalie's niece Ann, who will soon be visiting the Lanes. Patty overhears her parents discussing how to convince David to "get married to her right away" and flies into a panic thinking they're talking about her. David arrives, and despite being struck by his good looks, Patty does her utmost to convince him that the Lanes are highly dysfunctional, trying to dissuade him from marrying into her family. David quickly figures out the misunderstanding but plays along, finally telling a relieved Patty he couldn't possibly compete with her Richard—maybe he will marry Ann to get over his misery that things with Patty did not work out. Weaving together the allure of the teen dreamboat and the default alternative of Patty and Richard "going steady," the episode vaguely points to marriage as a possibility—but, once more, only for guest characters waltzing through a single episode—and a possibility moreover to be dreaded.

One of the series' oddest and most innovative episodes develops the anti-marriage theme by combining the stasis of sitcom structure with the show's doubling motif. "Fiancée for a Day" (S3E30) opens with Patty and Richard in a parked car, discussing the nice evening they've just had with some recently married friends. Richard says, "We're not getting any younger—let's get married!" Patty says yes, although she knows she won't have the nerve to tell her parents.

Two extremely stylized fantasy sequences about married life ensue. In the first, among a bubbly flurry of ribbons, bows, and polka dots, a somewhat upper-crust Patty affectionately greets an equally upper-crust Richard returning home from his rewarding white-collar job. He carries a doll for their adorable daughter Patricia (played by Duke—more doubling); and Patty happily tells him about her day as a homemaker. Back from this fantasy, Patty receives a visit from their young married friend Sally (played by Judy Carne, who became the "sock it to me" victim on *Laugh In*) who drops by to talk privately with Patty and confesses that financial woes have marred her marriage, as husband Bob "knows about as much about finance as I know about inter-ballistic missiles."

Once Sally leaves, Patty has another fantasy about married life with Richard. The camera is positioned in exactly the same place, and the characters assume their previous marks on what appears to be the same set, but now rendered as extremely run down with visual indications of poverty everywhere. There are intimations of violence; their child has a comically exaggerated overbite; and their dialogue—word-for-word identical to that of the first fantasy sequence—is delivered with such sarcastic resentment so as to utterly capsize its initial connotations. After this alternate negative fantasy, another rhyming scene occurs "in reality." Not unlike Sally's earlier lament to Patty, Bob now complains to Richard about Sally's excessive shopping, claiming "Women know as much about finances as I know about inter-ballistic missiles."

Rather than advancing the situation, the episode's twofold structure plays each potential outcome against the other. At once separate and shared, these fantasies cause Richard and Patty to lose their nerve and forgo their engagement. The episode's coda likewise mirrors its opening, with the two once again in a parked car, but now saying they're glad they're *not* like Bob and Sally. The installment entertains a fully doubled image of the future—what would it be like if Patty and Richard were married and have children?—to entertain it again with a completely different tone and meaning.

In "Going Steady" (S1E22), an earlier episode, Patty asks her parents to approve of Richard giving her his ring to indicate that they are going steady. Natalie and Martin reluctantly agree, as they expect the relationship to be short-lived. Richard takes their okay as an occasion to move into the Lane home, where he swiftly becomes an annoyance. Martin is appalled by the young man's food consumption, and Patty is horrified by his behavioral shifts when he begins dispensing edicts about her appearance and dictating their leisure choices. Martin's disapproval deepens and, unlike other episodes in which he jokingly points out Richard's limited "romantic" allure, here, he is truly annoyed. Discovering Richard eating voraciously once again, Martin snarks, "No wonder boys want girls to wear their rings: it solves their eating and housing problems." Cathy is troubled by Patty's surrender to Richard's domination, and soon the entire family is ready for this "going steady" phase to end, even Patty and Richard—although they won't admit it. Richard's father, who feels the kids are too young, comes over and everyone agrees that if they can convey the burdens that marriage entails, Patty and Richard will cease to "play house."

Martin talks separately to each of them, after which they have separate nightmares of what their marriage would be like. Both are dystopic fantasies staged once more with a profound theatricality, featuring two-dimensional expressionist decors of painted door frames without any backdrop. Both Patty's and Richard's imagined marriages entail endless labor at work/at-home to raise seemingly endless numbers of children while the other partner is out having a good time. Richard's nightmare vision is initiated by Martin coyly referring to Natalie as the boy's "mother-in-law," and, looking straight into the camera ridden with panic, Richard cries out "My mother-in-law!" before we move into his version of the nightmare (Figures 3.4a, 3.4b).

Appropriately, given their vibrant, even overwrought enactments of marriage-phobia, "Going Steady" and "Fiancée for a Day" offer The Patty Duke Show's boldest experiments with style and narrative. The theme threatens not only to upend domestic stabilities and teen antics, but also the series' usually plain, sober visual style, which some fans recall appreciatively as a non-flamboyant absence of pretension.

By representing amorous coupling, especially the kind that might point to reproductive, heterosexual marriage, as oppressive or nightmarish, The Patty Duke Show undercuts the desirability of this ideal. And while "Fiancée for a Day" perhaps most overtly dramatizes its marriage-phobia, its own, less stylized details also convey these points through Patty's parents' repeated insistence that she should be playing the field and their concern that Patty and Richard are getting too serious. And so it ends that, over its three-year existence, Richard's "pinning" of Patty is as far as The Patty Duke Show will

Figure 3.4a The Nightmare of Marriage: Richard's Version

Figure 3.4b The Nightmare of Marriage: Patty's Version

ever go. (Recall that even the show's later telefilm depicts them as divorced—beyond the sexual aspects of courtship and marriage.)

Such details elaborate the notable and near-total distance *The Patty Duke Show* kept from the nation's preoccupation with sex and sex roles at the time. In the Fifties, *Playboy* had created a lusty masculinist heterosexual culture; the following decade was inaugurated by the Pill and the publication of bestsellers such as Helen Gurley Brown's *Sex and the Single Girl* (1962). Yet even as the decade immersed itself in the shifting sexual mores for young singles, the FCC dictated that television could depict very little of this. The topics exist in highly displaced ways: the attractive woman of the cohabitating couple in *My Living Doll* was, for instance, not a fellow human, but an android robot companion for Bob McDonald, whose job as a scientist attempted to turn her into an object of study, not an object of erotic desire. Brassiere ads placed bras over tight sweaters on mannequins or humans, such as busty Hollywood stars like Jane Russell, often to humorous effect. It was the cinema, an industry needing to differentiate its product from the perceived rivalry of TV, that began to tackle more risqué material, whether through European imports like *Belle de Jour* (1967) or domestic productions such as *Lolita* (1962). By 1968, the motion pictures ratings system (G, M, R, X, originally) was introduced to catch up with the rapidly advancing explicitness of cinema's new vanguard.

Given the constraints of TV broadcast policy and industrial standards regarding the topic, the lack of erotic frisson between Natalie and Martin Lane, or Patty and Richard, is not altogether surprising. Yet its near-total absence suggests new ways of imagining male-female relationships that exceed prevailing norms involving sex and marriage, even turning a blind eye to romance. What goes on between Patty and Richard brackets out the idea of "love"—too strong a word, actually, for what is basically a holding pattern—from a sense of progress or narrative development. Just as Maxwell Smart and Agent 99 or Jeannie and Major Nelson should never have gotten married (which pretty much fed into their series's cancellation), Patty and Richard, as teenagers in a challenging world and as sitcom placeholders in a rather unchanging structure, never exceed the stability of the situation from which they started. The very term "going steady," which served as a song name in the contemporary Broadway and film hit *Bye Bye Birdie*, captures the steady-state nature of romance in teen sitcoms that is so fundamental to their broader stasis.

The fact that love manifests as a holding pattern rather than something to be sought after has several consequences for *The Patty Duke Show*. For one, Richard's constant presence as Patty's steady means that most of her intrigues and enterprises occur beyond the realms of love and romance. With amorous adventure pretty much off the table, she can turn her attentions to initiatives out in the larger world and, as we explore in Chapter 5, in civic, economic, and political arenas rather than those confined to home, school, or romance. This is no small achievement for a seemingly escapist, silly sitcom.

The Patty Duke Show's distance from more sexually expressive context may indicate a certain lagging behind or "squareness" of the show. Yet its transparent anti-marriage messaging would be difficult for traditional cultural commentators to champion. As a "hinge" work, it straddles a squareness that cannot really address the flamboyant energies of youth culture (sex, drugs, and rock and roll) but it also cannot endorse standard understandings of marriage as women's fate. The show is thus inscribed in its times, albeit in an ambiguous and often awkward fashion. That lack of erotic tension within the Lane household might even engage a potentially progressive dimension.

When the series aired, Eros was often being promoted as a valuable but underutilized political force, whether by Marcuse in *Eros and Civilization*; Wilhelm Reich in *The Function of the Orgasm* (both hugely influential for the Sixties, although first published before that decade); or even Susan Sontag in "Against Interpretation," the last line of which declares "we need an erotics of art."[43] Of course, much of what was touted then as the sexual revolution played to the benefit of straight men for whom the Pill and *Playboy* transformed women into docile playmates. Even would-be revolutionary groups such as anti-war activists and the Black Panthers did little to challenge this construction of femininity and its value. Male activists of all stripes would plan, supervise, and lead protests against the Vietnam war and corporate America, while their girlfriends mimeographed and made coffee at headquarters. In the early Sixties, Black Panther Stokely Carmichael infamously remarked ("joked," we are supposed to believe), "What is the position of women in SNCC? The position of women in SNCC is prone." (SNCC stands for the Student Nonviolent Coordinating Committee, which played a significant role in the civil rights movement.)

Without wanting to stretch the point too far, *The Patty Duke Show* does seem to free Patty from the restrictions of serving as a romantic, sexual, or familial object and enables her to make the forays she does into political, civic, and personally oriented realms of young adulthood. (And she was not "punished" for these initiatives or for her being too young, as Nash argues about the partially sexualized, partially diminished "Gidget," who, she maintains, was given a pedestal from which to fall, or an emptiness to be filled with familial approval.)[44] Patty Lane had no pedestal from which to tumble, nor was she diminished for embarking on her schemes and goals. Yes, they are presented comedically, as "hairbrained," and end with predictable returns home by the end of each episode. But that ideological and narrative resting place was often more restive than restful. In demanding nothing sexual of teenage girls during the "sexual revolution," *The Patty Duke Show* freed girls like Patty and Cathy to fantasize about or explore aspects of young female adulthood on their own.

PART II
TELEVISING AMERICAN DREAMS AND CONFLICTS

A Thematic Account

4

Twins, Doubles, and Their Others

Comic Openings in the Sixties

Life would be easier if there was only one of me ... but a lot less fun.
—Patty Lane to Cathy Lane in "The Wedding
Anniversary Caper" episode

As early as its fourth episode, *The Patty Duke Show* checks in on how things are going for the series, as if to ensure it is adhering to the centrality of cousins so "two of a kind" as to make you "lose your mind." "The House Guest" opens with Martin receiving a long-distance call from Cathy's father, Kenneth, Martin's twin brother in Scotland. The update on Cathy that Martin gives him obligingly reiterates the show's premise: "She and Patty are confusing the whole neighborhood. Reminds me of our youth. The twins bit all over again."

Although Martin's claim that Cathy and Patty are sowing confusion affirms that central gimmick, it contradicts everything that audiences had seen up until then. Previous episodes had contained little if any evidence that Cathy's and Patty's visual similarity had bewildered either the show's characters or viewers at home. Indeed, "The House Guest" later refutes Martin's throwaway remark when the eponymous house guest shows up and readily distinguishes, rather than confuses, the girls.

When the series depicts the cousins together, it presents them either side-by-side through split-screen optical effects or in immediate succession to one another through editing, creating another layer of doubling yet always making sure we know who is who. The side-by-side shot of the girls in identical clothes in the credit sequence is a sort of exception that holds no sway over episode plotlines where comparative techniques highlight the contrast between the twins, rather than the similarity that typical side-by-side placement for twins foregrounds, another move that is rather incongruous for a series that establishes its twin cousins as identical. The show's use of

The Patty Duke Show *and the American Sixties*. Caryl Flinn and Dana Polan, Oxford University Press.
© Oxford University Press 2026. DOI: 10.1093/oso/9780197667439.003.0005

make-up, wigs, and costume also deprioritizes the girls' physical resemblance to highlight their differences: Patty has a flip wig; Cathy's is a pageboy, and their behavior, comportment, accents and vocal deliveries are all distinct from the other's (Figures 4.1a and b).

For a series premised on identical twins, that lack of confusion between them is remarkable, and, surprisingly, it's sustained throughout the show with few exceptions, most of them fleeting and inconsequential. A rare instance in which one twin tries to pass herself off as the other occurs when Patty attempts a career as a fortune teller to her classmates—mystical regalia and all. Conducted at home, her business does too well for her to handle alone (another instance of entrepreneurialism running amuck) and she enlists Cathy to pretend to be her so that they can double up on paying customers. Patty changes out of her costume just as a bunko squad cop shows up, but when Cathy, garbed as fortune teller Patty, emerges in the same room, the jig is up. However, it's not the resemblance between them that matters to the policeman, just the fact that one girl's outfit confirms that illegal clairvoyance has been going on in the Lane home. This peculiarity—a show "about" twins that rarely makes use of that conceit—cues us to think about twinning in ways that deviate from conventional understandings, which tend to stress the similarities (especially visual ones) between twinned siblings—or cousins, as the case may be.

Just as audiences of *The Patty Duke Show* would not have been confused by the two girls, they would not have confused the twinned fathers during the phone call of the "House Guest" episode. Schallert portrays both Martin and Kenneth but, as Kenneth, he simply adds a mustache, making the man look less like an eminent journalist than a kid who'd plastered on a prop from a dollar store. Moreover, the men never appear in the same shot—they are geographically separated, after all.

In this installment, Kenneth had called his brother to warn him that their Aunt Pauline was planning to visit Brooklyn Heights and stay with the Lanes. When the intractable Aunt arrives, she initially remarks on the girls' resemblance, yet adds that Cathy has always been the prettier one. This immediately undercuts Martin's remarks about twinning as a source of confusion, and Pauline's hastily-made observation insinuates ready distinction into the girls' resemblance very early on in the series.

As it delves into its contemporary subject matter, *The Patty Duke Show* doesn't rely on resemblance to make the point: to the contrary, it needs viewers to recognize distinctions between the two girls and their

Figure 4.1a "Cathy's Hair" says 'Cathy!' "

Figure 4.1b "Patty's Hair" says 'Patty!' "

separate ways of attaining their goals. In this fashion, the series uses the twins' enterprises to project an idea of teen life that is comic in the fullest sense of the term: a celebration of the upbeat possibilities that await the girls. Here, *The Patty Duke Show* offers something special with regards to the dominant tradition in representing twins. For the series stands most as an ode to the differences between the girls instead of their sameness. Even more importantly, their opposing traits (regional backgrounds, levels of outgoingness, academic dedication, and relationships to American pop culture) remain surprisingly value-neutral and morally unjudged.

The Patty Duke Show presents a set of "identical twins" but opens the structure up to wider sets of identities and possibility. This, as we argue, is achieved through *doubling*, a term that builds off of but is not the same as twinning. Doubling captures a more expansive process that establishes a jumping off point to new cultural formations and potentials. Unlike, say, the horror genre, which was loathe to alter the formula of attributing cleanly oppositional ethical and moral valences to twins, another version of those dyads was appearing on television and movie screens that suggested the *comic* possibility of doubling without moral judgement.

Curiously, prevailing scholarship on twinning seldom engages with comic renditions. One wonders whether in contrast to that overwhelming emphasis on evil twinning, *The Patty Duke Show*'s presentation of twinning in affirmative, even buoyant, terms might help explain its near-total absence in that literature, which excluded the show in a dishearteningly similar pattern to its dismissal from most sitcom histories.

In this chapter, we examine prevailing theories, concepts, and ideas of twinning, in and beyond the Sixties, and consider how they operate in regard to Duke's quite distinct sitcom; in our view, these dominant claims fail to account for what the show actually accomplishes. We contend that, as an artifact of Sixties mass media and girl culture, *The Patty Duke Show* drops a literal concern with *twinning* to deploy a wider, looser sense of *doubling* that helps elaborate the series' interactions with its own social and historical moment.

The Dominant Story: The Negative Tradition of Twin Studies

As we noted in the Introduction, historians of the Sixties tend to divide the decade into an early conservative phase and a later, rebellious one and load each one up with its own clichés. And, as we discussed in Chapter 3, TV critics have created their own common history of the sitcom, with distinct phases sequenced in a similarly linear fashion. Likewise, commentators on twinning have generated their own standard story, a set of talking points that limit their analyses and conceptual frameworks.

Accounts that consider twins in terms of their relationship to singletons (the term for non-twins) exhibit the discourse's overriding trends most overtly. Moving across epochs and regions, mythic narratives and scientific studies, they note that singleton culture almost always imposes a function on twins that primarily serves the singleton observers.[1] The latter transform twins into omens of good or evil, bounty or losses, figuring them as freaks of human nature or informants on it. Or they are seen as preternaturally insightful, para-kinetic or psychic, as in the oft-touted twins who finish each other's sentences, or who seem to engage in telepathically shared acts and decisions despite temporal or geographical separation. William Viney and Hillel Schwartz pinpoint a key aspect of this pervasive perspective. As Viney puts it, "We are pillars of whatever difference or similarity or remarkable quirk you may want to see."[2] In fact, very little ink has been spilled on distinguishing twins from each other or considering them as fully separate beings.[3]

Forced to function as Doppelgängers or unusual examples of human subjectivity, twins seem always to present a conundrum to singletons, whether in cultural criticism or scientific research. Ultimately, the argument goes, they are there to teach dominant, singleton society something fundamentally existential about human life, be it the monstrosities lying just past the normal or the need to challenge those self-same norms. Twin studies teem with questions such as "What are the limits of human individuality?" or, with conjoined twins, "Where are the limits of a human body?"

Viney convincingly demonstrates that this line of questioning has long had a deleterious impact on the lives of twins, especially when twin study began in earnest in the Thirties, a period when eugenics was a popular area of scientific fascination. Rooting the scientific study of twins in such questions smacks of the laboratory treatment of primates; indeed, Viney cites twins researcher Tim Spector's chilling declaration that twins are "the closest we get to doing animal experiments on humans"[4] And when singletons turn to twins for insight, they often, knowingly or not, rely on highly individualized notions of the (singular) non-twinned self as a point of departure, a humanist concept that gained momentum in the late Renaissance and continued to reign throughout early capitalist and scientific eras when western concepts of human subjectivity privileged individual thought, achievement, and industriousness above all else. There's a telling paradox here: twins are blurred together in the dominant perception so that singleton individuality and self-integrity can be all the more secured. Conversely, though, Hillel Schwartz suggests a fragility to this fetishization of individualism by seeing twins and doubles as irremediably other to the unique self, writing of the early twenty-first century, "our culture of the copy mocks the romanticism which seeks out the irreproducible as the source of truth."[5] Whether this mockery foretells the collapse of the ideology of individualism is up to the reader to decide.

Many popular narratives trade in dualities and oppositions into which twins are readily inserted—good guys and bad guys, urbanites and rural folks, princesses and pagans, monsters and victims—but they figure most prominently in horror, signaling dominant culture's suspicion of them. The trend is true for fables both classical and contemporary, highbrow and lowbrow, and across media platforms. One of their most iconic cinematic iterations has been the ghostly twin sisters in *The Shining*, but others have filled screens for decades: *The Black Room* (1935), *Evil Twin* (2007); Bette Davis as twins in *A Stolen Life* (1946) and, twinning herself again a quarter century later, in *Dead Ringer* (1964), whose title is itself subsequently twinned twenty-five years later, in David Cronenberg's twin-gynecologist thriller, *Dead Ringers* (1989).

The list of good/bad twins in horror is endless—we're not even counting film traditions beyond North America—and likely to grow as AI and CGI technologies expand. Within "high" literature, the tradition is emblematized in Dostoyevsky's *The Double* (an inspiration for the 2013 film *The Double*), Dumas's *The Man in the Iron Mask*, Wilde's *The Portrait of Dorian Grey*, Poe's "William Wilson," and, most anointed of them all, Stevenson's *Dr. Jekyll and Mr. Hyde*. All of these stories erect strict dyads, apportioning moral features of goodness to one twin and of evil to the other. Their idea of a double takes on a metaphysical bent to suggest that, as a condition of being, everyone has a shadow life behind or beyond them.[6]

The organizing structure of the good and evil twins traces back in modernity to the Doppelgänger of German Romantic Literature that identified the dreaded figure of the double (literally, a "double-traveler") prominent in horror and its subgenres like the Gothic. Doppelgängers typically fall into two modalities: in one, a character double emerges from within, the dark side of a split figure, as in *Jekyll and Hyde*; in the other, an identical entity exists external to a person, an outsider who might compromise or spirit away the base individual's identity, fortune, or career.

Practically without exception, commentators on twinship invoke Freud's notion of the uncanny, which itself references E. T. A. Hoffman's stories of "The Sandman" and "Olympia" to exemplify the uncanny's floating sense of odd disturbance. Freud argues that its "excitement of dread" comes into play when something familiar (*heimlich*, or home-like) is perceived as alien or unfamiliar (*unheimlich*, or uncanny), as when "Olympia," Hoffman's feminized automaton, comes to life. Notably, Freud does not lean on the idea of twinning per se as creating this sense, but that of a self, location, or experience that has been doubled or vaguely repeated or shadowed by something not quite recognized, something at once familiar and different, such as an inanimate, human-adjacent form (a doll, statue, or puppet) that shadows the human. This explains the horror genre's penchant for dolls, turning them into creepy stand-ins for duplicated, inverted, stolen, or ghostly identities wrongly brought to life. In this way, Freud's uncanny isn't about twinning so much as doubling: a doll is not the twin of the human but an inanimate other. In fact, Freud only once addresses biological twinning as such in his work. In "The Psychogenesis of a Case of Homosexuality in a Woman," he cites the case of twin brothers, one successful in heterosexual romantic conquests, the other developing homosexual tendencies to avoid amorous competition with his twin. This, his one reference to twinning, has nothing at all to do with the uncanny.[7]

Writers and creators continue to connect twins to Freudian uncanniness and position them within polarities of moral goodness and immoral evil. In 2023, leftist cultural critic Naomi Klein released the bestseller *Doppelganger*, written soon after people began to emerge from the COVID-19 epidemic. She starts by noting how Naomi Wolf, her political opposite, had functioned as a "shadow Naomi" with whom Klein was often confused. While Wolf had initially become a feminist icon after the publication of *The Beauty Myth* in the Eighties, over time, her ideas took some unexpected dark turns as she began to espouse far right-wing conspiracy theories. Klein took note, chiefly because people were mixing her up with Wolf, due not simply to the parallel rise of their fame, but of online culture and its increasingly distracted interlocutors and their fast-paced flurries of posting and reposting, all augmented by the social isolations and political divisions of life under COVID-19. Contending that Wolf was functioning as the "mirror side" of her own career and identity, Klein considers the phenomenon as part of a larger "mirror world" that takes aspects of the real world to twist—and twin—them into a disturbing post-truth shadowland with its claims to alternative "facts," theories, and realities.

The Mass Reproduction of Sameness:
Twinning Goes Multiple

The authors of many twin studies glide smoothly, too smoothly, from focusing on literal twinship to quickly shifting their attentions to massive, multiplied sameness, as if twinness were the gateway to infinite replication. As art historian James Meyer writes, "The only certain attribute of the double, apart from twoness, is that it is endless—a mise-en-abyme of repetition, copying, splitting, inverting, mirroring, shadowing, twinning, juxtaposing, and opposing, to name some of its expressions."[8] The terms are often used interchangeably or teleologically, suggesting that one-on-one doubling leads inexorably to out-of-control multiplication, not unlike the entrepreneurial ventures Patty frequently undertakes. Even the trajectory of Hillel Schwartz's resolutely historical study of twinning and mass reproduction, *The Culture of the Copy*, follows this arc. His first chapter, "Vanishing Twins," is bookended by illustrations of doubling, such as a woman observing her reflection in a mirror, but it also includes a photograph of multiple, nearly identical mannequin hands left in a drawer, as Schwartz's account zips quickly from twinned images to cases of mass proliferation.

Proliferation, replication, and reproduction took on an intriguing variety of concrete forms across American products and media in the early Sixties. In 1960, the first commercially viable photocopier was released to the public. Having taken years to develop to the point of producing faithful copies, it effectively dislodged notions of originality or singularity as the sole bearer of communication and meaning. The machines not only enabled one-to-one duplication, but created new paths for visual reproductive practices to emerge, arguably culminating in Daniel Ellsberg's revolutionary use of Xerox in 1969 to photocopy the Pentagon papers from the Rand Corporation, and eventually releasing them to the *New York Times*.[9] Around the same time, as Schwartz notes, carbon-copying allowed typewriters to make near-exact duplicates, a process he provocatively calls a "re-enactment," in which a facsimile might serve alternative, mediated purposes more than the original did.[10] At the other end of America's fascination with proliferation was the

1960 arrival of "The Pill," which curtailed one sort of reproduction but provided people with increased options for their sexual and procreative choices. And, melding multiplicity with synchronicity, the Telstar rocket-satellite was launched in July 1962, enabling the simultaneous transmission of live television pictures trans-Atlantically.

As if guided by Marcuse or Adorno and other postwar leftists, progressive intellectuals and cultural commentators of the Sixties maintained that the human subject was but a cog in a preordained system of endlessly self-replicating mass production. No longer was there a self that confronted mountains of products; it had itself become a product of mass production. Selfhood had lost its agency, its particularity and its ability to control its own identity—or to possess an inviolate singular identity at all. From this critical vantage point, it seems reasonable to assert that mass culture embodied those social changes in structures and metaphors of replication, doing their part to leave lapsed subjectivity in their wake.

The left-wing intellectuals and creatives of the Sixties were intent on critiquing the unaltered conformity that, they maintained, was partly generated by an all-absorbing consumer culture—cue Pete Seeger's release of "Little Boxes," a song whose immediate target was the identical-looking suburban homes that were springing up like weeds after the war. In his blistering "How to Look at Television," Adorno maintained that the "hidden layers" of the new medium's ideological messages existed only to manage the mollified masses. In a curious invocation of both twinning and the uncanny, he wrote that formulaic TV shows produced "halo effects of previous experiences."[11] For him, the machinery of mass culture could not refer to anything new, but only to established patterns that are absorbed by consumers who lose their own identities and agency in the process of viewing them.

At the same time that left-wing theorists were blasting warnings about the creation of false, nonexistent choices in capitalist mass production, their politically opposing twins, the red-baiters of the Right, launched a curiously similar argument about popular culture. (It is not surprising that *Invasion of the Body Snatchers*, a classic of replication as destruction of selfhood, has been interpreted both as an American Cold War fantasy against Communist takeover and as a cautionary tale about human uniqueness being on the wane, with citizens becoming soulless members of a massified group.)

This brand of critics lamented how mass culture, especially the sort easily accessed by teenagers, women, and other "susceptible" subjects, served as an empty purveyor of vapidity, deforming what was once Real Art for Thinking

Individuals, who had now become sheep-like consumers. Right-leaning high art critics such as Harold Rosenberg, Dwight MacDonald, and Clement Greenberg viewed both Soviet Communism and American mass culture as evil proliferations of homogeneity that, replicant-style, threatened respected and established powers and values.

Whether from the left or the right, the castigation of mass culture as mass conformity had a palpably gendered dimension to it. As commentators saw it, mass culture promulgated a diminished sense of moral propriety encapsulated in a mythology of "uncontrollable" desires of young women in the public sphere. This view maintained that mass culture generated a feminized mass psychosis (consider "hysterical" female fans of The Beatles), implying the presumed proliferation of female hysteria everywhere.[12]

Concerns with—and about—proliferation thus encircled *The Patty Duke Show*'s initial broadcast years, and no more so when considered alongside other developments in girl culture. It tellingly overlapped, for instance, with the emerging fad of Barbie dolls, introduced in the United States in 1959, and which, by the Sixties, were ubiquitous in the homes of teen girls, a group which, as we note above, critics largely homogenized as a mindless flock of rapacious, passive consumers. Unsurprisingly, the endless array of molded dolls attracted no shortage of vitriol by cultural gatekeepers, and Barbies were the basis of many a joke and cynical eyeball roll and scarcely functioned as the proto-feminist role models Mattel asserted in its publicity crusades.

During the Sixties and Seventies, differentiated varieties of Barbies were manufactured, packaged and sold by profession, rather than by occasion or mode of dress: boxes of doctor dolls and biologists replaced those of dancers and beachcombers. Ethnically and racially diverse Barbies were soon planted on store shelves and, since then, have marched into ever-expanding categories (movie tie-in Barbies; "inspiring women" historical figure Barbies, including Helen Keller). Read through a less cynical lens, however, could mass-produced culture be carving out small (and admittedly highly commodified) entry points for girls to imagine futures of entering male-dominated careers? Severe critics of mass culture would undoubtedly dismiss the idea that a plastic doll—or the teen characters of *The Patty Duke Show*—could ever expand young women's horizons, and would see the items as further examples of the consumerist ideology subtending the Culture Industry, which, for Adorno and Horkheimer, fabricated minor distinctions between comparable goods to generate simply the illusion of choice and grant a false sense of particularity to each object, for example, this pop song versus that one; this car with fins, this one without; this Barbie versus the other one. The Culture Industry extended that contemptuous classification to those who purchased these objects, individualizing them only insofar as their common function as consumers came to the fore.

Sixties Mass Culture: Horrific Twinning and Replication

Unlike the metaphysical nineteenth-century Doppelgängers, the doubles in the Sixties who were taking over their hosts tended to be material and earthly, pragmatic in purpose, extending anxieties over computers replacing humans—along with Soviet invaders and the bombs that might also annihilate the American populace. Horror films held fast to the good and evil binaries of old, even as they moved from a metaphysical or supernatural realm to a more earthly one. Tom Tryon's 1971 novel *The Other* and its film adaptation a year later, were in many ways Sixties texts, featuring nice, placid Miles and the evil-doing Holland (depicted by identical twin brothers) complete with flashbacks showing the latter's wicked deeds as a child. The surprise revelation is that Holland had died in a freak accident and Miles had been channeling his deceased sibling. With its focus on bad seed offspring, *The Other* stands at the edge of another subgenre that emerged in the Sixties: monster progeny films. Prominent among them are 1968's *Rosemary's Baby*, *The Exorcist* and the *Omen* franchise, and the trend of tiny monsters they established has continued apace in film culture, with evil sometimes redirected to children's dolls—the later *Chucky* and *M3GAN* franchises owe a certain debt to E. T. A. Hoffmann. In its early incarnations, the monster progeny subgenre served as a backlash to the excitement of an engaged, youthful potential fostered during the Kennedy era, and even the edgier demands made by young protesters. This branch of the horror film presents kids as vicious obstacles to the future and not as the kind of auspicious gateways to adulthood that Patty and Cathy extended.

The sense of negative twinning was not simply a reaction to the Cold War or robots taking over the world. Since WWII, both American cinema's popularity and its institutional clout had been eroding, and movies of the time were often cloaked in the recognition that Hollywood had become a ghostly industry inhabited by fading figures—decrepit doubles of themselves.[13] Unsurprisingly, this was often played out on the bodies of female characters as well as the actors who played them, a keen reminder of Hollywood's abhorrent treatment of older women. (The trend was labeled, after all, "psycho-biddy" horror.) Of note here is another sub-variety of postwar horror films that cast aging glamour icons of the studio era (Joan Crawford, Bette Davis) as good/bad twins, or as sisters, as in Robert Aldrich's cult movie *Whatever Happened to Baby Jane?* (1962).[14]

The oppositions staged by films like this were exaggerated and familiar, so intense and exhausted, as to embalm them in a thick veneer of camp. The sisters in *Baby Jane* are not 'directly twins, but, for most of the film, Crawford melodramatically enacts the "good," or at least victimized, member of the pair, and Davis the sadistic torturer. Here both the sisters and the notoriously competitive stars who played them connote a depleted youthful force, a foregone fame and sensuality, a femininity past its prime. Other cinematic doublings around a faded Hollywood included the messy, campy homage to the iconic *Vertigo* in Aldrich's *The Legend of Lylah Clare* (1968), in which a washed-up producer tries to resurrect the success of a late actress with her newly arrived double—both played by *Vertigo*'s Kim Novak! Less known is the pilot for a sitcom that was never picked up, *The Ginger Rogers Show* (1961), in which the famous dancer of the studio era, in an attempt to stay relevant, plays twin sisters who pose as each other either to discourage or entice the other's beau-of-the-moment. Its own campiness, tired and sadly unintentional, is at once unbearable and overbearing.

Television and popular film of the Sixties took up the strained clichés about twins and doubles. Most depicted an externalized evil twin who absorbed or destroyed the original self, or a hidden identity dividing itself from within, not fully disposing of the horror tradition, but ushering it into the realm of science fiction, a slight movement away from the horror genre. Episodes of *The Twilight Zone* offer several provocative illustrations. In "The Dummy" (1963, aired shortly before the start of *The Patty Duke Show*), a ventriloquist's wooden dummy takes on a life of its own—a male Olympia that marches into the world of popular entertainment—and eventually takes over the ventriloquist, who is reduced to acting as his wooden puppet in the tradition of the vanishing or absorbed twin. An especially sardonic episode, "The Mind of the Matter" (1961), strikingly reiterated the doubled self as source of dread: an irritated, misanthropic grouch (played by standup curmudgeon Shelley Berman) yearns for a world populated solely by people like him and, when this literally occurs, finds the infinite stream of grumbling Shelley Bermans unbearable (Figure 4.2), Unlike the dystopian fantasy of one-on-one replacement in *Invasion of the Body Snatchers*, the terror here

Figure 4.2 Endless Bermans

emerges from the endless multiplication of one's self, not unlike Huxley's vision of birth in *Brave New World* in which infants roll off an assembly line. Yet even as it revises Sartre's dictum "Hell is other people" to "Hell is other yous," the episode concludes with a moralizing lesson: assaulted by the unpleasantness of his overabundant selves, Berman's character curbs his crabbiness and learns, much as Naomi Klein will, the importance of acknowledging the self in the other. In the quantitative tradition that "The Mind of the Matter" exemplifies, something unnerving and uncanny occurs via the proliferation of self, something we also see in Diane Arbus's iconic photograph, "Identical Twins" (1966/67), on which Kubrick would later base his twin girl-ghosts in *The Shining*.

The Gendering of Replication

High art of the period was an active participant in the decade's obsession with duplication and serial replication but, notably, as a supposed antidote to insipid, mass cultural groupthink. Seriality, for instance, was adapted from

European modernism (as in music) and some of the era's most elevated artists appropriated mass-generated objects and icons of popular and day-to-day culture such as comic strips, soup cans, and the like.

This thirst of rarified gallery-based art for popular and common, everyday objects produced a curious paradox. Despite the melding of these mass reproduced artifacts into their own art, the artist doing that blending was conceptualized in terms of an antiquated, Romantic notion of a *lone* creator, whose being, beliefs, or process his work purportedly expressed. Thus the world of high art in Sixties America was still holding fast to the centuries-old idea of individualized creators *even as* it was trying to break free from the shackles of established, European modernist art. More pointedly, that American artworld was increasingly exploiting the potential for the duplication or serial extension of its own creations. Jasper Johns, for instance, produced nearly forty versions of his 1954 "Flag." But that series remains a "Jasper Johns" work and retains its value through that provenance alone. It goes without saying that the individuated artists at the basis of such highly valued pieces, singular or multiple, were overwhelmingly male.

Masculine Prowess: Fantasies of Extension and Comedies of Diminishment

The Patty Duke Show offers its own playful encounter with American modernism in the episode "Our Daughter the Painter" (S3E5), in which Patty brings home a painting she made at school, a canvas of what she calls "Op Art" that's essentially a widening spiral in a frame. Everyone, including high-cultured Cathy, views the painting as an unsightly blotch. When someone predictably states that they don't "get it," Patty explains that it's because they're looking at it upside down. Cue the laugh-track.

Other girl "artists" at Brooklyn Heights High (note that they are grouped, not individualized as were real-world male gallery artists) warn Patty that her family will try, as theirs did, to purge the painting from her home. To be sure, this is a sitcom set-up, but at the same time it hints at the chasm between the "serious" work of actual, highly vaunted male painters outside the show and the fictional teenage girls within it, a chasm that characterized the actual contemporary art scene. The deprecating exclusion of women from the upper echelons of "op art" as producers is wryly commented upon in

Stephen Sondheim's classic, "Ladies who Lunch," in which an embittered middle-aged Manhattanite toasts her fellow under-stimulated socialites:

> *Here's to the girls who stay smart*
> *Aren't they a gas?*
> *Rushing to their classes*
> *In optical art . . .*

In the same vein, Patty's efforts at high abstract art cast the painting as an empty effort whose meaninglessness, or lack of pretentious self-referentiality (not to mention its sitcom context), keep it far beyond the category of Real Art but typical of what a girl might come up with. Its presence is a joke aimed to amuse the middlebrow, befuddled characters of the series and its presumptive audience members, denying either group the interpretative agency or ability to handle ostensibly sophisticated Art. Of course, *The Patty Duke Show* wasn't alone in ridiculing nonrepresentational, contemporary art—middle-brow stand-up comedy, television shows and skits, print articles and cartoons, and satirical publications like *Mad* magazine often treated it as little more than a laugh-line.

But it's not clear who the joke of modern art is on. Certainly, Patty and her girl artist cohort are ridiculed for slavishly following a fad (girl artists!?!). Yet the episode also insists on the value that the painting comes to have *for Patty* who becomes quite earnest in her defense of her artistic ambition. Unable to tell Patty the truth (that they can't stand her Op Art), Natalie and Martin lie and declaim how downright masterful her artistic effort is. When the piece is accidently put up for auction, Patty's parents, Richard, Cathy, and Ross, enlist friends and acquaintances as accomplices to keep bidding up the price so as not to shatter Patty's belief in her artistic mastery. (The bidding tellingly starts off at twenty-five cents). As in the "Author, Author" episode discussed in Chapter 3, where the family conspires to maintain Patty's assumption that she is a successful novelist, "Patty, the Artist" ends with her *not* being disabused of her illusion about her artistic talents. It is, however, revealing that the bidders whom the Lanes, along with Richard, recruit to raise the price of Patty's painting are all men, as if to align the making of art with the feminine, and the making of art's *monetary value* a sham perpetuated by men, rewiring once more the conventional gendering of production and consumption.

During the era, artistic cultures high and low championed the idea of male prowess, locating it either in the artist, the energies of the artwork, or the endlessly replaceable cavalcade of women often taken as subject matter, ranging from rock singer Stephen Stills's 1970 "Love the One You're With" to the *Playboy* culture of lookalike Bunnies to Warhol's serialized portraits of female icons. At the same time, however, corners of popular culture seemed to retaliate, constructing masculinity and men as endlessly replaceable figures, a point that even feminist critics of mass culture overlook. This extends beyond the infinite array of Ken dolls, Barbie's steady, lifeless boyfriend. Consider the James Bond franchise, whose first 007, Sean Connery, certainly had brought a forceful, down-to-earth masculinity to the role. Yet once George Lazenby and Roger Moore were cast as subsequent Bonds, even the iconic Connery became as substitutable as the Bond girls who bounced in and out of each of the films. At the same time, the "Tammy" movies bestowed the character's male suitors with a certain replaceability. Yes, different actresses played Tammy in successive films, but the recasting of the men was more pronounced as the series cycled from *Tammy and the Bachelor* to *Tammy, Tell Me True* (featuring a professor as beau) to *Tammy and the Doctor* to *Tammy and the Millionaire*. The franchise arguably operated as the gender-bending converse of James Bond: *Tammy* moved from amorous partner to amorous partner giving no man any staying power. She simply enjoyed the short-term romance of the moment, whoever the guy.

The Patty Duke Show playfully participates in its own objectification of male characters by putting them into a string of replication that potentially renders them substitutable, replaceable or even disposable. Constantly, Patty falls for dreamboats, sometimes without name, who pass through single episodes and barely function as full characters—as is spotlighted in "The Invisible Boy" (S3E31), whose anonymous yet desired title character is so generic and replaceable that his face never appears onscreen. We see but two legs protruding from beneath a car he keeps repairing (Figure 4.3). And in relegating Richard to the role of the steady companion, ready to be tossed over for a momentary amorous whim and in presenting other men as passing fancies and placeholders for imagined but impermanent romance, the show undercuts the special uniqueness typically given to masculinity. This is true even for its male guest stars, who spark interest for a time and then disappear. One episode takes this a step further. In "The Boy Next Door" (S2E6), Patty gives up on her paramour of the moment to return to Richard, saying that "I'd trade Scotty for Richard and two Beatles albums," turning her suitors

Figure 4.3 Interchangeable and Barely There: The Boy Next Door

into objects replete with exchange value. Thus, even in the shadow of the more elevated art of high modernism that upholds a virile masculinity, the popular culture artifact *The Patty Duke Show* offers up a modest critique by rendering masculinity as replicant sameness while keeping the identical twins firmly distinct, with vibrant personalities in their own right. In its own fashion, *The Patty Duke Show* presents masculinity as a massified emptiness—not unlike teen icons like Bobby Sherman and Troy Donahue, whose faces were endlessly put into rotation on the covers of girls' magazines of the time such as *Tiger Beat*.

Two-Way Doubling in the Arts: Crossing Established Lines

The boundaries of high and popular art were, and have always been, more permeable and less steadfast than one might imagine even as gatekeepers of high culture insisted on keeping those distinctions in place. In the Sixties, the boundaries were beginning to meld in productive ways.[15] The obvious examples are the museum-grade Art pieces that referenced and showcased commodity culture and even replicated their own works through reproductive materials and techniques. The boundaries of high and low were blurring, whether critics, merchants, and artists wanted them to or not.

But the critical discussions of High Art raiding popular ostensibly low art forms overwhelmingly position the phenomenon as one-way, perhaps due to the fact that High Art is the kind that makes it into art history classes. However, as *The Patty Duke Show*'s "Op Art" episode demonstrates, lowbrow cultural forms, even something as base as a silly sitcom, were making their own raids into the upper sanctums of high art. Otherwise put, the traffic between these ostensibly mutually opposed, doubled worlds moved across a two-way street. Perhaps *The Patty Duke Show* seems an unusual place to find such a well-founded elaboration of popular culture raiding high-end culture. It's also unusual for not simply quoting or parodying it, as other comedic media and popular acts would do, but to use that borrowed material in ways that asks us to consider how those worlds collide, how they are intermeshed, and even poses the questions of gender and authorship within aesthetic production and consumption.

Some traditional art critics such as Harold Rosenberg and Clement Greenberg were so displeased with what they saw as the spoiling of pure art by mass concerns that they maintained that nearly all forms of contemporary art had become so debased as to enter the category of kitsch, not true art. It's not incidental that such definitional debates (what in fact is True Art?) were anchored in the specialized world of high art (and supporting institutions such as museums, galleries, classrooms, and taste-setting journals like *Artforum*). Popular television usually stood exempted from such debates, or rather, was forced to, because for most critics, it wasn't an Art form at all, and when it was attended to, was met with derision.

In addition to poking into the high realm of gallery art, television sitcoms were adopting forms of adjacent mass culture for their subject matter, in a lateral rather than top-down appropriative fashion, as with Pop Art. *The Addams Family* came from cartoons, *Batman* was derived from comic books, *Lost in Space* referenced science-fiction cult classics, *Get Smart*'s shoe phone mocked the absurd gadgets Q devised for James Bond. And so the doubled raids of television sitcoms involved not only the movement between high and low art worlds, but between TV's sideways turn to other, usually preexisting, popular media forms. To be sure, that lateral, intermedia doubling began in the early days of broadcast television (in which many successful radio shows were turned into TV series), but it hit a pinnacle of sorts in the Sixties when showrunners turned to new tricks that not only borrowed content from other media, but recycled tired clichés, both textual and ideological, to inject the impression of novelty into outmoded genres.

Tricia Jenkins notes the sheer number of spy shows running in what she calls "The Year of the Spy," 1965. So familiar to audiences was the genre, she contends, that producers were willing to relax some established conventions, allowing female and Black performers to have leading roles (*Girl from U.N.C.L.E., Get Smart, I Spy*), combining retreads with the impression of revitalization in order for the genre to sputter on. Given that staid images of the nuclear family had saturated entertainment and journalistic media, it is hardly surprising that its clichés were beginning to grind down, and the gimmickry of sitcoms at the time can be taken as evidence of that very erosion.[16] While some may rightly view these reworkings as a cynical (and lazy) attempt on the part of media industries to innovate, others might see it, equally reasonably, more productively as camp.

Sitcoms: Camping up Clichés

Camp had existed for over a century among gay and queer cultures, where it was used as a sort of code legible primarily to insiders. But in the Sixties, it boisterously entered the mainstream. It was inaugurated—perhaps even "legitimated"—by the 1964 publication of Susan Sontag's "Notes on Camp," a piece that offered a copious, if unexplained, list of examples taken from across cultural and aesthetic divides: Richard Wagner and Tiffany lamps on the one hand, and *King Kong* and *The Enquirer* on the other. Of greater interest for us here are the current practices that were bringing its hitherto marginalized practices into the fold, whether through the works of Lichtenstein and Warhol or *I Dream of Jeannie* and *Batman*. It doesn't take much work to see how TV's "silly sitcoms" of the era could become easy camp targets, with their overwhelmingly superficial, ridiculous premises and their lack of anything remotely resembling real "content." Yet, for us, *The Patty Duke Show*, the ostensibly silly sitcom, does not fit the category.

In many ways, camp works as another doubled phenomenon. On the one hand, it is a production practice, whose stereotypical example is the drag queen, but easily extends to artifacts as varied as opera, comic books, melodramas, used car ads, and acting styles—texts that often produce camp intentionally. But most people understand camp in its second form, as a mode of consumption and of reading, or, more precisely, of *re-reading.* (As commentators from Sontag on have asserted, camp puts dominant cultural forms and norms "into quotation marks.")[17] Camp twists conventional, or "original" meanings by amplifying features that might have seemed insignificant at first blush. (Adrienne Rich argued much the same for feminist re-readings of existing texts). An example might involve a media star whose attributes and meanings shift radically after, say, a scandalous secret or exploit that is made public, thereby making it impossible to read their pre-scandal appearances in the same ostensibly innocent way. This is one way in which the initial production of the camped-up artifact is relatively immaterial; it is the reinvigoration that imbues it with campiness. At times, this aspect of camp, what Sontag labeled "unintentional camp," can take on an almost vicious, accusative form: a laughing at a text or person unaware of their campiness. It is such "failed seriousness" that fueled the reception of *The Valley of the Dolls.*

Whatever the genesis, rather than extinguishing the artifact's initial or conventional interpretations, camp builds upon them, creating a sort of generative re-reading not completely unlike the way doubling operates in *The Patty Duke Show,* where the features and goals of one twin never obliterate or triumph over those of the other, but rather work together to produce more than two blandly identical characters or goals. Camp requires a point of origin from which to jump off and rework, just as TV shows of the Sixties were reworking older representations of domestic life and the gender roles assigned within them

It's worth noting that, over half a century after the publication of Sontag's "Notes on Camp," critics still kneel before it as if it housed the true, authoritative meaning of camp-—despite camp's hardy demolition of the idea of "truth." An otherwise useful recent anthology, *Camp TV of the 1960s,* includes a piece entitled "Can TV Music Be Camp?," as if asking permission for acoustic phenomena to be acceptable as camp (the answer, as we'll see, is "yes"). This, and Sontag's, "is it or isn't it" line of ontological questioning has grounded an endless series of camp criticism, although, happily, more nuanced approaches and studies have begun to emerge.[18]

More recently, TV scholar Quinlan Miller pursues the idea of camp as a recycling center, yet another a form of doubling insofar as an original object, style, or self-presentation is repurposed and gains a secondary meaning. He is not the first to deploy the metaphor, but his particular focus falls specifically on playfully exaggerated, outmoded performance styles as the key purveyor of camp in US television. According to him, the flamboyant, histrionic guest stars of *The Patty Duke Show*—Paul Lynde, Robert Q. Lewis, Charles Nelson Reilly, and, especially, Kaye Ballard—lodge queerness into the series. (Miller tends to use the terms queerness and campiness interchangeably.)[19] He goes on to maintain that queer qualities in fact infiltrated nearly *all* sitcoms of the pre-queer (indeed, pre-LGBT) era when they use established, stand-up comedians who based their schtick routines from earlier traditions of vaudeville exaggeration, rapid-fire one-liners, and performative delivery styles.

However, while the queer moments Miller extracts from *The Patty Duke Show* might gesture toward playfully exaggerated and even alternative ways of leading one's life, the cameos on which he focuses are only an intermittent presence in the series, never sustained beyond a single episode. They are scarcely numerous enough to mark the series as camp, and even when they appear, they never overshadow the show's quieter form of comedy. To us, the series' overall tenor, look, and performance style scarcely flirt with the consistent and blatant camp aesthetic of *Batman*. Duke's series reworks television's old clichés in a subtler, less stylized fashion, as in its marginalization of the bland *pater familias*. Schallert's Martin Lane may be a bit feckless, but little about his performance is campy.

To be sure, though, *The Patty Duke Show* does seem to provide glimpses of blink-and-you'll-miss-them camp moments centered around high stylization and heightened performativity. Curiously, most are acoustic, emerging from a soundtrack unafraid of clichéd musical cues or of unusual instrumentation—an entire episode is devoted to Patty's attempt to learn to play the tuba, and the bagpipes Cathy plays are hardly commonplace in television scores. Periodically, highly noticeable uses of percussion overtake the soundtrack, as when snare drums played in a military fashion accompany the numerous groups of potential renters that march through the Lane home when the family plans to move to France (discussed in Chapter 5). The unusual sounds direct and even demand our attention to them in a way that softly played strings almost never do. But these are isolated moments.

Camp exaggeration seems quite secondary to moments of the series that entertain serious thematics and feelings of adolescence, and that enact some of the sincere affective investments that camp typically derides. Such instances trade not in cheeky, eye-winking camp, but in the mini dramas of everyday life. These sober, dramatic sides of the series are typically manifested in scenes involving meaningful family interaction and that appear pointedly without music, without laugh-track.

For instance, after Cathy and Aunt Pauline have a contretemps in "The House Guest," the laugh-track drops out for six minutes. There is no background music, no canned guffaws from an imagined audience as Martin tries to get a disconsolate Cathy to come down to dinner, nor when Cathy goes to Aunt Pauline's hotel room to attempt a reconciliation. Only when the scene finally ends does music reappear, and the laugh-track resurfaces once in a brief coda when Pauline returns to the Lane home, accompanied by a silly dash of underscoring as she tries to conduct the family in some awkward music-making.

Numerous episodes can be read not as cheeky, eye-winking camp, but as small dramas of everyday life, replete with the serious thematics and feelings of adolescence: a daughter distraught that her father doesn't believe her when she says she didn't violate curfew; a father distraught at thinking his daughter might be running off to elope; a mother who feels her family is taking her for granted; a teen who recognizes the deprivations in developing countries; and so on.

Comic Possibilities in the Sixties:
Twinning Reenvisioned through Doubling

Pushing the tradition of twinning as horrific to the side, popular culture of the Sixties capitalized on notions of doubling and twinning to connote something unusual, valuable, and fun. Even in advertising, as Hillel Schwartz argues, twins were used to underscore the excitement of a product by staging them side-by-side, as if to "doubly" endorse it, whereas a second option, which pit twins against one another, implied that using a product would benefit the twin who had turned to it, leaving the other behind. Even the sensational "before and after" pictures of weight-loss programs took to the trend. TV viewers and magazine readers were also exposed to doubling in ads for things like bras, or for Doublemint gum ("It's two, two, two mints in one!").

Likewise, made-for-comedy twin acts in theater, television, and films of the time sprang largely from platforms of playful masquerade and mimicry. While imitation and impersonations, always a form of doubling, have rich, established histories in comedy and especially satire, the Sixties seemed especially susceptible to them.[20] Routines fed off of asymmetry putting them into valences of straightlaced/wacky, as in the Smothers Brothers (siblings, not twins), in which older brother Tom played the goofball and Dick the straight guy, just as George had been the straight man to Gracie Allen in radio and TV. Neither was good nor evil; comic duos were no longer fraught with opposing moralities or valor: what was once malice was now simply mischief. Philosopher Helena de Bres, herself a twin, notes that singletons always ask, "well, who's the quiet one?," a cliché exploited by *The Patty Duke Show* by positioning Patty as the scheming mischief-maker and Cathy as the smart, rational "quiet" one.[21]

Another televisual form of imitative doubling entailed casting performers who physically resembled each other, or who were actual twins or siblings. Hungarian-American icon Eva Gabor, of *Green Acres* fame, was always dubbed the "nice one" in contrast to her sister Zsa Zsa, who was more famous for being rich and uppity than anything else; Jerry, the younger brother of the eponymous star of *The Dick Van Dyke Show*, resembled his sibling enough to appear as Rob Petrie's irresponsible brother Stacey in several episodes of that show. Much of the comedic mimicry of Sixties sitcoms, including *The Patty Duke Show*, untethered twinning from the idea of close visual mirroring.

Not unlike traditional accounts, Sixties popular culture often used twinning as a path to multiplicity. Notably, it was comedy that provided the foundation of this movement. By the late Fifties, comic multiples were bestowing delightful difference onto sameness, as when Peter Sellers or Jerry Lewis played three or more roles in a single film. This trend, perhaps inaugurated in 1949 with multiple Alec Guinesses in *Kind Hearts and Coronets,* would reach a pinnacle of sorts in *The Mouse That Roared* (1959), in which Peter Sellers starred as three of its leading characters, including a Duchess. In the following decade, Sellers impersonated James Bond in *Casino Royale* (1967), a parody in which numerous characters pretended to be the "real Bond," including, of all people, Woody Allen. In general, these movies in which single actors played multiple roles tended to use fewer special effects than *The Patty Duke Show*, their characters didn't optically join in single shots so much as chat in shot-reverse-shot formations. Moreover, in *Mouse*, there's no narrative point to the twinning or tripling; it's simply a showcase for a talented actor, as was the case in *Dr. Strangelove* (1963), in which Sellers portrayed military figures from Germany, the United Kingdom, and the United States, voicing different accents with bravado.

While primarily appealing to kids and French intellectuals, Jerry Lewis's doubling films surpassed the simple delights of mimicry to comically present a range, albeit narrow, of masculine identities. In *The Nutty Professor* (1963), he plays an endearing scientific naïf, Professor Kelp, a Jekyll to a Hyde-like obnoxious alter ego (Buddy Love) that emerges by way of experiment. In *The Family Jewels* (1965), Lewis assays *seven* roles—six zany uncles plus the unrelated chauffeur of an orphan who must choose one of her uncles as her new father. Predictably, she opts for the honest, caring chauffeur over the self-absorbed, vain uncles, privileging the mirage of supposed authenticity over adornment and excess. Unfortunately, the denouements of these films frequently uphold a sentimentality that celebrates the related idea of being true to one's presumably singular self.

Elvis Presley's musical *Kissin' Cousins* (1964) features two distant relatives, both played by Presley. As a comedy, it eschews the "good and bad" dichotomy of horror but doesn't abandon duality altogether—it renders the hillbilly Jody more brutish and intellectually slower than his army cousin Josh, who, of course, is the story's favored twin, in part due to Presley's own highly publicized recent stint in the US Army. Early on, Josh romances two sisters and sings of "One boy, two little girls," but by story's end, having had to choose one, he croons, "Once is enough," with twinning itself seemingly threatening monogamy. Despite his considerable prowess as a singer, Presley fails to do well at depicting multiple forms of himself (Warhol did this better with his silkscreens of the performer). Weirder still was Max Baer Jr.'s cross-dressed depiction of his "twin sister, Jethrine" in eleven episodes of *The Beverly Hillbillies*. Possessed of a relatively deep voice and standing at a sturdy 6'4", Baer sports an ill-fitting Shirley Temple wig of cascading blonde curls while the rest of the family cluelessly reads the goofy Jethrine as Jethro's actual sister, letting only the television audience in on the joke.

Most prominent, and prominently remembered, within the Sixties cycle of twinning movies is Disney's 1961 *The Parent Trap*, a near contemporary of *The Patty Duke Show*, with young teen Hayley Mills (daughter of actor Sir John Mills) playing the double roles of sisters raised separately by divorced parents. (Some TV viewers we've talked to contend that *The Patty Duke Show* fully ripped off *The Parent Trap*.) The more refined daughter lives in Boston, where her mom and grandmother are denizens of its haute Brahmin society, while the other lives on a California ranch, a location presented as Boston's earthy, authentic alternative.

When they meet at summer camp and learn that they are sisters, the girls conspire to rekindle their parents' feelings for one another in order to reestablish an intact nuclear family, that childhood fantasy we noted that

Figure 4.4 Hayley Mills Meets Hayley Mills in *The Parent Trap*

was promulgated by other films of the time (Figure 4.4). Mills's great skills at impersonation and the movie's special effects create an impressive array of visual fantasy, granting the twins an almost magical sense of power. To young viewers with fractured or distanced families, *The Parent Trap* was sheer wish fulfillment, led by a teen star, and teen girls, powerful enough to orchestrate a happy family reunion.

To be sure, some Sixties sitcoms deployed the twinning motif in the conventional way of moral opponents even as they moved in comic directions: Jeannie (played by Barbara Eden), the lead of *I Dream of Jeannie*, has an evil twin, imaginatively named Jeannie II (also played by Eden), who periodically arrives for an unwelcome visit, as was also the case in *Bewitched*, in the form of Samantha Stevens's evil twin, Serena. (Eden's switch from blonde hair to black wig as Jeannie II is no more convincing than Schallert's mustachioed Kenneth.) A weightless sense of performance slightly overtakes the good and bad attributes of the twins in both sitcoms, whose pairs deliver nothing remotely threatening, just an excuse for already-contracted actors to stretch their legs a bit. Nor does their wickedness ever cross the comic boundaries of their shows to tip them into horror—the nonstop laugh-tracks and the campy vamping by the bewigged twinsters make sure of that. It would seem that more than easy visual doubling is at work here, for both shows untether twinning from the idea of close visual mirroring—why else the deliberately ill-fitting wigs of Max Baer or Barbara Eden? At the same

Figure 4.5 What a Difference a Wig Makes: Jeannie x Two

time, though, however comedically and campily rendered, the sets of twins on those sitcoms all position one of the "pair" as more desirable or morally upright than the other, apportioning ethical worth to one twin over the other, something that *The Patty Duke Show* eschews (Figure 4.5).

The Patty Duke Show is indeed unique in not prioritizing one twin over the other. In "The President" (S1E9), a rare episode that pits the two cousins against the other, Cathy and Patty compete for the presidency of Brooklyn Heights High's Girls' Club. Like "Patty, The People's Choice," in which the twins support an upstanding, JFK-ish candidate, "The President" tutors Patty and Cathy on the ins and outs of campaigning and voting. When Cathy proposes a debate in class, a fellow student reminds us of the show's historical context by calling out, "A debate got a president elected!" and, well-versed in US history though she may be, Cathy responds, "Yes, Lincoln and Douglas!" A classmate laughs, "you *have* been gone for a long time."

Predictably, the twin candidates have competing platforms: Patty promises to make school life breezy and fun; Cathy wants to advance culture and the joys of classroom learning. Underscoring those differences are alternating montage sequences showing each of them presenting her policies at a school assembly, along with a third candidate who simply says, "Vote for Me." As ever, the cousins are clearly distinguishable.

Neither of their political platforms is privileged over the other's; school, it is implied, should be both fun *and* educational. As if to avoid taking sides, the campaigning concludes with the vapid "Vote for Me" classmate being voted in. With this nearly senseless victory, the storyline implies that it's the fact of running for office that matters more than getting elected. At the same time, it turns out that once elected, the platform-less "vote for me" girl actually has some ideas: her first action in office is to organize a clothing drive for the poor, and former rivals Patty and Cathy now team up to realize this higher, collective civic endeavor.

Another first-season episode also spurns the idea of confused twin identity to great effect. "How to be Popular" (S1E12) starts with Patty playing host to a swarm of energetic teens, flailing about at a party in her living room in weird dances like "the Hammer." Dialogue overflows with exaggerated youth slang: one of the rare comprehensible lines comes from a boy who asks Cathy, standing alone in a corner, if she's Patty's cousin "from Cutesville," to which she cluelessly replies, "No. I'm from Europe."

From that same corner, Cathy frets about her unpopularity, and watches sullenly as even Tiger, the family dog, dances with a human partner. Patty, who is "losing control" as she is wont to do while dancing, worries about Cathy, and tries to convince a boy named Henry to dance with her. Henry refuses, telling her, "to get someone else to water your wallflowers." Overhearing the exchange, a forlorn Cathy sneaks up to their bedroom to order a "You Can Be Popular" manual from "Aunt Jane," an advice columnist for teens at Martin's paper.

Carefully following each of Aunt Jane's advisory tidbits—be helpful to others, be honest to others, ask questions of others—Cathy skates through a disastrous succession of failures. When Patty later learns that her cousin had sought advice through a self-help book ("Holy moly!"), she doubtlessly imagines that she, the Queen of Teen Popularity, could have done better. Patty's own, slangy advice is, "Don't be 'dual,'" and, when Cathy asks for elaboration, she tells her, "be yourself." Given how sedulously the producers work to enforce the trope of "being dual" in the show's very premise, Patty's advice is somewhat jarring.

Ultimately, she suggests that Cathy consider dancing (for her, a catchall cure), ignoring the fact that Cathy's popularity problems started at a dance party. After some thought, Cathy recalls a "tribal dance" she and her father had encountered in Africa, claiming to find similarities to some of the American dance crazes. Cut to Cathy downstairs, instructing Patty's friends in the details of this "tribal dance," a series of frozen poses for the most part, quickly landing the popularity she had hitherto only dreamt of. Irritated by Cathy's newfound magnetism, Patty's jealousy even extends to Richard, who has also been won over on the dance floor. Having taken a hit in both pride and confidence, Patty stomps off to the bedroom where she, too, writes Aunt Jane, asking for advice regarding her cousin's newfound popularity.

The episode stands out for several reasons. Less stylistically constrained than others, it includes ostentatious panning shots—one rising from Patty's party to the ceiling, above which the crestfallen Cathy worries in bed about her wallflower status—and another scene begins with Cathy's offscreen face reflected in a mirror within the larger space of her bedroom. The most extended formal play occurs in a dream/fantasy Cathy has of descending the family staircase in gauzy gown and tiara (not unlike the credits) and arriving at Patty's party to find that the boys are all desperate to dance with her. Aloof from the fray of her doting fans, she declines, so that she can meet her date for the evening at the door, who turns out to be no less than Frankie Avalon. With Cathy on his arm, the entertainer mimics Patty by playfully calling the roomful of teens "beasts" and leaving the house with Patty's practically copyrighted "bye-ee." This is Cathy's story, and between fantasy, formal experimentation and drama of teen despair, Patty needs to be narratively sidelined—literally pushed to the side during her cousin's crowd-pleasing "tribal dance" and then isolated in her bedroom as she writes to Aunt Jane as cousin Cathy had done.

The episode is also among the few that contain external shots, when Cathy leaves the house to read her advice book in private and, later, to accompany schoolmate Craig (subsequently to be enlisted in the dressmaking episode analyzed in the previous chapter). When Cathy walks with Craig, everything demarcates her from Patty. Unlike her outgoing counterpart, Cathy must rally her nerves to talk with him, and her attempts to overcome her awkwardness are rendered somewhat pathetically, as she literally chases after Craig to demonstrate her interest in "learning more" about him, only ultimately to outrage him. He blows up when he interprets Cathy's ongoing questions ("to show interest" in him, per Aunt Jane's advice) as intrusive bids to delve into his family's scandal, involving a bigamist uncle, thus sustaining the twin motif. Cathy's brief forays into the external world were not only rare in the series, but among the few that were shot on location in

Figure 4.6 Cathy Braves the Suburban Outdoors

New York, thereby bestowing a potential sense of actuality in a series with an otherwise low-stakes interest in street realism (Figure 4.6). It's revealing that this occurs in a relatively dramatic moment that foregrounds Cathy's emotional dejection. As if to acknowledge the shift in visual style once she is outdoors, the underscoring takes on a jazzier, less whimsical sound, with prominent woodwinds that are vaguely reminiscent of Leonard Bernstein's then-contemporary score for *West Side Story*—as if to assert that this story, too, is set in the streets of New York.

"How to Be Popular" disinvests in the idea of the girls' identical twinning, displacing it onto structures of doubling, even through formal mechanisms. The opening party scene, for instance, cuts between Cathy standing to the side of the room and Patty maniacally dancing in the middle of it. Later, as Cathy beguiles the group with her African dance, we cut to inserts of her jealous cousin, standing alone at the edge of the group, positioned much as Cathy herself had been before. Cathy's fantasy of having boys wanting to dance with her is doubled by her ultimate success in doing so. Each girl writes to the advice columnist; Cathy goes outdoors twice; there are two dances; and two (earlier) scenes involving Cathy attempting to compliment Natalie in another bid to follow Aunt Jane's sketchy advice.

Confusion and Competition:
Exceptions to Prove the Rule

Due to its premise, *The Patty Duke Show* was obliged to treat twinning as a matter of mistaken identity in some episodes, although, as we have noted, these are fewer than one might imagine. In an early one, revealingly entitled "Double Date" (S1E10), Cathy accompanies a cowering Patty to the doctor for her annual flu shot. Cathy enters the doctor's office to warn him about her cousin's fear of needles, but he gives her the shot meant for Patty before she can open her mouth—the episode's first confusion of the cousins. Predictably, Cathy is bedridden from adverse reactions and Patty, feeling badly that Cathy will miss her first dance competition, schemes up a plan to play both twins at the dance. As she plans her deception, though, she worries that even *she* might confuse herself about who she is at any given moment, a hokey unlikelihood given her careful planning. At the party, Patty frantically splits her time between Richard and Ted, Cathy's erstwhile date, by running into the kitchen where, to the bewilderment of the maid (Margaret Hamilton of *Wizard of Oz* fame), she changes back and forth between the cousins' outfits and hairstyles. Believing that Patty is Cathy, Ted tells her that she is much prettier than Patty, just as Aunt Pauline had done. When Ted and "Cathy" win the dance contest, Patty grows annoyed that anyone could possibly imagine Cathy to be a better dancer than she is, and protests. Her own impersonation ultimately has her confusing herself: flustered by her perceived defeat, Patty refers to herself as "Pathy" and "Catty."

More than any other episode, "Double Date" highlights the cousins' mistaken identities and its impact on characters around them. Yet viewers are spared any confusion, receiving clear-cut clues as to who is who thanks to the in-between kitchen scenes of Patty changing in and out of identity, along with cutaways to a bedridden Cathy upstairs.

The admittedly few scenes where one girl pretends to be the other unfold often in what may be called backstage preparatory moments, where one twin readies herself to slide into the role of the other. In one episode, audiences are privy to this when Cathy subs for Patty, who had been given the role of Cleopatra in a school play but is now laid up in bed with laryngitis (actually, stage fright). Suddenly rallying after the play starts, Patty rushes to school and barges onstage while Cathy is already in a scene, so that now there are two Cleopatras declaiming the words of Shakespeare, much to the delight of their audience. By maintaining consistent screen direction in this sequence, the episode keeps clear which girl is which, despite identical stage dress and jet-black wigs. The layered theatricality of this doubling (Cathy as Patty and each as Cleopatra) not only directs viewers' attention to Duke's immersive acting skills but also nudges us to reflect on ideas about performance and performativity in general.

The aforementioned "The Boy Next Door" also thematizes competition and confusion between the girls as Patty and Cathy compete for the same guy. Heartthrob Scotty has just moved into the Brooklyn Heights neighborhood (Richard is conveniently away visiting relatives) with charms that attract each girl. Cathy is struck by his interest in *Moby Dick* and Laurence Olivier; for Patty, it's his good looks and athleticism. Although they fall for him independently, the twins soon learn that each one's new "boy" is one and the same. For his part, Scotty always knows which cousin is which, except when he is somehow fooled by Cathy's impersonation of Patty at a picnic in one of her few devilish schemes. Cathy had pretended to be Patty at the latter's behest: Richard had come back from a vacation, and Patty needed her cousin to take Scotty on her scheduled date. Bad move on Patty's part: Cathy, a surprisingly fierce adversary from the beginning of this episode, had actually called Richard to get him to return home, and then uses the picnic date to pick a fight with Scotty *as Patty*. In this way, the dastardly Cathy succeeds at breaking up Scotty and Patty, but audiences are left to wonder how her plot succeeded given that Scott had hitherto shown no confusion about the twins.

"The Boy Next Door" and "Double Date" demonstrate *The Patty Duke Show*'s ability to twist grandiose assertions about twins of the negative traditions to serve its own purposes and amuse audiences, instead of leaving them to contemplate the profundities of the philosophical limits of human existence. There is nothing uncanny about the Lane twins, separately or together; as Patty repeatedly insists, she's just "an average American teenage girl."

Digging less into the stereotypes of twinning, or its literalness, *The Patty Duke Show* moves into other, more generous conceptions of doubling. Even objects participate in doubled structures. "A Slight Case of Disaster" (S1E30) revolves around a pair of outfits for an upcoming dance. Patty insistently goes on the prowl for just the right dress and locates one she can't afford. But she buys it on credit anyway, planning to return it post-prom. Unbeknownst to Patty, though, Cathy borrows the pricey dress for a music recital, and blackberry punch accidentally spills all over it, instantly turning the dress into a failed copy of itself—no longer wearable but, also, no longer returnable.

Doubled objects also ground "The Friendship Bit" (S1E29), which opens with the two cousins facing each other and comparing their emotional debts to each other. All of a sudden, Patty can't stop sneezing, and a doctor determines that she's developed an allergy to her cousin (!). The girls must keep a physical distance from each other—leading the episode to curtail its special effects since the two can no longer share a tight televisual frame together. Cathy, predictably, starts reading up on allergies and psychology and discovers that some allergies can be psychosomatic and begins to wonder if Patty isn't unconsciously jealous of her. Perhaps Patty's miffed that Martin and Natalie had given Cathy a pin for doing so well at school. Based on her research, Cathy offers Patty a public diagnosis of "schizophrenia" and clarifies, "That's a person with two personalities." Like Patty's admonition to Cathy in "How to Be Popular" to not be dual, Cathy's labeling here of Patty gestures to the fact that the series has one actor playing "dual" roles. Everything, of course is worked out. To blot out any jealousy in Patty, her parents buy her a pin just like the one they had given Cathy, and it transpires that the pin, not the girl, was the source of the allergy. It is revealed also that Cathy had deliberately failed the same test to help Patty get over her supposed jealousy, and the episode ends with even more doubling, of allowing Cathy to retake the test and, of course, acing it.

Thus, in contrast to the critics of popular culture, especially those who argued its deleterious impact on young girls, *The Patty Duke Show* steers clear of the bleak sameness of replication to turn its sights on differences created through doubling. Rather than being pitted into good and bad models, the Lane girls offer glimpses of what might lie beyond the constrictions of twin sameness and forced conformity. To be sure, those glimpses, as we shall see, often required the use of rose-colored glasses.

Legacies of *The Patty Duke Show* in Popular Culture

Defined as the show is by doubling and twinning, it's no accident that references to *The Patty Duke Show* after the end of its run gravitated to this premise. Because the memorable song initiates that theme even before the storylines, it's scarcely surprising that "Cousins" is probably the most prominent reason that *The Patty Duke Show* has endured throughout popular culture, its memorable music and lyrics extending well beyond activating boomer nostalgia but re-booting it for later generations. Some pop culture revisions rework the lyrics but retain the tune. *Rocko's Modern Life*, a successful, adult-oriented TV animation series from 1993, reworked "Cousins" to distinguish between Bloaty (a tick) and Squirmy (a worm), figures who are both "blood-sucking filthy vermin, different as night and day" but with enough shared features that "you can lose your mind/ when parasites are two of a kind."

Sixty years after *The Patty Duke Show* aired, queer online activist Randy Rainbow, who updates classic pop and show tunes with new, politically charged lyrics, transformed "Cousins" to "Buttons" in a joint attack on then-first-term president Donald Trump and Korean dictator Kim Jong Un. The video, like the show, was shot in black and white, and Rainbow used split screens to pair the two men as unstable, mercurial leaders who at any moment could put their tiny fingers on nuclear triggers, the "buttons," where the word "cousins" was initially used. Employing the "Cousins"' melody, he vocally enumerates the two tyrants' loonier traits in a manner that neatly twins them.[22]

In perhaps the most hilarious reference to *The Patty Duke Show*, the working-class domestic sitcom of the Eighties and Nineties, *Roseanne*, reflexively used the song—and the *Patty Duke Show* credit sequence as a whole—to poke fun at the casting change of a major character, the older of the family's two daughters, Becky. Teenage actor Lecy Goranson had been replaced by Sarah Chalke when Goranson's studies began to interfere with her commitment to the role, but she subsequently had a change of heart and was rehired, only to find her schedule again overstretched, leading her to be replaced once again by Chalke for several episodes. (In a bit of cheeky reflexivity, in Chalke's first episode as substitute Becky, the Connors compare the merits of the two "Darrins," the husband who had been played by different actors on *Bewitched*.)

Roseanne had never had a theme *song*, just a generic instrumental tune, but in this one-off episode, its closing credits directly borrow the melody, tempo, dynamics, instrumentation and some of the lyrics of "Cousins" to relay its tale of the show's two Beckys:

> Meet Lecy, the one you used to see
> From '88 to '93
> But Sarah came and took her place
> Because she had a similar face
> That's . . . our TV [lyrics unintelligible]

But they're Beckys
Nearly identical Beckys
All the way
One pair of matching actors
But only one part to play . . .

Still they're Beckys
Nearly identical Beckys
And you'll find
They walk alike

They talk alike
Abruptly leave the show alike
You could lose your mind
When Beckys
Ain't two of a kind

Duplicating *The Patty Duke Show*, the sequence features the two teenage girls side by side in a split screen: one Becky regally descends a staircase while the other dances wildly to rock music; one pretends she's in front of a mirror while really facing the other, etc. Everything is taped in black and white, and, in a witty final touch, the sequence closes with a cut to Becky's dad (John Goodman) observing the shenanigans while standing next to Patty Lane's dad, William Schallert, in a time-warped twist.

Another hilarious parody of "Cousins" exists on vinyl. Rhino Records released an LP entitled "Rerun Rock: Superstars Sing Television Theme Songs" (in print as of this writing) that offers versions of classic TV theme songs performed in the style of famous pop and rock singers. A track is given to *The Patty Duke Show*, whose "Cousins" sounds exactly as if it were sung by Bob Dylan, his nasal, gravelly voice and distinctive phrasing engulfing our ears, the song orchestrated in the distinctive style of "Like a Rolling Stone," organ and all. (We once played it to a small group of film and media scholars, and even those who understood the unlikelihood of the song's authenticity were reluctant—or too puzzled—to admit it was a fake.)

Beyond the song, *The Patty Duke Show*'s twinning theme has also been taken up in later films and TV series. While it's beyond the scope of this book to track down every one of these later references, several are worth noting. A few episodes of the classic 1994-2004 series *Friends* invite Ursula, the identical, estranged twin of Phoebe (both played by Lisa Kudrow), into the group's world. One episode has them sitting in their apartment where, in the background, a TV set tuned to a Spanish-language channel is showing reruns of American shows. For some three seconds, *The Patty Duke Show* appears onscreen, causing Phoebe to go ballistic and demand that it be turned off. Another brief but explicit reference to the series appears in the movie *Shriek if You Know What I Did Last Summer* (2000), a straight-to-video send-up of the *Scream* franchise, pitched largely to adolescents. The conclusion reveals that its serial killer was the twin cousin of a hapless high school cop. Learning this, the students declare how much the two men resemble each other, only to be told that one likes "the minuet, the ballet russe, and crêpes suzette," and the other "likes to rock 'n roll" and a hot dog causes him to "lose control." The teens' collective reaction?: "What a wild duet."

In a more sustained fashion, *Jessica Jones*, a Netflix series that ran for three seasons in the 2010s, involves a complex, thematically oriented replay of narrative motifs from *The Patty Duke Show*. Orphaned as an adolescent in a car accident that also gave her superpowers, Jessica was adopted into the family of single-mom Dorothy Walker and her daughter Trish, destined to become a child star in a fictional sitcom called "It's Patsy." Though not twins, their relationship unfolds after one girl (the one with more "alien" skill sets and features—not unlike Cathy) is moved into the established household of the other. Duke's own career is referenced through the character of Dorothy Walker, who, like Ethel Ross, is a domineering stage mother who will do whatever it takes to make Trish a child star, including changing her name from "Trish" to "Patsy" (!) and brutally managing her public image and private life. Dorothy's invasive machinations hamper Trish/Patsy's development, making it virtually impossible for the girl to mature, landing her in a world of unworthy gigs, drugs, booze, and years of therapy.

Disney's award-winning *Liv and Maddie*, a late-twentieth century sitcom that rivaled *The Patty Duke Show*'s female teenager marketing campaign, references its predecessor in a credit sequence that pairs twin sisters Liv and Maddie (both played by Emmy-winner Dove Cameron) in front of a mirror through split-screen special effects.[23] Through the credits, we learn that Liv had become a child star and left for Hollywood, only to return home to her family in the Midwest. But Hollywood has made her narcissistic, crass, and superficial whereas Maddie has just stayed home and become a tomboy who is quite successful in sports, perhaps a reboot of *Billie*.[24] A third season episode, "Grandma-a-Rooney" explicitly confirms *Liv and Maddie*'s debt to

The Patty Duke Show. Liv is about to receive an award, and her globetrotting grandmother Janice, played by Patty Duke herself, is due to give it to her. Before her arrival, the girls' mother shows them a picture of Janice and her twin sister Hilary as teenagers, using a photo of Cathy and Patty Lane from *The Patty Duke Show.* Maddie had always believed that she was Janice's favorite, so when Janice arrives and ignores her, she starts to suspect that Janice is, in fact, Hilary. She attempts to trick the elderly woman by saying she's planning to serve her favorite dish but deliberately doesn't name it. "Grandma" immediately responds "crêpes suzette." Just before the award ceremony, it slips out that Janice actually *is* Hilary, stepping in for Janice, who had been stranded overseas. Eventually, Janice shows up and, in split screen, proceeds to squabble with Hilary over who had been *their* grandfather's favorite. Observing the two, Maddie quips, "what a crazy pair," a line she repeats over the closing credits.

Doubling Down on Context: Twinning and Proliferation Across the Decades

The Sixties and Beyond

The Patty Duke Show handled twinning in a way that situates it comfortably within a historical moment marked by dualities, be they in the worlds of art, political and ideological thought, in race and gender relations, in media forms labeled both "serious" and "frivolous," and even in left- and right-wing critics' shared belief in the brain-deadening effects of proliferating mass culture. The decade of the Sixties bristled in other ostensible face-offs, between defenders of established institutions and norms and those who advocated change—including changes in representation. And there's even a doubling in the historical habit of dividing the decade itself into halves, or of asserting that dueling generations were each somewhat homogenously marked by presumed social and political positions. But despite *The Patty Duke Show*'s premise of twinning, its notion of getting past notions of similarity and moving instead into doubling was a resonant and rather far-reaching act.

At the end of the twentieth century, twinning enjoyed a discernable resurgence in popular culture. Yet unlike its presence during the polarities encouraged by Cold War ideologies and the struggles over cultural expression and identity in the early to mid-Sixties, the latter fad was largely divorced from the obsessions and sociocultural structures of that earlier era and lacked the resonance of its predecessors from which it borrowed so heavily. Many of these later mass media releases were retreads of established, popular twin texts—films most blatantly—and were simply byproducts borne of an entertainment industry in panic, and whose focus on profit was as conspicuous as it was transparent. Audiences at the time were being siphoned off by cable television, video rental stores, and the ability to produce visual and acoustic media at one's own home. Entertainment industries grew cynical, fearful, and were becoming blatantly risk-averse, lazily turning to franchises and—more apposite to a book on twins—reboots, most notably of the already "doubled" films of the Sixties, such as *The Parent Trap*, remade in 1998, with Lindsay Lohan; two years earlier, Disney had released *The Parent Trap II,* in which Hayley Mills, who had depicted the original twin daughters, now portrayed mothers.

Imagine how baby boomers could now enjoy reboots of their favorite childhood shows with their own children, not unlike Disney's lucrative marketing formula. By the turn of the century, remake culture had overtaken Hollywood, television, and even Broadway, where transmedial adaptations became increasingly common. Established TV series and cartoon strips became stage shows (*Buffy the Vampire Slayer, Spider Man*), old TV shows became new movies (*The Addams Family, Bewitched)* or glitzy stage musicals (*The Little Shop of Horrors, Sunset Boulevard*). The cravenly reiterative nature of these revivals did not go unnoticed, and even *The Patty Duke Show* was not immune to the cynicism behind the ploy. In its scorching review of the reunion show, *Variety* called it, "just an uninspired excuse to wring a few bucks from a long-deceased franchise."[25]

To be sure, a number of late twentieth century popular culture texts pushed the theme of twins and doubles into new directions; bigger budgeted efforts include *It Takes Two* (1995), featuring the Olsen twins, and the meta-doubling of *Big Business* (1988), in which Bette Midler and Lily Tomlin each played twin roles of themselves (four years prior, Tomlin played half of a split self along with Steve Martin in the classic *All of Me*). The Young Adult book series *Sweet Valley High,* launched in 1983, featured two Southern California identical twin sisters whose salacious adventures would have had left Patty and Cathy clutching each other in panic. Whatever their popularity at the time, however, few of these twin comedies endured in the popular imagination like the original *The Parent Trap* or *The Patty Duke Show*. In fact, as we've already seen, many raided the latter to animate or even authorize their later, anemic recycling of the theme.

For by this point, the concept of twinning had become so worn and over-done as to become the source of parody. How else could bodybuilder Arnold Schwarzenegger, a man who takes up so much space, and Danny DeVito, who takes up so little, be "twins" in their film of the same name in 1988? 2023 saw the release of the deliberately bad taste *Dicks: The Musical!*, a campy, low-budget movie led by two male actors playing identical twins who bore no physical resemblance whatsoever to one other. Promoted as a queer re-make of *The Parent Trap*, the film has the brothers not only wanting to re-unite their divorced parents, but ending up becoming sexual and romantic partners themselves, humorously and lasciviously upending the incest taboo that, as Constantine Verevis has argued regarding the Sixties *The Parent Trap*, had shielded the twin sisters from any inklings of same-sex desire.[26]

Another resurgence of twinning and proliferation characterized a number of mass media forms in the first decades of the twenty-first century, abetted by ever-developing digital and AI technologies, which, even offscreen, have facilitated rather effortless creations of twinned or multiple beings, of making copies that can eclipse their originals or not having an original to begin with. A double—even in something as basic as an avatar—may or may not correspond to anything human, much less the idea of a particular indi-vidual. Yet it's ultimately unclear how these features induce popular culture's revived turn to twinning in such times.

The most compelling effort to find the historical and cultural ground-work for these newly "twinned" media texts was offered in 2025 by Natasha Shimon. Shimon takes the phenomenon of doppelgängers, twins, or doubles in acclaimed movies like *The Substance* (2024), Bong Joon Ho's *Mickey 17* (2025), and the TV series *Severance* (2023) as readable in terms of a *splitting* of self, especially in response to social pressures and promises of personal benefit. In *The Substance*, for example, a middle-aged actress is divided into a second, more corporately valued, younger version of herself. In *Severance*, a disturbingly underdefined-employer "severs" the lives and minds of its workers from their non-work existence; and in *Mickey 17*, Robert Pattinson portrays an astronaut that evil, higher forces send on dangerous assignments that kill him over and over again, and after each death is repeatedly revived—"printed" in the parlance of the film, into a numbered clone. Unlike previous "split personality disorder" films (*Psycho*) and *Split* (Shyamalan, 2016), which formulaically deployed a psychologized notion of the split, "the terror of these [2020s] movies," Shimon asserts, "isn't the atrocity of their actions when their 'other self' takes over—it's the fact that they don't have any autonomy in these moments." Fundamental to this splitting, Shimon maintains, is "coercive consent" in which vulnerable subjects have no choice but to submit themselves to an unmalleable power (a political group, institution, or ideology) in order to survive. *The Substance* literalizes the perception of aging women as worthless "monsters"; *Severance* shows the life-sucking demands made of employees by corporate entities; *Mickey 17* enacts the disposability of members of the working class. Shimon astutely notes that these texts do less to horrify by pitting one twin or replicant against the other (the good-evil dyad) than to comment on the power dynamics at work that force splitting and twinning—the ostensible loss of self and of agency—upon characters unable to decline the proposition. Her conception of twinning thus invokes a removal, rather than an additive, surplus feature.[27]

Shimon's focus on coercion and power brings material awareness and nuance to a structure that had, for ages, been largely construed as a horrific abstraction (what we termed the "existential bent" to classic narratives of doubling). At the same time, the sense of coerced labor behind her notion of splitting, while aptly describing recent working conditions in recent times, is scarcely exclusive to this period since such alienating divisions routinely characterize capitalist operations and ideology. Indeed, as we noted in relation to twinning narratives of the Sixties, there was a discernible shift from the metaphysical to the worldly. Are there then other factors that might also account for the return to twinning, splitting, duplication, and replication since then?

Having a single performer assume multiple roles has always been a showy, conspicuous way to headline their talents and to stress the feat of their performance, in the tradition of Guiness, Sellers, or Lewis. To take but one of many examples: in 2025, singer/actor Cynthia Erivo appeared as *five* identical characters on the TV show *Poker Face* (2023–25). But the lure of these texts of duplication and replication typically lands less on the performers than on the special effects that makes their proliferation possible. In *The Alto Knights* (2025), for instance, Robert DeNiro plays twin characters whose twinness is not only inessential to the plot but does little to showcase the actor's fearsome talents. What is the movie's most impressive moment? A scene in which one DeNiro simply walks seamlessly around the other.

That same year, *Sinners* featured Michael B. Jordan as twin brothers who return to the Jim Crow South to establish a juke joint for Black patrons.

Critics tended to overplay the distinctive, even opposing, features of the two men, whereas thematically, the film uses doubling, or splitting, more as a means to separate the musical styles, economic success, and sovereignty of Black versus white social groups, and to foreground the threat posed by the latter in appropriating and killing the former (in the dyadic horror structure of zombie/human). Even so, *Sinners,* like its advertising campaign, remained intent on flaunting the technology that was able (unlike *The Patty Duke Show*) to place the twins, side by side, 'crossing the line' as one brother hands a cigarette to the other, as if to say, "look what at what we did"! (That this moment occurs at the outset of the film, soon after the brothers are introduced, suggests an instruction to viewers not to let their attention stray far from its technological achievements and effects.)

Unlike *Patty Duke,* whose use of twinning was apace with the cultural preoccupations of its time, and unlike even the Nineties, when twinning could be tracked back to an entertainment industry mired in panicky retreads, it is ultimately difficult to find a throughline between twinning in early twenty-first century popular culture and any contemporary zeitgeist. To be sure, Americans have been awash in sundry positions and obsessions over digital technology and AI, but it's not clear how the doubled and multiplied characters of the moment were in fact generated by a new "structure of feeling." Those doubles—common to these films and others, and to acclaimed anthology TV series such as *Black Mirror*—seem to have sprouted from digital gimmicky itself, rather than a socially situated preoccupation or sensibility, offering little in the way of thematic resonance. Thus, AI and digital technologies may, for the most part, have simply revived earlier audiences' fascination with the ability of optical technologies to present duplicated illusions, enabling viewers to be delightfully bewitched once again by the question of "how did they do it?" with attention directed to technical prowess over social and historical relevance.

Conclusion: Youth Must Be Heard

The Patty Duke Show's emphasis on twins each going their own way, even while working on the same project together, showed the potential that twinning can offer, whether in structural or narrative form. Many episodes, especially in the first two seasons, featured the two teenage girls peering into rewarding, even political, opportunities.

A telling case is "Patty, The People's Choice" (S2E7), all about the electoral process and the ways it can be used and abused. It's yet another episode in which the cousins are not confused with each other, and that illustrates the power of doubling over literal twinning. It begins with Patty and Cathy deciding to campaign for T. J. Blodgett, an old family friend (and trustee of Martin's newspaper), for election to Congress. Blodgett and his campaign manager refer to the girls as "pretty," a remark that, rather than confusing *or* differentiating the twins, simply stereotypes them as a couple of attractive but inconsequential teenage girls devoid of political worth or agency. The girls soon switch their allegiances to his more deserving opponent, Clark Williams, when they find actual substance in a speech he delivers (it doesn't hurt that Patty thinks the young Williams is handsome). Senatorial candidate Williams—clearly modeled after JFK—exudes vim and vigor and promotes a liberal agenda, promising to fight unemployment and to increase financial support to schools and foreign aid. In addition to his current job as a professor, Williams had served on MacArthur's staff in Japan, an undisguised allusion to JFK's military past. Blodgett promises the same funding aims but unrealistically claims that they will be achieved by lowering taxes. When the girls question him on the point, Blodgett confesses he has no real platform but will say anything to get elected, opening their eyes to his hypocrisy and his efforts to court voters by any means possible.

At home, Cathy starts to say, "What I think . . . " Patty finishes with, "I think so, too," conveying their mutual decision to switch their campaign support. Although this sharing of thoughts and finishing the other's sentences is a dusty stereotype about twins, it's one of only a small handful of times *The Patty Duke Show* uses it. In actuality, the fleeting moment carries no hint of an uncanny telepathic connection: it's less about the shared identity of the girls than their mutual coming to an impactful political decision. Their overlapped thoughts still distinguish the cautious Cathy, who was initially reluctant to back Blodgett, from Patty, who had heard her cousin's suspicions but hadn't heeded them, and who has now converted to Cathy's position. As their awareness of Blodgett's shortcomings increases, their political astuteness about the approaching election also grows and becomes more active and actually helps his competitor win the election.

"Patty, the People's Choice" begins and ends with Blodgett at the Lane home, bookending the episode with the sitcom's desiderata of stasis and its reestablishment. But that reestablishment has been revised. Precredit, Blodgett was shown trying out a speech on the family and receiving enthusiastic support, with Martin the only one concerned about the hollowness of his campaign promises. The finale begins with the family worrying that, when Blodgett arrives this time, he will be angry with Patty and Cathy for redirecting their support and helping Williams get elected. Instead, the blustering loser announces that he's not cut out for politics and should remain what he's always been: a businessman and gentleman farmer in Dutchess County. He thanks the girls for helping him see the light and the episode concludes with him taking them out for ice cream. The twins not only have read him correctly but are rewarded for it!

Earlier in the same episode, Cathy had lectured her high school class about the American electoral process, reciting facts about the organization of the US government and laying the groundwork for her fuller Americanization on the show. Such civic-minded lectures recur throughout the series and emphatically highlight Cathy's rich educational background. But as the episode unfolds, a larger, more significant lesson emerges as well: girls need to explore *and take action*, rather than just deliver or listen to dry lectures on American politics. And the twins make this happen.

By its doubling of Patty and Cathy, "Patty, The People's Choice" shows how teenagers working together constitute a more potent political force than they would have been separately, despite the title's unfortunate reference only to Patty (a trend that mars most episode titles). The twins' likeminded teamwork reveals neither a mindless sameness nor blunt, moralized opposition, but a wider field of options that seem to align with the progressive agenda of Kennedy and immediate post-Kennedy years (the Blodgett-Williams campaign would have taken place in 1964, when Kennedy's term would have ended). Even the name of the civics program on which the Lane girls question the two candidates is rather Kennedy-esque: "YOUTH MUST BE HEARD." Taken as a whole, the girls' active endeavors have little to do with literal twinning, and everything to do with doubling, and the power that arises from their joint efforts.

5

Playing with the Political

"Patty, The People's Choice" and "The President" arguably present Patty and
Cathy Lane at their most political. Whereas "People's Choice" shows the girls
working in tandem on a congressional campaign, "The President" installment is more representative of the series' somewhat unusual take on twinning in which the twins share a goal but approach it through unshared means.

Both episodes imply that young women might be capable of harnessing
a certain form of agency within social and political realms. In "People's
Choice," Cathy and Patty's work ends in success, helping the more qualified
candidate, Professor Williams, win the election. Just as importantly, though,
their initial support of his less principled rival exposes them to the darker, less
upstanding machinations of political operations, with the episode retreating
slightly from a full-throated idealization of the American political process.
In "The President," the cousins gain first-hand experience by running their
own campaigns and, even though they both lose, the show encourages us to
cheer on their enthusiastic efforts (the episode in fact cannot allow them to
win, for that would give one twin value at the expense of the other, which the
series was largely keen on avoiding). Here, it's the experience, not the outcome, that matters. For as modestly as *The Patty Duke Show* might present
the political efforts of its teen characters, the fact that it begins to articulate
doubled, "collective" action carries weight in a series broadcast during the
JFK and early LBJ era.

On top of these politically themed installments are others that feature the
cousins engaging in additional forms of civic service, such as Patty wanting
to join the Peace Corps or initiating a pen pal correspondence with a Soviet
official or Cathy intending to marry a Prince from a fictional developing
country to improve living conditions there. These episodes, which move
beyond the domestic space of the Lanes' home, afford peeks into larger, sociopolitical worlds, and the series consistently treats the girls' desire to participate within those adult worlds with a measure of respect. In fact, *The
Patty Duke Show* was rather unique among TV sitcoms of the time for *not*
ridiculing either its teen protagonists or their goals. Compare, for instance,

The Patty Duke Show *and the American Sixties*. Caryl Flinn and Dana Polan, Oxford University Press.
© Oxford University Press 2026. DOI: 10.1093/oso/9780197667439.003.0006

with *Gidget,* whose lead was countlessly concocting schemes to get to the beach or to date cute boys. That sitcom, over the entirety of its run, contained only two references to Gidget's desires to make a difference in the world, and trivialized both. One has her protesting the inequitable pricing at the local movie theater; the other has her running a campaign to save a beloved hamburger shack threatened with demolition. In contrast to Patty and Cathy, Gidget's engagements with social "activism" beyond the home are not only few in number, but are construed as little more than misguided attempts on her part, creating fluffy fodder for sitcom jokes.

The earnestness and zeal with which Patty (and sometimes Cathy) pursue their goals, even as these fall comically apart as they must, suggest something different: even a "gimmicky sitcom" can reveal preoccupations and aspirations of its larger political and cultural context. *The Patty Duke Show* constructs the energetic, youthful America of the era around a network of supporting themes such as public action, go-getter entrepreneurialism, naive but well-meaning drives to do good or to make a mark in the word, and even some forward-moving experimentation, as with gender roles. The realm of action for teenage girls, the series implies, can lie beyond domestic norms (consider also the negative depictions of marriage as social institution). As we note below, its focus on engaged citizenry and opportunity aligns with the Camelot spirit of the times.

Youthful Visions of JFK: Doing Good in the World and on TV

Even before he was elected president, John F. Kennedy generated a sense of youthful optimism and desire for change. At his nomination as presidential candidate at the Democratic National Convention in Los Angeles, he announced, "We stand today on the edge of a New Frontier, the frontier of the 1960s," stressing the nation's commitment to space exploration. NASA flourished during (and after) his presidency, culminating in the American moon landing of 1969. (As Lynn Spigel has observed, TV flagged the importance of space exploration through the occupations of many a sitcom man [*I Dream of Jeannie*'s astronaut Tony Nelson, and *My Three Sons*'s aeronautics engineer Steven Douglas] and several sitcom premises [*Lost in Space, My Favorite Martian, The Jetsons*]).[1] Richard Nixon, the conservative Republican candidate running against Kennedy, was not terribly forward-thinking, in an almost literal sense. His vision was not about voyaging boldly into the future but about entrenching anxieties Americans had long had, stressing, for example, the need for citizens to remain vigilant of past and on-going threats posed by the Soviet Union.

Kennedy became the nation's youngest president when he was elected at age forty-three. His rhetoric, platform, and policies were all characterized by charismatic youthfulness, and rather than falling on the cliché of adults needing to improve the world for the future, he included younger genera-tions by calling on them to be active participants and citizens of the nation and the world. In other words, it was less for parents to improve the world for future generations, but for youth to forge some of those new directions.[2]

In his inaugural address of January 20, 1960, before his oft-quoted "Ask not what your country can do for you, but what you can do for your country," the new president emphasized the transitional nature of the period the United States was entering: "Let the word go forth . . . that the torch has been passed to a new generation of Americans . . . Let us begin anew, remembering that civility is not a sign of weakness." As Lynn Spigel puts it, JFK pressed a "re-start button" not only with the new frontier space program but by appealing to so many other promises of new beginnings and new forms of involved citizenship.[3]

Quickly dubbed "the television President," much as F.D. Roosevelt had been called the "radio President" in exploiting the then-new medium in his Fireside Chats, Kennedy had an instinctive sense of how to use television and mass media, making himself widely available for interviews and photo shoots. He gave the impression of being as modern as the medium of televi-sion itself. But, as many commentators knew (Norman Mailer most notably) this image was not one of an organic "authenticity," but one that was carefully and meticulously choreographed.[4]

Kennedy's best-known TV appearances occurred in the four Great Debates with Nixon, which boosted Kennedy's campaign by amplifying the men's contrasting appearances. In the first debate of September 26, 1960, the young, photogenic senator, wearing makeup, gazed directly into the televi-sion camera while Nixon, only slightly older and still ill after a recent hos-pital stay and refusing makeup, appeared utterly lacking in visual allure, his face covered by five o'clock shadow and small whirlpools of sweat. (Said Chicago Mayor Richard J. Daley, "My God, they've embalmed him before he even died.")

Kennedy was burnished with such a magical patina that the media des-ignated his time in office the modern Arthurian era of Camelot, what jour-nalist Theodore White called "a magical moment in American history when gallant men danced with beautiful women, when great deeds were done, when artists, writers, and poets met at the White House, and the barbarians beyond the walls held back."[5] In 1960, Lerner and Loewe's musical *Camelot,* based on T. H. White's *The Once and Future King,* debuted on Broadway and quickly became the president's favorite show.[6] Jackie recited some of the more nostalgic lines from the musical's eponymous—and John's favorite—song in her famous interview with Theodore White soon after her husband's assassination. The near-mythic Arthurian dimensions defined the short but glistening tenure of the young president.

President Jack and First Lady Jackie Kennedy—in name, nearly another set of twins—became instant cultural icons on the eve of the new decade, with Jack, not unlike Patty Lane, standing as the all-American of the pair, a former war hero and congressman who tossed footballs on the White House lawn, and Jackie (a smoother, more charismatic version of Cathy?) forging strong bonds to Europe and beyond with her urbane style, education, and support of the arts (Figure 5.1). The key pipeline was to France, where she had studied and whose language she spoke: the President famously quipped at one point that he was "the man who accompanied Jacqueline Kennedy to Paris."

For her part, Jackie, a former journalist ("Camera Girl," as a 2023 biography terms her) was just as shrewdly aware as her husband of the importance of media image-making.[7] As early as 1953, she and Jack appeared on Edward R. Murrow's hugely popular TV show *Person to Person,* in which the eminent journalist interviewed prominent celebrities in their homes. Jackie often selected which appearances the two should make as a couple, and which she would make on her own, as in the quirky and breathless but widely watched televised tour of her newly redecorated White House.

Prior to Kennedy's campaign and election, broadcast television had been under siege, and his sustained use and promotion of it helped revive the floundering medium. In the early Sixties, over 90% of American households owned at least one television set but its status as a new media form was hardly secured. (The country's economic slump of 1957–58 scarcely helped matters.) By the end of the Fifties, network television had passed its first phase of experimental live shows, sitcoms, and live theatrical and musical performances broadcast from New York City for national consumption. By decade's end, most of the anthology shows were gone, few series were broadcast live, and conventions in genres like the sitcom were beginning to ossify. Instead of the ethnically diverse, community-oriented urban sitcoms that characterized its earlier output, the sitcom had morphed into stale,

Figure 5.1 Another Set of Matching Bookends. Courtesy Alamy Images

individualized white bread families, and its popularity was outstripped by the less adventurous western genre (*Gunsmoke, Bonanza, The Virginian*) which skewed to white, masculinist fantasies of glory and old Americana.

Interference by regulators, censors, sponsors, and competing film and re-cording industries also paved a bumpy road for the still-fledgling medium. The Quiz Show Scandals of the Fifties, in which Duke was involved (see Chapter 1), brought opprobrium to the medium, and when FCC chairman Newton Minow attacked the medium as a "vast wasteland" in 1961, his words struck a chord. Letters of public support poured in, and for the next few years, defensive broadcasters nervously produced a slew of educational shows and documentaries that helped aid the ascendency of television's respectability that Kennedy was ushering in.[8] Gerald Jones speculates that *The Patty Duke Show*'s Peace Corps episode and several socially minded installments of *The Dick Van Dyke Show* may have actually been produced in reaction to Minow's condemnation and to what he calls the "totally unbeliev-able families" of American sitcoms.[9]

Although it was Kennedy who had appointed Minow, the president's em-brace of the new medium starkly contrasted with his FCC Chairman's con-tempt for it. Kennedy had actually begun to elevate TV's status even before his election by using it as a political and moral tool rather than one solely aimed to entertain. He also understood its power to generate libidinally charged images, especially for women and girls, presenting a sort of more serious, accomplished, and grown-up version of the young stars gracing the cover of *Tiger Beat*. During his political campaigns, Kennedy, along with his family and handlers, worked sedulously to generate the appearance of the young politician as one of the country's most eligible bachelors. His mother, Rose, held weekly teas with female constituents to help manufacture a fantasy of access to Jack, who didn't propose to Jacqueline Bouvier until he entered the world of politics, when it was understood that a wife and potential family would boost Kennedy's image as a family man rather than as a philanderer. Certainly, the charismatic politician provided a more exciting and vibrant version of the bachelor dads on television who, as Betty Friedan argued, were expected to stimulate the fantasies of housewives and other female voters.

Even in death Kennedy was the television medium's star. In an unprec-edented move, the three American networks worked in tandem to broad-cast his funeral, pulling virtually all of their regular programming. A special, abbreviated edition of *TV Guide*—really an expanded pamphlet more than anything else—reflected on that coverage. The flyer was stuffed with favor-able reviews and self-congratulatory affirmations regarding the unqualified success—and newfound maturity—of the television medium in handling the events.

Three months after the assassination, The Beatles premiered on *The Ed Sullivan Show* and quickly conquered America, in no small part because, as Susan Douglas persuasively argues, they served a compensatory func-tion as idols for girls and young women who needed to redirect their hopes, desires, and even erotic energies away from Kennedy. Douglas notes that a chief draw of this English group for female fans was the reassurance they provided to girls and women, rather than hints of real exoticism, eroticism, or threat. Their masculinity was gentle, with more balladic love songs than other British groups like The Who or The Rolling Stones, whose "foreignness" lacked any softened, mollifying edges, and whose songs didn't coddle female listeners so much as objectify then.[10]

Sitcoms and Camelot Cosmopolitanism

Though clearly pitched at girls who hadn't yet reached voting age, *The Patty Duke Show* was informed by the alluring social and political changes that the charismatic JFK had brought to bear on the national landscape. (When Patty Duke herself met the young president, she called him "spellbinding, the sexiest man ever."[11]) Assassinated just two months after her series began, he served as a structuring absence to it, one that, not unlike a god, could not be named or directly presented but whose calls to service Patty could follow. Evidently, producers had filmed a dream sequence for "The President" episode in which one of the cousins received an official certification from the president, who was depicted in a rocking chair, face hidden from the camera. After his assassination, producers pulled the scene.

Patty Lane clearly embodies the vibrant, upbeat spirit of the era, as her character continually sampled various professions, activities, and identities available to her as a young white, middleclass American, many in the mode of the active citizenship that Kennedy extolled. In this vein, and contrary to the histories that assume Sixties popular culture existed as a fluff-filled world apart from the political goings-on of the time, even a sitcom with a preposterous premise like *The Patty Duke Show* could elaborate how mass cultural artifacts actively engaged with and even constituted the social and political concerns of an era.

To be sure, *The Patty Duke Show* funnels those engagements through the broad lens of sitcom comedy and the often-outlandish roles Duke's character tried on in every episode. Yet, as we've noted, a number of identities require her to venture beyond the home, even as others involve her attempting to reboot her fundamental Americanness. In "The Perfect Teenager" (discussed in the Introduction), in which a quiz informs Patty that she is *not* a typical American teen, she works overtime to reestablish those credentials, oddly, and anachronistically, by attending a charm school class.

Patty Lane's can-do spirit leaves its stamp on nearly every episode, but its most distinguishing feature is the good-willed *American* energy behind it. We see this in her drive to join the Peace Corps in Africa, when she proclaims her intent to bring "American know-how" along with her. Phrases celebrating "American know-how" and "American can-do spirit" run conspicuously across the series and are usually issued by Patty or her father. In one case, though, a Crown Prince from a faraway, fabricated country uses it to explain to the Lanes what he expected to get out of his visit to the United States, suggesting that the world at large knows about, and envies, this desirable American energy.

That specifically all-American spirit is evident in entrepreneurial episodes like "The Tycoons," in which Patty twice attributes "American know-how" as the key to her success with her dressmaking enterprise. Another, tellingly entitled "Can-Do Patty" (S2E14), opens with Cathy's teacher informing her that she's bound to win an oddly named "The student with the most can-do school spirit" contest. Patty, loafing around the house, gets a lecture from her father that "it's better to say yes to life's responsibilities than no." She responds by going all in, getting involved in too many projects in brash, American corporate style, farming out the work to Cathy and Richard as she busies herself with expansive fantasies of becoming the first female US President. (There's a glitteringly queer moment when someone at school wonders out loud about Richard's place were Patty to be elected, "He'd be First Lady!") Later, Martin praises his daughter for her "can-do spirit," yet adds that Cathy has been performing the actual work and deserved to win the contest. Patty, realizing the right thing to do, consequently gives her classmates a speech endorsing her cousin, who wins the title by unanimous vote.

It is worth noting, as an aside for now, that the ostensible foreigner seems to require the advocacy of an American to succeed in a contest of "can-do" spirit. As we dig deeper into the ideology that fuels this cheerleading for all things American, the privileging of Patty over Cathy in the series becomes unmistakable. That orientation intensifies over its three-year run; starting in Season 2, there are increasing episodes with titles like "Patty and the . . .," underscoring the declining importance of Cathy and of twinning itself. Yet it is not a smooth or fully linear evolution since *The Patty Duke Show* never posits either girl as "the good one" or the one who has traits and skills that outdo or better the other's.

As we demonstrated in Chapter 4, Patty and Cathy, "different as night and day," work not as oppositional twins (such as Samantha and Sabrina or the two Jeannies) but together in difference. In so doing, as we argued above, *The Patty Duke Show* transforms the format of twinning into one of doubling and diversity, an expansion rooted in outward, differentiated movements rather than a duplication dependent on internalized, binding ones. Even in episodes that place more narrative attention on one twin over the other, the storylines dramatize how an individual can be doubled by another version of herself that she might strive for over the course of the show's twenty-five and half minutes. If Patty frequently fails in her projects, it's not the initiative that is critiqued but, more typically, the way it balloons out of control. Most of her failures—wanting to date her doctor; to cook, look, or write like a French girl; to be an American folk singer—are due to the fact that the modes of being that Patty tries out are not yet available to an American girl of her age.

By rendering twinning as differentiation, the series creates a gentle optimism about not needing to be a singular thing or having to live a particular way. Of course, that fantasy, like all fantasies, is determined by the social conditions of its times, in this case, Kennedy's emphasis on an active youth and, in more nascent form, feminism's explorations into new roles for women. Interestingly, and in spite of her ultimate criticism of it, Susan Douglas observes that *The Patty Duke Show* offered numerous "possibilities" for young women, and notes that, generally, one of the "most important legacies for female consciousness [generated by mass media at the time was] was the erosion of anything resembling a unified self."[12] For Douglas, "*The Patty Duke Show* reinforced the notion that a girl was a grab bag of traits and masks…that could be deployed in different situations."[13] She goes on to note, however, that the series' fantasy of changing identities, "show[s] the pitfalls of such impersonations," focusing not only on the comedic renderings of these efforts, but their abandonment at each episode's end which brings the girls back to square one, an emphasis on narrative conclusion that we have noted in other scholars of girl culture. While those endings can be seen to close the door on Patty's zest for adventure, we find significance in *The Patty Duke Show*'s budding hope of nonconformity, iconoclastic futures, and alternative identities.

In this way, while Patty's pursuits suggest political endeavor, her show (like any other sitcom or series) cannot directly represent, much less reflect, specific events of its times. Otherwise put, the political undertakings invoke the era but offer no rigorous purchase on them. But through mechanisms of displacement and Williams's "structures of feeling," it's clear that the show engaged with social issues, if only at the level of fantasy. *The Patty Duke Show* unquestionably participated in a larger tradition of TV shows revolving around spirited, outspoken characters (from *Our Miss Brooks* to *The Golden Girls*) and/or quirky misfits (*Ugly Betty*), not just to entertain viewers, but to activate dreams in which their lives might be differently led, providing ephemeral escapes from the rules, norms, and pressures of everyday life.

Historians have singled out a different, less teen-oriented sitcom, *The Dick Van Dyke Show*, as the quintessential "Kennedy series." The show depicts the experiences of an attractive, self-achieving young couple, Rob and Laura Petrie, who seem to encompass the suburban version of the American dream. In her slightly bouffant flip and capri pants, critics have noted, Mary Tyler Moore even looks a bit like Jackie Kennedy (Figure 5.2). The Petries are presented as progressive adults, unwilling to take advantage of their privilege and concerned about equal opportunities for all. Gerald Jones clarifies the analogy: "The Petries were not sitcom versions of the Kennedys, but small-time folks *trying* to be like the Kennedys," noting, that for all the good taste evident in their home decor, Rob constantly trips over the ottoman, allowing

Figure 5.2 Rob and Laura Petrie: TV's Jack and Jackie. Photo by CBS via Getty Images

national audiences to access the fantasy of Camelot without feeling subordinate to it.[14]

The series did, in fact, dip its toes in modestly politicized situations (in one noted episode, Rob's comedy show receives an award for its depiction of Black people), thanks largely to the openly liberal stance of writer/producer Carl Reiner. Yet more than directly invoking Kennedy-like political actions, it comically dramatized some of their "structures of feeling," including the effects generated by a handsome young couple. Some of these sentiments were also fed by, and fed into, dreams swirling around achievable middle-class glamour, optimism, and domestic stability.

In a two-parter, Rob is encouraged to run for New Rochelle city council and quickly learns that campaigning involves creating favorable impressions with outright disregard for political depth or authentic commitment. As Rob attracts the attention of voters, especially female ones (again, not unlike JFK), he comes to realize that his opponent, an unglamorous dweeb (played by that go-to unglamorous dweeb Wally Cox), actually offers well-researched positions of substance. Yet, just as the episode seems to be barreling toward its conclusion (will Rob step aside for Cox's more capable candidate?), it ends with Rob winning the race. While Rob's efforts at engaged citizenry summon analogies to Kennedy and the New Frontier, the abrupt ending of the episodes forecloses even a minimal notion of politics: there's no stock-taking, no wondering what Rob's undeserved victory means, or what comes next. His political venture is a one-off, and that newly assumed position as councilman never comes up again. Here as elsewhere, as Jones maintains, the series does less to sustain a New Frontier than to generate the impression of one.

Other sitcoms of the time often had characters running for office in quick, slapstick endeavors in which they briefly attempted to move out of their habitual worlds and wear shoes too big for their feet. *Green Acres*, for example, had Lisa and Oliver run against each other in a local election, conducting stunts such as Oliver donning a Beatles wig and Lisa imitating Lady Godiva nude on horseback to court the male vote. Yet for all its teenage hijinks, *The Patty Duke Show* situated its campaign episodes within a *sustained* interest in public engagement and of moving energetically forward into possible roles and identities. As Gerald Jones puts it, *The Patty Duke Show* "did for teenagers what *Dick Van Dyke* did for young marrieds: It attempted to seize its moment and bring the forward-looking energies of young Americans into line with mainstream systems."[15]

America's Cosmopolitan Turn in the Sixties

During WWII, Americans perceived their connections between their home nation and other countries as entailing self-sacrifice, an effort viewed as a necessary mission to assume and fulfill. As David Farber writes, "In this new world, in which old differences of ethnicity and religion and region were downplayed, the binding ties of an imaginary national culture magnified. The great events, WWII, the Korean War and the Cold War . . . contributed to this nationalization."[16] Federal policies of the Fifties, as we have noted, tended to prod that sense of unity into protective measures both outward (supervising the rebuilding of Axis countries) and inward (advancing new consumerism and familial organizations).

The outwardly-directed focus of the Sixties dovetailed with policies that largely eschewed prior political harshness, shifting to softer public relations efforts that entreated citizens to help populations beyond American borders, usually impoverished regions deemed undeveloped—that is, not industrialized or under the full sway of US-styled democracy—pursuits that allowed the United States to aid others while simultaneously asserting its superiority in being able to do so. That selfsame sensibility informs the fundamental premise of *The Patty Duke Show*, in which the Lanes welcome their Scottish niece into their home, a situation that seems to suggest the ease and desirability of America's expanding cultural boundaries. Later in this chapter, we discuss ways in which that perceived cosmopolitism informs episodes in which the Lanes only *appear* to confront the world at large.

Although plenty of Cold War anxieties continued to plague the nation, America's engagement with foreign lands was giving rise to shifting perspectives, policies, and fantasies. For many Americans, foreign lands and cultures now fostered curiosity about places that extended promises of luxury, sophistication, enjoyable lifestyles, new products and sights, in short, escape from the everyday. Take, for example, the Fifties fad for Calypso and Caribbean music in Harry Belafonte's popular "Banana Boat Song," or Marilyn Monroe's steamy performance of "Heat Wave" in *There's No Business Like Show Business*. Even Hollywood beefcake Robert Mitchum was given the green light to record the rousingly campy LP, "Mitchum Sings Calypso."

For better-off Americans, such visions of cosmopolitanism seemed increasingly within reach, thanks in part to an enticing mix of economic stability and technological developments that had been built on established fantasies of armchair colonialism. Flying, for example, had been a luxury for most people during the Fifties, but by the Sixties, airlines aggressively vied for middle-class consumers, developing jingoistic phrases broadcast across radio and television: one airline promised "friendly skies," while others had names alluding to global travel (Trans World Airlines, Pan American). By the time of *The Patty Duke Show,* sitcoms and other mass media were leaning into the period's interest in foreign cultures and global connections which seemed ubiquitously represented across media, businesses, universities, and tourism such as safaris, cruises, world fairs, even theme parks like Disneyland, with their jungle rides, "Tomorrowland," and "Small World" exhibitions. Even for Americans who simply stayed home and watched TV, the world and its events were but a console away.

In a way, *Gilligan's Island* cashed in on the craze, by stranding a ragtag group of sightseers on an island after their boat tour had gone awry. It, and *The Patty Duke Show,* coincided with a set of tourist movie comedies in which Americans visited foreign locales, for example, *Paris When It Sizzles* (1964) and *Dear Brigitte* (1965), a trend that continued to the end of the decade, as in 1969's *If It's Tuesday This Must be Belgium.* Perhaps these fantasies constituted "the New Frontier" for average Americans.

These desires, though, did not always involve a venturing out or outwards. During the decade's early and hinge years, American cultural curators eagerly imported foreign culture into the United States, in realms both high and low. Julia Child introduced French cooking to millions of American chefs at home,[17] and the celebrity "New York Intellectual" Susan Sontag brought awareness to urban readers of challenging French directors such as Robert Bresson and Jean-Luc Godard. Along with Jacqueline Kennedy, Sontag was one of several influential young American women who had ventured to France, often in their "junior years abroad" to bring its culture back to the United States. (The very phrasing of "junior year abroad" nods to the resumption of life back home in America once that finite adventure is over: one goes abroad to return, laden with cultural riches ready for homespun adaptation.)[18]

By introducing a foreign cousin into the Lane household, *The Patty Duke Show* galvanizes the prospect of global involvement, and numerous episodes explore the possibilities of family adventures in France, Argentina, Africa, the Middle East, and beyond. Frenchness in particular gives a zesty flavor to the basic sitcom format in "What's Cooking, Cousin?" (S2E33). The episode opens with Patty learning that classmate Gloria has been taking French cooking classes, enticing Richard away from Patty's all-American hamburgers—and from Patty herself. She attempts to counter Gloria's culinary seduction by enlisting European-savvy Cathy to prepare French foods (*fruits de mer*, even those renowned crêpes suzette) that Patty will fob off as her own. Of course, all goes haywire: Cathy gets called to an unavoidable dinner at the French consulate with a friend of her dad's, Monsieur Honoré, and is thus unavailable to cook the winning dinner. Scrambling, Patty calls a frozen food delivery place (that hangs up on her), and then, with a thick accent, a French restaurant (that can't produce her meal in time). When Richard arrives, he immediately announces he wants to try Patty's promised French fare, as he's fed up with her burgers. Panic. But in a crosscut to Cathy out at dinner, Monsieur Honoré saves the day. As she recounts Patty's dilemma to him, he asserts that the classic French reputation is on the line (shades of "The French Teacher") and uses his influence to have a French meal of haute quality delivered to Patty's kitchen. Ironically, and after all that, the coda has Richard declaim that he has had his fill of rich French cooking and wants nothing more than Patty's venerated burgers. The episode trades in heavy-handed clichés about Frenchness: seductive accents, culinary heights and honor (as in the very name of the Gallic benefactor), only to drive home the satisfying superiority of the down-to-earth ways of the United States. That is the norm to which one wants to return, and the storyline scores a comic victory for the American way of life after having flirted with French culture.

Cosmopolitanism Turns Inward

In a way, the liberal cosmopolitanism on display in *The Patty Duke Show* was a geopolitical phenomenon, one the series produced by the structure of international doubling through Cathy and Patty. Positioning them as counterweights is one of the show's most evocative forms of differentiation, connecting the series to the fads, fears, and preoccupations of the Sixties. In Cathy's introduction of foreignness, gently and safely rendered, into the Lane's American household, she serves as an avatar of the expanding view symbolized by the Camelot era. But it starts to fall apart in Season 3, when Cathy's influence, and indeed her presence on the show, starts withering away. In episode after episode, the cosmopolitanism she represents loses out not just to the United States and US-centrism (for Cathy is unquestionably Americanized over the show's three years), but to the show's depiction of the United States through the location of Brooklyn Heights, which Patty, the American cousin, energetically embodies. And, throughout the show's run, Cathy remains a symbolic rather than active participant of most of the girls' projects, leaving most of the scheming, dreaming, and forward momentum to Patty. In doing this, *The Patty Duke Show* at once adheres to and undermines the ideology of an American global fervor peacefully coexisting with the country's sense of home and its self-proclaimed "can-do" spirit.

For instance, "Patty Joins the Peace Corps" (S2E9) has Patty signing up, unbeknownst to her parents, for the agency Kennedy had recently established. "I fudged my age a little—it's the spirit that counts," she informs Cathy, adding, in an announcement so absurd it receives the freeze frame that leads into the opening credits, "I'm going to Africa!" (Later, Patty will justify her misrepresentation of her age by saying, "I'm doing this for my country" and it's "the American thing to do.") To demonstrate to her family that she's sort of ready for this assignment, Patty grabs some bongo drums (somehow lying around the living room) and pounds away, claiming that the music signifies, "Take me to your leader," clichés of both music and dialogue that were typically reserved at the time for outer space creatures and Native Americans. Indeed, the prism through which Patty's do-good story is told is awash in racist and regional stereotypes (Figure 5.3).

To prepare for her work, Patty decorates her room in masks, shields, and spears and swaddles her beds in animal skin patterns. She begrudgingly eats homemade grass soup but won't go so far as to consume the fresh salamander Ross procures. Dreamily fantasizing about the sounds of wild animals, Patty dances hectically to music heavy with the acoustic bromides of pentatonic music and an emphasis on tom tom-like drums. She utters preposterous, stilted phrases that she claims to be in Swahili (of course they aren't), assuming that the language is spoken across the entire continent. In this move, the episode's writers join other Americans of the time by treating Swahili as laughably comic due to the word's sound more than anything else. The writers also have her declare that Ross would "make a great shrunken head." But ultimately, Patty is dissuaded from leaving. She is reminded of the importance of her volunteer work at a local orphanage, whose kids she knows individually and whom she clearly enjoys. The moral is this: Patty's American wards need her help every bit as much as the African "natives," as Patty puts it, so she'll start by saving North America and think about the Peace Corps when she's "older."

Figure 5.3 Co-opting African Otherness in a Brooklyn Bedroom

As an indication of the limits of the liberal desire of doing good in the world, *The Patty Duke Show* twice uses "Africa" as a plot device to signify a land of primitivism in need of American help. Along with the installment in which Cathy becomes popular by teaching her classmates a tribal dance, the Peace Corps episode is bloated with this vision as Patty declaims, "I want to shine a light in the darkness." Even the ostensibly worldly and knowledgeable Cathy instructs the Lanes (in what can only be called imperialist language) that "Africa is a fascinating *country*," trying to rev up the enthusiasm of Patty's family for her cousin's possible assignment.

Kim's Adoption

Sitcoms, like many of the stories in mass culture, often repressed more than they revealed, even, and perhaps especially, when they appear to be tackling specific concerns of the era. In "Patty the Foster Mother" (S131), Patty's effort to be a global citizen results in her filling out what she thought was paperwork for a symbolic sponsorship but ends up being for the actual adoption of an eight-year-old Korean orphan named Kim. By offering "Kim," a common Korean family name, as a (genderless) American first name, the episode renders that name at once more casual and less significant. The same heedless flattening of foreign identity also informed the casting: Kim was depicted by the young Delfino De Arco, a non-Korean actor.

Kim arrives at the Lanes' doorstep and becomes a veritable family mascot as the Lanes whisk him away on an undepicted whirlwind tour of metropolitan New York, as if that suffices to introduce the child to the American way of life. Ultimately, however, when the adoption agency catches its error, the Brooklyn Heights door shuts just as quickly as it had opened: Kim had been promised to a GI and his Korean bride. (The boy's backstory is unclear, but judging by the actor playing him, his likely age implies he had been orphaned during the Korean war.)

Such details harbor the darker components of the era's armchair (and actual) excursions of global travel and assistance by encouraging the colonialist mindset underpinning "white savior" stories and actions. Thus while "Patty the Foster Mother" attempts to portray suburban white people as open and welcoming, its narrative bluntly ensures that these American families be kept uniformly white. From the start, the usually self-absorbed Patty, believing in her ability to do good, leaps at the idea that "her" foreign orphan—a project more than a person—needs to be Americanized (before he even shows up, she sends Kim a tennis racket). The episode further enforces that messaging with its heavy-handed conclusion: Kim must be removed to restore the white, American norm of the sitcom's narrative base and stasis.

With Kim whisked into the Lane home and almost as quickly dispatched from it, the adoption episode captures a significant ideological feature of *The Patty Duke Show*: its cosmopolitanism and engagement with other regions, especially in undertaking good deeds, are really about nurturing the American ego and shoring up its domesticity (Figure 5.4). The snapshot of Brooklyn as a small-town place in which the home is central produces a much less neutral world than the show's producers may have been aiming for, and creates a sense of placelessness, a concept to which we now turn.

Brooklyn: Ground-Zero of Placelessness

As a hinge year text, *The Patty Duke Show* followed in the footsteps of many instructional sitcoms: its nuclear family is set apart from their neighbors in

Figure 5.4 Inviting and Expulsing the Foreign

a barely defined, much less depicted, neighborhood. *Father Knows Best*, for example, took place in the blandly named town of Springfield (something reprised decades later in the long-running animated sitcom *The Simpsons*).[19] Although the Brooklyn Heights setting of *The Patty Duke Show* refers to an actual geographical location—one stressed in the show's theme song, "Patty's only seen the sights/a girl can see from Brooklyn Heights"—it is made to be as empty and generic as the make-believe Springfield. Where, exactly, are Mayfield and Hillsdale, home to the Cleavers and the Reeds, respectively?

In 1979, a side-splitting *Saturday Night Live* skit riffed on the generic, interchangeable look of sitcom settings by creating a black and white episode of *The Twilight Zone*, replete with creepy underscoring and a deeply serious male voice-over. Guest host and former sitcom child actor, Ricky Nelson (of *Ozzie and Harriet* fame) enters the same door of the same kitchen set three or four times calling out, "Mom, I'm home" each time, and each time he is greeted by three sitcom "moms," all played by Jane Curtin, differentiated solely by the theme songs of their respective shows. But when the last mom responds with an offscreen "Ricky, is that you?" Gilda Radner enters as Lucille Ball, chaotically burning dinner for *husband* Ricky (Figure 5.5).

Figure 5.5 Lost in Sitcom Space: Ricky Nelson goes Home on *Saturday Night Live*

Channeling that generic placelessness, *The Patty Duke Show* does little to situate its action in Brooklyn Heights or the greater New York metropolitan area (in contrast with the solidly New York-based of *The Honeymooners*), converting its geography into an abstraction. What few shots we get of the city mostly are filmed from the Lanes' front door, usually involving an obviously painted backdrop of the skyline across the river. Others are taken from stock footage. Unlike Rob Petrie's workplace on *The Dick Van Dyke Show*, Martin Lane's Manhattan newspaper office is seldom depicted, his vocation as a newspaperman primarily signified by a tucked paper under his arm at home. The spaces of teen action are not much different: as we discussed in Chapter 2, few exterior shots of Brooklyn Heights High or the shake shop show up, especially in the first two seasons. Even the credit sequence eschews an establishing shot of the neighborhood or the Lanes' house, deviating from a convention established in domestic sitcoms like *Leave it to Beaver* and *The Munsters*. Only rarely does *The Patty Duke Show* employ location shooting, although, as we've noted, once production moved to Los Angeles, the series shows a few more outdoor shots that it awkwardly tried to fob off as Brooklyn Heights.

Brooklyn Heights exists less as a place than a placeholder, a signpost of a suburb defined primarily in opposition to the larger metropolitan area—its flipped double, if you will. The Lanes are more isolated and confined in their home than the characters of many other hinge-year shows like *Dick Van Dyke*, *The Beverly Hillbillies*, or *Gidget*, who respectively went to work, the bank, and the beach. *The Patty Duke Show* constructs Brooklyn Heights as a universe away from the concrete jungles of Manhattan. Less than a handful of references are made to "going downtown," and even "Brooklyn" is simply a vagueness resting beyond their front door, rather than a destination of any note. The occasional glimpses of actual cars parked outside the house work to constitute Brooklyn as an abode for commuters, but most of the Lanes' stories play out in their home's interior.[20]

This choice to downplay Brooklyn likely reflects the pragmatic budgetary concerns and time constraints of filming a weekly sitcom. To quote Paul O'Keefe, "all their energy was spent on the special effects."[21] Other industrial factors may also have motivated the unsituated, placeless aspect of *The Patty Duke Show*. Like the other broadcast networks, ABC was trying to attract as wide a national demographic as possible and, by the mid-Sixties, when TV had become an established, lucrative medium, the industry avoided shows launched at specific social groups or regions. As we have seen, networks were going wide. And for them, wide meant generic, and generic meant a bland, white, suburban middle class living in a nowhere intended to mean everywhere.

All the same, these industrial concerns don't fully resolve why *The Patty Duke Show* paid so little attention to the region, especially given the popular rural sitcoms of the era (*Green Acres*, *Mayberry RFD/Andy Griffith*, *Petticoat Junction*) that firmly relied on locations, albeit ones fictionalized and mediated through clichés of an imaginary, rural America. The nondescript nature of *The Patty Duke Show*'s Brooklyn, a borough of New York known for highlighting its local flavor and perky can-do particularity, contributes to a different, though not unrelated fantasy and ideological project: bathing the world in Americanness. Placelessness seemed a good place to start.

In her study of Sixties American television, Victoria E. Johnson raises the importance of the concept of heartland to it. It points, she argues, both to an actual region (typically, the Midwest) and a state of mind, not unlike Williams's "structures of feeling." Yet *The Patty Duke Show* has a slightly complex relationship to these sorts of topics. Obviously, it possesses a "heartland" in sensibility and feeling, but it images the urban site of Brooklyn as the cornerstone of small-town Americana.

It's significant that one of the few depicted places beyond the home is the shake shop since, in a way, it harkens back to heartland images of the soda fountain (it's where George commits to Emily in *Our Town*) and elaborates the respectability of hard work (consider the episode in which Patty takes a job there). Not fully a symbol of old-style Americana, since its space features not only a jukebox but characters of color, the show's version of the soda fountain is nonetheless not modern in any hip sense, like the beatnik coffee shop where Patty works in another episode. *The Patty Duke Show* thus extols heartland values like family, personal entrepreneurship, responsibility, etc. and in this way proffers a "suburban heartland," by presenting Brooklyn in a small-town, lightly contemporized way that Johnson's 'heartland' is not.[22]

In some cases, the Lane home is a sort of tabula rasa, as when aspiring teen writer Patty transforms the attic into a writing garret to channel a *La Bohème*-inspired Françoise Sagan, or when the family uses Japanese decor, dress, and design to bribe a baseball coach (whom they had been told was a fan of Japanese culture) into bringing Ross onto the team. Tellingly, these performative inscriptions of the larger world into the home don't last beyond single episodes. More frequent is the situation in which the Lanes simply refuse to move outside of their house, even as Patty's exploits often, though temporarily, leave that home behind. Anchoring the show's focal point on the suburban home pointedly compromises the sense of cosmopolitanism to which it otherwise gestures.

The Patty Duke Show's lack of forays into the community ensures the absence of regular characters from the neighborhood, no nosy neighbors—in contrast to many of its contemporaries such as *The Dick Van Dyke Show*'s Millie, *Bewitched*'s Gladys Kravitz, *I Love Lucy*'s Ethel and Fred Mertz, comic sidekicks all. Aside from Richard, who is constantly inviting himself inside, few people cross the family's threshold. Similarly, as much as Patty's popularity is trumpeted, she has no important recurring friends or schoolmates beyond Richard and school rival Sue-Ellen, whose name appears more often than her actual character (in a further dismissal of detail, she is depicted by two different actors).

Even the speech of members of the Lane family enforces the show's sense of placelessness. Ostensibly unmarked (void of any New York accent, Brooklyn or otherwise), their voices convey a false sense of neutrality. This is not illogical, given the narrow parameters of the series' cosmopolitanism, for accents convey the existence of difference, of potential outsiders and of other groups, cultures and countries. Outsiders were only brought into *The Patty Duke Show* through the tiniest clutch of characters—and they were almost always colorfully distinctive and vocally non-"neutral": a Greek grocer; Patty's French teacher, Cathy's prince from that fictional country. Imprinting the dialect of Brooklyn Heights with the bland neutrality of "unmarked" American voices helps burnish other characters with a stylized, noticeably material presence, depicted as outlandishly other through their exaggerated accents. Ultimately, Patty's "Byeees" and "Holey Moleys" drew attention to her not as a New Yorker but as a teenager.

Demonstrating the extent to which the series turns inward on itself, several episodes feature additional twinned family members, with accents that stress less any actual regional differences than the performance of them. In one, a cousin of Cathy and Patty's, Betsy, a boy-crazy girl from the South (a "Confederate Cleopatra," according to a petty Patty), comes to live with the Lanes since her own parents are being "too busy with their store." Predictably, Duke depicts this third twin. Whenever Kenneth, Cathy's father, appears, Schallert dons that cheap mustache; but when a separate episode introduces a third Lane brother, "Uncle Jed," whom Schallert also depicts, he is made to be quite the rube and embarrasses Martin (After all, Jed shares the same name as Jed Clampett of *The Beverly Hillbillies*). Far more than Kenneth, Jed is vocally and visually rendered an outsider, not just by dint of his abstractly "rural" origins, but by his speech, buried in an untraceable accent that Schallert later described as a "Nor'easter" but that, to our own ears, comes from nowhere, sounding more like the block-headed rendition of the non-Anglophonic languages we hear in other episodes. Each of these occasional visitors introduces a sense of ethnic, national, or cultural otherness that extends a temporary departure from Brooklyn Heights, but notably, their regional difference *intrudes* into the space of the family home. They are not figures whom the Lanes actively seek out.

In sum, the placelessness of the nonentity of Brooklyn Heights is not as neutral as it may seem. For what's left vague or undepicted works as a presumed norm—something so taken for granted that it doesn't *need* representation or attention drawn to it, in contrast to the caricatured stylization of characters who enter its fictional space as ambassadors from worlds beyond. Ultimately, *The Patty Duke Show*'s retreat from establishing a sense of place naturalizes and reinforces the series' Americanizing impulse.

The family's Brooklyn Heights home is handled as a base of operation from which Americanism radiates outward in a quixotic balancing act between the local and the global, as conveyed by the lyrics of "Cousins": "Meet Cathy who's lived most everywhere/ from Zanzibar to Berk'ley Square/ But Patty's only seen the sights/ a girl can see from Brooklyn Heights." Yet *The Patty Duke Show* largely skips over those "sights" just beyond the Lane doorway to move into the global, or more precisely, to be given the opportunity to encounter and then retreat from the global.

This is elaborated most tellingly in installments that raise the possibility of departing from Brooklyn Heights to travel to foreign lands, only to "return" home by never leaving it to begin with, reaffirming a domestic life without risk or genuine exchange. In this way, *The Patty Duke Show* shows that the possibility of leaving the States was ultimately less important than declining that opportunity, a double negation whose contorted logic restores power to the country of refusal.

Cosmopolitanism Uncovered

In an episode tellingly called "Cathy Leaves Home, But Not Really" (S3E14),[23] Cathy applies for a study-abroad opportunity in Argentina only to decline it when she discovers she'll be dispatched to an isolated rural community, aptly named El Fin del Mundo. Rather than seeing the assignment as a chance for western modernization/improvement of a developing region (as going to Africa would have been for Patty), Cathy first expresses dismay at the prospect and, as if channeling her social cousin, admits that she had originally applied to the program to meet boys in the big city of Buenos Aires. The "do good in the world" premise of other installments is slightly refocused here by adding a layer of domestic tension: Cathy has begun to fret that the Lanes have grown tired of her, especially when they feign enthusiasm about her acceptance into the program abroad, believing that this is what she wants. When Cathy decides against going, the Lanes are demonstrably relieved, and the episode ends—just as it had when Patty, deciding against the Peace Corps, said, "I've got to stay here and solve the problems of North America."

In "The Princess Cathy' (S1E14), the heavily exoticized young "Kalmere," crown prince of the fictional country of Bukanistan ("near India," we're vaguely told), proposes to Cathy. Kalmere is played by young pop singer

Richard Caruso, a casting choice that fictionalizes the character's ethnicity as much as his country's, just as we had seen with Kim. Once Cathy realizes that Kal's inordinate wealth, which she initially found off-putting, could be used to underwrite some needed infrastructural projects, she is prepared to accept his proposal and move to his country. (When the prince gives Cathy a priceless emerald as a token of his affection, her interest in it is unrelated to its value as a luxury commodity, but as something she can sell to raise money for the improvements she wants Kal to bring to his impoverished country with her at his side.)

That do-goodism is promptly extinguished once Cathy learns that, by accepting, she would become the first of what Kal expects will be a long list of brides. Against this foreign custom, she defends monogamy, "That's the way of *our* people," "In America, girls like it *our* way . . . one to a customer," confirming her Americanization in humorously consumerist terms. Moreover, Cathy's use of the first-person plural is a clear signal that the British cousin might be becoming "ours" as much as "Our Patty, [who] loves to rock 'n roll" had always been.

The Patty Duke Show's patina of interest in the cosmopolitan thus folds back into a deep-seated insistence on all-Americanism, a reversion that is among the series' most prominent ideological traits and that exposes some of the tensions underlying American attitudes around national and international engagement of the time. Retreating home after exploring other, ostensibly more exciting worlds and dreams—or having the possibilities of exploring them—is a time-worn American tenet that has been promoted many times across popular media. Among the classics are Dorothy in *The Wizard of Oz*, "If I ever go looking for my heart's desire again, I won't go looking further than my own backyard, because if isn't there, I never really lost it to begin with," and *Meet Me in St. Louis*, in which Mr. Smith's family is overjoyed that they won't have to relocate to New York City, despite having spent most of the 113 minutes of the film excitedly preparing for the move.

The Patty Duke Show has its own *Meet Me in St. Louis* episode, "The Continental" (S1E20), which opens in the family living room with Natalie, Patty, Cathy, and Ross completely bored and complaining about the various tasks each has to do. The camera turns to Martin just as he comes home from work, anxious about news he must deliver: J. R. wants to transfer him to the newspaper's bureau in Paris. To his surprise, his family is thrilled (exclaims Patty, "Yippie!"; Ross, "Boy, I can't believe it! I'm going to be an international!") and the episode follows the Lanes packing and making preparations to expand their cultural horizons. Cathy leads the family in French lessons and Patty tries to show Richard how love can play out in other lands by impersonating French, Spanish, and Hungarian lovers, intimating how seductive she can be in all three languages. (How this might reassure the poor boy is anyone's guess; but once again, it flaunts Duke's gifts at foreign accents, just as when, depicting Cathy, she tutors the family in French.)

Other devices of the episode have the outside world penetrating the family's enclosed world before the Lanes even leave for Paris. An unusually large number of local characters traipse through: Mr. Pavadapalous, a Greek grocer (seen only in this installment), brings Natalie a basket of fruit and tells her how much he and the never-depicted neighbors will miss her, and Ted and Nicky, occasional suitors of Cathy and Ross, respectively, come to bid their adieux. Realtors parade a steady stream of boisterous potential renters through the house, the soundtrack accompanying each group with the sound of militaristic snare drums, as each makes its march throughout the homestead. These gauche invaders of the Lanes' guarded interior spaces go even further, freely criticizing Natalie's décor and helping themselves to Mr. Pavadapalous' fruit basket. "You know, Mommo," laments Patty, "I don't like the idea of strangers living in our house," evincing unease about the newcomers who might be taking over their space as well as the strangers that the Lanes will encounter once they depart.

By mid-episode, no one (except Martin, now sporting a beret) is excited about leaving (Figure 5.6). When Natalie tries to summon Ross's earlier enthusiasm, the boy flatly repeats, "Yippie, we're going to Paris." But not to worry: the Lanes will not be moving forward—they will not be asked to meet new people or alter locations. Doubling back on itself, the penultimate scene again starts with Natalie, Patty, Cathy, and Ross moping about their imminent departure in the living room. A worried Martin enters, repeating the exact lines from before, concerned about the bad news he must break to his family: J. R. has changed his mind, and Martin will not be transferred to Paris after all. His family jumps for joy. In the episode's subsequent coda, Natalie and the children are positioned in the living room exactly as they'd been at the start, doing the very same things they'd been complaining about but now performing with excitement: addressing PTA envelopes, learning lines of a play, preparing for a Boy Scouts' meeting. "Suddenly all of us appreciate everything more," Natalie muses, and Patty embraces her "marvelous" father, who quips, "Suddenly I'm marvelous. And you know what I did? I didn't take

Figure 5.6 Monsieur Martin's Beret

my family to Europe." And so the local seems to come into play only when the threat of leaving it looms.

Rather than voyaging abroad to experience the pleasures of global engagement, the series demonstrates the pronounced American ideological preference to import those joys into controlled domestic environments, often to dampen them. "Other" lands and cultures matter (to Patty, to the family) not in the classic sense of the ostensibly altruistic, Kennedy-esque cosmopolitanism, but in terms of what outsiders can do for you.

Consider the very characterization of Cathy. By presenting her as a demure relative from the United Kingdom, the series renders traditional upper-class, western European values as quaint and unthreatening—a charming product for Americans to safely assimilate or exoticize. It's not difficult to sense that Cathy's higher culture might need to cede to the fun and youthful energy Patty represents. This (admittedly nonlinear) process begins as early as the end of season one. Effectively ratifying her time thus far in the States, Cathy reviews photos of her first day in America, and comments with dismay on how "foreign" she looked. Another first-season episode confirms how much Cathy's has already joined the New World when she comes to the aid of a basketball player who is failing his US literature class, coaching him in the facts of American literary history of which she, of course, possesses instinctive knowledge. When the jock can't remember any details of her lessons, Cathy translates them into numerical basketball moves that Patty and her cheerleader friends set out to chant outside the exam room. The implication here is that Cathy's intuitive intellectual awareness (of American literary facts) needs conversion into a lively, all-American sports idiom.

In fact, *The Patty Duke Show* continually asserts that the United States possesses a more contemporary, hip young vibe than Cathy's Britain, even as the series attempts to absorb the worldliness to which the latter gestures. For example, in "Patty Pits Wits, Two Brits Hits," (S2E23) British pop guest stars Chad and Jeremy garner success in America only because of Patty's home-grown acumen when she sneaks them onto a Brooklyn radio station, which of course turns them into local celebrities.[24] The episode begins with the duo performing to acclaim at Brooklyn Heights High, and goes into flashback to chronicle the story of their absorption into the American scene.

Moya Luckett has keenly noted how the series disconnects Cathy from the contemporary "mod" scene in London and the "British Invasion" that were actually very important to American teen life of the early and mid-Sixties. That particular culture is put aside in order to tie Cathy to dustier notions of upper-crust Englishness and an elite, imperial past that was fast fading from view. The appreciation of the energies of rock and roll and swinging pop culture is transferred onto the figure of Patty.[25]

Others from Within

The sense that middle-America must confront its otherness also informs *The Patty Duke Show*'s treatment of racial, economic, and cultural differences *within* the American population, as its presentation of Uncle Jed suggests. But we'll see that *The Patty Duke Show* never took the social, racial, political, and cultural groups considered "outcasts" or "minorities" of the United States all that seriously (truth be told, few national sitcoms of the time did), giving it a backwards-facing pathway.

For instance, two episodes feature oh-so-hip "beatniks," a demographic that enjoyed less cultural capital by the mid-Sixties than it had earlier. By then, mainstream culture and media had reduced the hip movement into campy, bongo-playing jokes. In one episode, Patty tries her hand as a folk singer at a cafe, where a pretentious, beat-styled performer takes the stage. A more sustained exploitation of the beatnik-as-joke appears in "Anywhere I Hang My Horn is Home" (S3E19), in which Dick Gautier (Conrad Birdie from the original stage production of *Bye Bye Birdie)* portrays unemployed jazz trumpeter Gate Garrison, whom Patty meets as he is about to lose his apartment and invites to move in with her family (Gate is enough of a laughingstock to disqualify him as potential boyfriend material for Patty). The guest proves to be a bull in a china shop, breaking things and cluelessly playing music too loudly.[26] Like the "accented ethnics" that weave in and out of the series, Gate is fully out of place in the bourgeois world of the Lanes, and, as sitcom viewers could anticipate, must be removed by the episode's conclusion in order to resecure it. Thus it is no surprise that, at the last minute, Gate tells his hosts that he has landed a job, though not a home, performing with his band on a cruise ship.

Unlike the placelessness of the Lanes and their neighborhood, Gate's is determined by the material lack of a home due to financial difficulties—along with his stated desire for "cool" work, a comic shield against taking his economic condition seriously. The Lanes' situation, in all its financial and ideological stability, is, as we have noted, conveyed to be normal enough so as not to require sustained emphasis. Gate, on the other hand, cannot be taken for granted: he is a colorful, disruptive character, and his unhoused, unemployed status presents another form of difference brought to the Lanes' home only to be expelled from it when he is transferred into another vaguely middle-class world (the cruise ship) where his difference from the tourists will be every bit as conspicuous. But for the series, his life is now safely out of sight.

That sense of being out of view had considerable resonance at the time. In his influential 1962 *The Other America,* Michael Harrington made the case for Americans to take heed of the poverty that existed throughout a country that was flaunting its prosperity. Repeatedly, he cast his metaphors in terms of visibility, as in wanting to "lift the veil" on poverty, to shed light on the "socially invisible" people who lived in its grip, and so on. The book's reach was so great that in January, 1964, President Johnson delivered an influential speech stressing the need to face the problem of American immiseration, and one of the major tenets of his Presidency would be "the war on poverty." Creating an out-of-work, unhoused character may have been a decidedly indirect way to recognize "the other Americans" facing economic hardship. It's a stretch, to be sure, but it is possible that, through significant displacement and a broad comic lens, the show is giving a slight nod to this trenchant social issue. TV critic David Marc concurs with Harrington's observations about domestic issues never making it into the "unreal" worlds of the sitcom. For him, it was genre that engaged in an "ideological smokescreen operation" concerning the kind of people sitcoms elected to include and exclude, and how they were represented, if at all.[27]

About American race relations, The Patty Duke Show is even more quiescent, especially given the times in which it ran. Martin Luther King had delivered his "I Have a Dream" speech to over a quarter million people only a few months before the series premiered; his famous Selma to Montgomery March occurred in 1965; President Johnson signed the Civil Rights Act in 1964, and the following year signed the Voters Rights Act. Black struggles for equality and voting rights preceded, coincided with, and followed the run of The Patty Duke Show, one of the broadcast world's unequivocally white sitcoms.

Unsurprisingly, policies of commercial television impacted the viability, and visibility, of Black-oriented shows. In 1952, the FCC had decided to freeze the number of new broadcast licenses, creating, as Alan Nadel argues, a deliberate scarcity of channels that led to tighter governmental restrictions concerning what existing stations could say. The stoppage effectively froze the TV world of the moment—one that had permitted the tiniest of spaces for alternative voices and viewpoints of minorities. Now they were kept to the bare minimum. As Nadel argues, the South served as a key demographic at this point: "any network found that alienating viewers in that region was a risk it could not take. It was fear of Southern backlash, for instance, not the complaints of the . . . NAACP, that led to Amos 'n' Andy's cancellation."[28]

For a show to include people of color, even as extras as The Patty Duke Show did, meant a conscious casting decision, which Paul O'Keefe acknowledged in our conversations. Exceptions included American variety and anthology shows such as The Ed Sullivan Show and The Twilight Zone that showcased Black talent in isolated episodes. Beginning in 1963, several TV dramas featured recurring Black characters (East Side/West Side, The Defenders, Mr. Novak). And, as we note above, The Dick Van Dyke Show was among the rare sitcoms of the time to feature African American characters several times; The Patty Duke Show, by contrast, acknowledged Black existence only at the margins. Nearly all of its Black characters were students, usually uncredited background figures in Brooklyn Heights High, the teenagers' dances, or the shake shop.[29]

Given the still-unfolding history of American school desegregation—begun with the 1954 Brown v. Board of Education decision and, in 1957, the calling of the National Guard to forcibly assist in integrating nine Black students into a white school in Little Rock—the show's inclusion of Black students, rather than in other roles, is intriguing. For, in contrast to the contentious process of actual school desegregation, *The Patty Duke Show* presented relations between Black and white students as quietly harmonious, with Black students dutifully silent as Patty or Cathy obstreperously took center stage. (In one episode, Patty says Hi to Mary, an African American student passing by in the school hallway but Mary, perhaps predictably, is given no dialogue in return.) And while African American presence in the series might indirectly point to the ongoing process of desegregation in US schools, their relative passivity renders the real-world violent struggles involved with desegregation efforts of the times as insignificant or already resolved. Still, while it is unlikely to have been even remotely on the minds of the show's creators, the Black characters appearing in the shake shop might offer a very modest, unintended nod to the counter sit-ins that began in 1960 in Greensboro, North Carolina.

The Patty Duke Show's casual placement of Black characters into white spaces meshes with the liberal intentions of the time with a colorblindness that fails to challenge its fundamental whiteness. Only once does a Black student have a speaking line (depicted by Tom Scott, who would go on to guest star in shows like *Sanford and Son* and *Marcus Welby, M.D.*). Another blink-and-you'll-miss-it single line is spoken by another minor Black character, the city hall clerk who gives Patty and Richard the fishing license that J. R. and Martin confuse for a marriage license. Union rules required that actors who spoke dialogue had to be credited and be members of the Screen Actors' Guild, so the lack of dialogue from the show's few Black characters reflects a parallel lack of diversity in SAG membership of the time.

An African American actor would not lead their own television series until *Julia*. Among the few sitcoms that featured a Black cast member was *Hogan's Heroes*, which followed the comic/heroic antics of a small group of Allied prisoners in a WWII German POW camp. Ivan Dixon, known for his stunning performance in the 1964 drama *Nothing but a Man*, played "Kinch," the cast's sole Black member. (A Black extra appears in several episodes, but never speaks—SAG rules again?) Dixon was dissatisfied with his experience and quit the series before it ended. Just one episode had centered on his character, one that pairs him with a Detroit woman in Germany posing as an

"African Princess," played by iconic Sixties/Seventies Black actress Barbara McNair. Kinch convinces her to return to the United States to fight for Black liberation there (recalling Patty and Cathy's need to stay in the States to conduct their social work).

In contrast, and in what is arguably the best installment of *The Patty Duke Show*, a famous Black performer takes things by storm. "Will the Real Sammy Davis Please Hang Up?" (S2E25) is a bit of a one-off (and the only time in which a singer performs live in the series), and veers away from the standard sitcom formula to prioritize the excitement of show and spectacle. Moreover, most of the action takes place largely outside of the Lanes' homestead, and Cathy's minimized presence eases the audience's ability to enjoy Davis's star turn.

The episode begins with an unusual degree of self-consciousness. Davis, as himself, gazes into the camera to welcome viewers to *The Patty Duke Show*, reassuring them that they're in the right place, before a dissolve takes us to the girls' high school (Figure 5.7). Patty is charged with finding an entertainer for the prom and, predictably, starts with a few panicky, failed efforts to land a celebrity (she even considers LBJ when Martin mentions

Figure 5.7 Sammy Davis Jr. Headlines the Show

that he will be in town to address a convention of journalists). In a rare scene in which she is shown outside of Brooklyn Heights, Patty carries a picket sign to Shubert Alley searching for an entertainer to play at her school dance.[30] During that time, Sammy Davis was on Broadway, starring in *Golden Boy* (in which there was a controversial interracial kiss—Broadway's first) and, in the episode, he spots Patty from above in his dressing room for the production, with a poster of *Golden Boy* prominently displayed on the wall. The star appreciates the girl's initiative and intends to accept the invitation, but Patty leaves in defeat before Davis's manager can reach her outside. The girl ends up being the subject of a human-interest story in *Variety* whose editor writes admirably about her "pluck." Davis reads the piece and recommits to doing the high school gig but now can't get through to Patty on the phone. (When the line is not busy, and she answers, she's sure it's a prank caller and hangs up). After several farcical missed connections, the episode ends with Davis at the dance performing his 1962 hit "What Kind of Fool Am I?" He crushes it.

In a curious, freighted moment, however, when Davis first appears onstage, he announces his plans to start the show with a Ray Charles number, which produces a failed call and response from the unresponsive, nearly all-white audience—a joke moved through so quickly one could easily miss it. And then, after his performance, Patty goes up to him with a coy, "I don't know how to thank you, Mr. Davis," to which the singer responds, "Oh I can think of one way [*very* awkward beat] . . . don't pay me that $15 [for being the guest at the dance]."

The space of that uncomfortable beat intimates that full thanks cannot be given. Duke, who was not only a white female but a minor, could only thank the dynamic Black performer with a handshake. The moment contains ghostly traces of a television special that had aired three years earlier in which white singer Petula Clark (whose special it was) and Black singer Harry Belafonte caused a scandal when Clark touched his arm during a duet, eliciting offended panic from the show's sponsor, the Chrysler Corporation (the network had fiercely debated Belafonte's appearance before it even extended an invitation to him).

"Will the Real Sammy Davis Please Hang Up?" is the only episode of *The Patty Duke Show* that does not have Blackness recede into the background. Davis's Black band members and assistant appear as prominent guest figures, and a greater number of Black characters appear in the background (albeit only as extras), gathering as fans in the star's dressing room and as students at the dance (one enthusiastic African American classmate, Mary [the same classmate Patty had greeted in the school hallway] actually gets to stand next to Patty in the foreground!). Although racial difference is not the primary focus of "Will the Real Sammy Davis Please Hang Up?" it pervades the episode.

Other social concerns and situations of the Sixties were peppered across *The Patty Duke Show*. The ongoing Cold War between the United States and the USSR haunts the one in which Patty fulfills a civics class assignment to write a government official: she writes a person whom she calls the "Premiere" of Russia. She's unaware that her letter, which had inquired about the country's freeway system, was received by the Russian authorities as a coded request to meet. The State Department, having flagged the correspondence, sends an official to go to the Lanes' home and asks the young girl to continue the exchange with text provided by his agency as a tactic to handle the diplomatic agitations her missive has engendered. Episodes like this elaborate how political sensitivities hovered over the series, again creating an inchoate sense of then-current "structures of feeling" at the time rather than a program of direct representation. True, bits of dialogue referred to then-President Johnson, but the nation's substantive issues were sequestered under thick layers of disguise.

The Christmas episode, "Auld Lang Syne" (S1E16) features another displaced reference to current events. Kenneth is fired by J. R. for ignoring an assignment to cover instead the breaking story of a developing country in revolt and subsequently being arrested there. But Kenneth redeems himself and renews his reputation as journalist-explorer by snagging an exclusive interview with the rebel leader who, after successfully overthrowing his country's dictatorship, agrees to be interviewed only by Kenneth Lane, an old acquaintance. Initial viewers would have easily connected this detail to CBS's already-famous 1959 televised interview with Fidel Castro that helped transform him into a revolutionary icon across the globe even, and especially, to Americans—Castro was, after all, trying to overthrow the dictatorship of Fulgencio Batista. Of course, by the time *The Patty Duke Show* hit the American airwaves after the Cuban Missile Crisis, Castro's status had taken a different turn.

Perhaps the most stunning—and again, surely unintentional—reference to a relatively recent historical event occurs in "Patty, the Candy Striper" (S3E12), in which a hospitalized Martin wants to interview his German roommate after learning that he is in fact "Dr. Schroeter, a famous rocket scientist . . . working on a book to colonize the moon." Schroeter's location in the United States calls to mind the many German scientists, including former Nazi party members, whom the United States recruited after WWII for their expertise, most infamously, Werner von Braun. At one point, Patty catches the man in the closet smoking an off-limits cigar; she tries to bring Schroeter back into the room where he commands her not to open the blinds. After he says with alarm, "Don't. From here, you can see the incinerator," he tries to clarify, "You expect me to watch all that wonderful smoke pouring out of that chimney when you won't let me smoke a teensy cigar?," an awkward line that tries to foreclose interpreting the incident as anything Holocaust-related. It is among the series' strangest moments.

The Patty Duke Show is vague about wartime in general. On several occasions, Martin mentions his time in "the war," references clearly aimed to represent the *paterfamilias* as patriotic, conventionally masculine, and authoritative. But the specifics about his military experience are firmly kept under wraps (which war? WWII? Korea?). One thing it is assuredly not about: the country's military involvement in Vietnam during the run of the series. "Can-Do Patty" features the show's only direct reference to it when a Brooklyn High School teacher explains a student's absence by saying he had enlisted.

Few installments mention the military, although the tie-in novel *Patty Goes to Washington* has the cousins surrounded by cadets aplenty. One episode of the series shows Patty with a crush on a young cadet she has just met, setting up another threat to poor, beleaguered Richard. Like the few government officials who appear here and there, the character is treated respectfully and, overall, the series seemed disinterested in lampooning military or government authority, in complete contrast to the military sitcoms running at the time. As Jones says, "In 1965, four years before Johnson implemented the draft, it was still possible for Patty to become infatuated with that handsome military cadet without branding herself as a hawk or even evoking the present situation in Southeast Asia. It was probably the last moment in which a sitcom about teenagers could still pretend to be hip while endorsing the status quo."[31]

Mocking and Minimizing
the Other: Ditching Cosmopolitism

In Chapter 2, we outlined some of the possible industrial reasons behind ABC's decision to make the 1965–66 season the show's final one. Reviewing that year's output, it's clear that the series had detached itself from almost any social engagement and lurched into sillier, inconsequential endeavors. Patty's forays were no longer aimed at "doing good" and were increasingly reduced to juvenile hijinks such as sneaking kittens into the house, working on a screwy spy caper, evading the "Mob," or chasing a runaway canine she had been dog sitting.

While we've maintained that *The Patty Duke Show* was never only about twinning, the series—or rather, its writers and producers—seemed to have retired the idea of doubling in this third season. Cathy appears less and less her cousin's equal, and her function as crisis resolver or mediator further wanes as Patty's father steps in to absorb those responsibilities. The show even displaces that function onto characters from outside the family. In "Sick in Bed" (S3E10), a male schoolmate comes over and mouths Patty's lines as Joan of Arc in a play that Patty is likely to miss due to an illness. The new duality between Patty and the boy elaborates how just how far the sense of the show's doubling has traveled. Cathy is out of the picture.

With buffoonery and mockery becoming the prevailing comedic norm by the show's last year, along with its retreats from exploits beyond Brooklyn Heights, its sense of serious engagement with the global had evaporated. The potential for international sophistication that Cathy had always represented became so insignificant that her character was appearing less frequently, in throwaway scenes or absent altogether, with family members briefly informing audiences that she's "in Paris" or "visiting her father." Such lines may have continued to position the British cousin as an icon of worldliness, but they are also pointing to her absence and her lagging importance to the show. Had Patty's "all American teenager" absorbed the "other," the foreign twin?

The Patty Duke Show had initially been gilded with the glow of Camelot, yet it somehow lost its way as the Camelot dream itself faded out. To be sure, LBJ's notion of "the Great Society" maintained some of JFK's progressive messaging, and the new president accomplished far more for civil rights than Kennedy ever had. After inaugurating the "war on poverty," Johnson took concrete steps toward making that goal by expanding Medicare with Medicaid, broadening access to food stamps, and establishing early educational programs like Head Start. More than a handful of episodes of *The Patty Duke Show* include respectful references to him. Nevertheless, Johnson was a hard-ball career politician who lacked the youthful idealism, hopefulness and dashing magnetism of Kennedy, whose impact had galvanized American youth.

Accompanying the series' retreat from cosmopolitanism was a growing willingness to ridicule nonwhite ethnicities, countries and cultures. In embracing facile, race-based humor, it inflated the importance of a specifically white Americanism. Its representations of racial difference, never levelheaded in the first place, took a dive, evincing an embarrassing intolerance to a number of races and ethnicities.

In one of the show's endless puns-for-titles, "I'll be Suing You" (S3E8), Patty covers for Richard after he gets a fender-bender in his dad's car. When a lawyer calls Patty for her eyewitness account, she avoids speaking to him by pretending to be an Asian houseboy at the "Ranes," answering the phone with a faux-Chinese (?) accent while squinting her eyes. When he calls again, she tells her interlocutor that "this isn't Pearl Harbor, you know," a weird response even when construed as a joke. When the lawyer shows up in person, Patty dons thick glasses and feigns poor eyesight, invoking Mickey Rooney's controversial 1961 yellowface performance of "Mr. Yunishi" in *Breakfast at Tiffany's* (and, in a more detached way, demeaning Duke's portrayal of Helen Keller). Martin just happens to be writing a news story on "Red China" in the same episode, and, following on its heels, the season's next installment has Patty dismissing a suitor with a "For all I care, 'Number One boy' can go take his rickshaw and go back to Mongolia," cramming Asia's diverse cultures and countries into a single grab-bag of laughs for white viewers.

While *The Patty Duke Show* had never evinced anything but a white, US-centric view of the world, these last-season barbs at ethnic and racial difference stand in marked contrast to the humor of earlier seasons, which usually burnished other lands—especially France, its fetish of choice—with rich desirability, even as that culture also served as the basis of clichés and jokey shorthand, such as Patty's homemade brioches or Martin's beret. By Season 3, however, even that superficial respect disintegrated, as depictions of difference were conducted through stereotypes patently constructed by and for an America-first gaze.

Such is the retreat that *The Patty Duke Show* made over its three seasons, pulling back from what had initially seemed to be an altruistic concern and curiosity regarding other countries and cultures. More to the point, though, its final season demonstrates that the series' flirtation with active, altruistic global citizenry had been a bit of a mirage all along, rooted in a fantasy of American power and privilege. Informed at its start by the outward-leaning vision of the Kennedy era, *The Patty Duke Show* ultimately participated in an equally pronounced "made in the USA" modality in which citizens were expected to interact with the rest of the world by, counterintuitively, turning inward. Duke's sitcom accomplished this by othering non-US cultures, whether by treating them as in need of white, western rescue (the kids of Africa and Korea); commodifying them (with French or Japanese-themed dinners); flirting with them (Cathy and the Mideastern prince, Patty and her French teacher); or treating them solely as jokes (the vague "Asianness" described above).

While there are no direct through lines between a historical moment and the media that emerge from it, no shortage of writers have argued that as the optimism of Camelot slipped from view, displays of cynicism and suspicions about the nation's ability to do good at home or abroad were coming into greater public awareness and focus. For Sixties historian David Farber, "By the end of the decade, the failure of Kennedy and other leaders to admit that American interests in the world were driven by motives more complex than neighborly good will or moral purity would radically undermine the faith of missions in their government." Farber thus rewrites the decade's division into discrete parts to argue instead that a "American-first mentality" tracked through its entirety.[32]

For, to recall Norman Mailer, even the golden gloss of Camelot was nothing more than an image concocted for the public from the outset and filled with contradictions and secrets under its radiant veneer.[33] For example, the same year Kennedy established the Peace Corps, he formed the Green Berets, the Army's feared special forces unit. Roughly coincident with the run of *The Patty Duke Show,* Americans learned of numerous military maneuvers that had been covered up by the CIA, the FBI, and the government itself: the Bay of Pigs, the extent of the country's involvement in Vietnam, the role of the United States in assassinating the democratically elected Prime Minister Patrice Lumumba of the Democratic Republic of the Congo (and the suspicious death of progressive UN Secretary-General Dag Hammarskjöld at the same time). At home, the formal surveillance of anti-war groups (including during the first national anti-war protest in 1965 in Washington DC); and the violent, often fatal attacks on members of the Civil Rights movement weren't as cloaked as official channels may have wished, due, in large part, as we noted earlier, to the coverage provided by the mass media of the time. But even on that latter point, as Heather Hendershot has argued, the country's faith in print and televised journalism as reliable purveyors of the 'truth' started spiraling downward and was irremediably ruptured after their timorous handling of the riots in 1968 at the DNC (Democratic National Convention) in Chicago.[34] Susan Douglas points to similar contradictions in what TV screens were feeding American viewers, "As the Sixties progressed, television became increasingly divided against itself, a schizophrenic medium that during certain portions of the day [and, one might add, certain kinds of shows] pretended there were no such things as social problems but at others shoved these problems right in our face through new reports and exposés like *Harvest of Shame*."[35]

Again, we are not claiming that *The Patty Duke Show* mirrors or doubles such shifts across US social and political events of the Sixties, especially in any linear, literal way. Rather, it rehearses some of the reframing and revision of social and political contradictions that had been operative in it from the start.

In "The Cousins" (S1E36), which was the episode that concluded Season 1, Cathy and Patty reminisce about Cathy's first year stateside. The installment re-uses clips from the unaired pilot, inserting them as the cousins laugh about Cathy's naivete in her new homeland (this is where she exclaims, "I look so . . . foreign!"). Flashbacks establish her initial ignorance about American teen culture; when first entering the cousins' shared bedroom, Cathy hadn't recognized some of the pop singers whose records and pinups Patty had scattered across the room. But as her character grows more Americanized, so does her ability to identify the teen icons of the moment; by the time Frankie Avalon shows up on the family's doorstep in Season 3, Cathy easily identifies him.

The final season, which also saw the retrenchment of Natalie and Martin into outmoded gender stereotypes of the domestic sitcom, confirms that Cathy Lane had achieved full-blooded Americanization, making her character somewhat beside the point in relation to the all-American Patty so central to the series. The globalized engagement of the Camelot era that Cathy seemed to initiate, like her character itself, was falling from view. To that degree, the shifts across the seasons confirm an impression that viewers likely had from the start: that despite the twinning premise, the series was most about how the two girls lived the American experience and that meant above all that Patty and not Cathy took center stage. Patty's character is the key avatar for the Americana on which the series and its premise were based, even as she seems to move beyond its strict parameters more than most sitcom characters. This afforded young viewers with important glimpses into paths not taken. But this all-American teen had to work repeatedly at learning the constraints and lessons of American ways and mores—work that ideology always requires, whether tied to progressive agendas or not.

Coda

Undoing "Cousins"

For a study of a television series centered on twinning, pairs, and doubling, it is only fitting for us to conclude by returning to where we began: *The Patty Duke Show*'s theme song. During the version of "Cousins" that played in the first two seasons, Cathy and Patty's differences were visually conveyed through discrete hairstyles, outfits, character bearing, and movements. While Patty tears down the household stairs in capris, Cathy steps down daintily, a bedecked princess in miniature.

We noted in our Preface that "Cousins" itself partakes in the themes of twinning and doubling in the series. Its lyrics reinforce the distinctions between the two girls, describing Patty as the all-American teen, energetically enjoying the sumptuous pleasures of mass culture ("rock 'n roll," "hot dogs"), and vaguely linking Cathy to upper-class clichés of Old Europe ("Ballets Russes," "crêpes suzette"). With images and lyrics carefully divided between Cathy and Patty—even the amount of their screen time is relatively balanced—"Cousins" seems at first to present a pair of opposing yet equal characters, "different as night and day."

But imbalance is part of that equation. Patty Lane's world is a recognizably American one, and in this way firmly implies that she is the show's grounding force. Through her, and throughout the series, the normative model of American teenhood is continually established and reestablished, even as she zips in and out of possible alternatives to that model. That "Cousins" introduces Cathy first, as someone we are invited to "meet" suggests that she is the interloper, the newcomer entering an already-established household. Perhaps the doubling in the credit sequence is not nearly as impartial as it first appears.

Unlike the visual aspects of the show's credit sequence, "Cousins" was scarcely distinct musically from other TV theme songs of the time. It was arranged in what music critics call the big band sound—not the big band

The Patty Duke Show *and the American Sixties*. Caryl Flinn and Dana Polan, Oxford University Press.
© Oxford University Press 2026. DOI: 10.1093/oso/9780197667439.003.0007

of swing jazz, but a generic catch-all category that gained popularity in the mid-twentieth century. Familiar to older radio and adult TV audiences, this style of musical arrangement had been cemented in TV programs such as *The Lawrence Welk Show* (1955–71). The sound typically relies on brass instrumentation and is conducted in an upbeat and even tempo, with little in the way of unexpected harmonies, chords, cadences, phrasing, or modulations. Unlike jazz, this middlebrow big band sound doesn't use improvisation or solos, prioritizing instead the idea of a group performing together, apportioning more weight to band leaders or arrangers than to musical soloists or specific musical sections, such as horn or rhythm sections.

Media and music scholar Josh Morrison aptly describes big band tunes like "Cousins" as the "protestant hymns of television: catchy enough to be interesting and memorable but very much accessible for the 'common person' without much or any musical training to sing along to."[1] "Cousins" was obedient to this brand of popular "hymnal" music, composed in an upbeat, major key typical of the sound and adhering to the style's focus on horns, heavily mixing saxophones and trumpets together. Like its distant relatives jazz and swing, "'Cousins,'" Morrison adds, "features (a slight) emphasis on the offbeat, especially the trombones and trumpets, and a slight delay or swing pause during the vocals of 'they're cousins/identical cousins.'"[2]

Such musical details immediately raise questions about the twinning concept that the song's lyrics (and the sequence's imagery) work so diligently to enforce. First, for a sitcom based on teenage girls and that narrated most episodes from their perspective, "Cousins" oddly eschews the R&B, folk, pop and rock music that dominated vernacular youth cultures of the time. And when the lyrics tell us that "Patty likes to rock 'n roll," the music is emphatically *not* rock and roll; The Skip-Jacks simply sing a little louder. Second, why doesn't "Cousins" exploit the opportunity to use soloists to distinguish Cathy and Patty, instead of relying on the lyrics and the images to perform that labor?

One small musical detail does work to differentiate the teens a bit. As Cathy descends the stairs, dreaming of minuets, a flute flourish (supported by clarinets) trills several times. Flutes are not fundamentally connected to the minuet or any other traditional European dance or musical form, and their appearance here provides a fleeting, momentary break from the big band sound, which typically eschews woodwinds. Its frilly sound also creates a moment of gentle ridicule of her pose of "fanciness." In fact, at the end of the last bar of that phrase, a barely discernible beat from the trombones—a slightly glissando sound—punctuates the sequence with a campy little "wah wah" that furthers the flute joke at Cathy's expense, before quickly pivoting back to Patty and the sound of an all-American vibe.

Throughout this book, we have noted how Cathy is molded through the stock images of a dusty imperial Britain. Representing her this way during the high point of the British Invasion dissociates her from the "Swinging London" scene (its music, fashion, and so on) that she might have well symbolized. In so doing, the show fiercely aligns youthful pop culture and vitality—that "can-do spirit!"—with the American music, dance forms, values, and products that Patty embodies. Thus the theme music of *The Patty Duke Show* helps deprioritize the global, aspirational cosmopolitanism that Cathy symbolizes, the worldview that the show seemed to have initially taken under its wing during JFK's Camelot. That movement appeared to open windows onto America's engagement with the cultures and mores of other countries at the time, only, as we have seen, to close them down. The music of "Cousins" suggests that in the series, the process actually started at its very outset.

The representation of Patty herself creates a discordant tension. Because "Cousins" is arranged in the familiar big band style of mid-century America—a "big, brassy sound . . . [that] is basically as quintessentially American big band as one could get"—the opening sequence essentially hands itself over to Patty, the "all-American teenager."[3] And while that big band style is in step with other theme songs of its historical moment, it utterly fails to line up with American teens of that same time. After years of enormous changes in popular youth music, few mid-Sixties teenagers would have been caught dead listening to their parents' music (why does Patty have a Paul Anka record in her room?). They would have been far more likely to be holed up in their bedrooms playing records or radios with Motown, soul, R&B, dance music, folk music, rock, and pop, and the hits that made the American Top 40, a weekly list of top-selling singles that circulated widely. Thus, even as the music of "Cousins" asserts the American nature of the show, it also renders all-American teen Patty, and the series at large, as resoundingly out of touch with their time.

By its final year, *The Patty Duke Show*'s modified credit sequence, including the reworked theme song, foreshadows the season's increased sense of American-centricity, spurning the series's provocative use of pairs, extension, and difference. Recall the significant closing image of the first two years' credits that had Duke, as Patty and Cathy, playfully "reflecting" each other at

Figure C.1 Brooklyn in Los Angeles: Patty on Her Own

the mirror—a sequence whose iconicity was underscored by its renewed appearance in the 1999 reunion movie.

Yet, as we noted, the final image of the newly generated opening for the 1965–66 season features a medium shot of Patty, alone with her books, walking down a SoCal sidewalk, Cathy nowhere in sight. Perhaps Patty's contemplative look reveals a character wondering where her cousin has gone.... (Figure C.1).

The new credit sequence also reworked the footage of Cathy descending the staircase. Now clad in a contemporary formal dress, tiara pin and flouncy shawl abandoned, she seems to be departing for a date in anywhere-USA, rather than for a waltz in an old European dance hall (Figures C.2a and b).

In some ways, the musical modifications of "Cousins" didn't change much: its lyrics were unaltered and, despite having been reorchestrated and rearranged, the song still sat comfortably within the big band tradition. Yet a few telltale signs reveal significant, if modest, shifts. Individual instruments briefly pop up and out of the big band's ensemble-based style. Whereas drums played a part of the unit in standard big band music, the updated version of "Cousins" has a new, conspicuous drumbeat, putting

Figure C.2a Cathy's Couture, Seasons 1 and 2: The Old World

Figure C.2b Cathy's Couture, Season 3: Outfitted for America

the rhythmic more than the melodic line into relief, enabling listeners to draw easy connections to contemporary rock. The drum plays in an offbeat rhythm, much like the rock and roll of the period, but does so inconsistently and intermittently—not enough to place the piece truly within a rock style. The revamped "Cousins" also has a more pronounced bass sound and foregrounds electric guitars and horns, other moves that imply rock music without doing the actual work of producing it.

Unlike the first version of the credits, in which Patty danced to rock and roll in a living room bustling with other teens, she now dances alone in her bedroom upstairs, with a drum-kit implausibly extending into the left frame (Figures C.3a and b). The instrument was a significant choice since, by this point, American audiences who had seen rock bands performing on TV, like the 73 million who watched the historic stateside premiere of The Beatles on *The Ed Sullivan Show* on February 9, 1964, had been made *visually* very aware of drum kits. Drums were positioned prominently onstage, so that viewers could easily see the band's name emblazoned on the side that faced the cameras, a staging tradition that has endured for decades. Representing Patty alone with the drums in her bedroom positions her (literally) above other characters, from whom she has now become spatially isolated, much the same way that the music itself has drifted toward individual instruments over a collective sound.

Duke's modified dancing style is also noteworthy: her bodily movements are jerkier, and her face has an almost manic expression that calls to mind those mass media depictions of "hysterical" female Beatles fans. This is not to question the veracity of actual fans' joyous, intense reactions to these and other musicians of the era, but to note how journalists frequently used this type of imagery to pathologize and patronize them, positioning photos of screaming young women alongside pieces that asserted that the fans were possessed by an uncontrollable sexual energy.[4]

Clearly, the revised song and opening sequence were a bid to update *The Patty Duke Show*. It cost the show's producers little to do so—it was cheaper for them to reorchestrate a TV theme song than to relicense its original recording—and, as we've noted, by this point, ABC was disinclined to invest much of anything into the series. So perhaps budget issues explain the shift, although we cannot definitively affirm that. Both Bob Wells, the lyricist of "Cousins," and Sid Ramin, its composer, retained screen credit, but in small print now, and *following* the name of Harry Geller, who was prominently listed as the show's new composer and music producer. Yet Ramin's melody

Figure C.3a Patty Loves to Rock 'n Roll: Seasons 1 and 2

Figure C.3b Patty Loves to Rock 'n Roll: Season 3

still anchored "Cousins" as well as the lion's share of the incidental music used in the episodes (films and television shows commonly use variations of their key musical themes throughout).

The more pronounced sounds of individual instruments in the revised "Cousins" function in another way; they widen the gulf between the twins. Predictably, when Patty is onscreen, we hear the mock-rock of drums and guitars whereas other instruments attend to Cathy. The flute trills that always underscored her descending the staircase are now accompanied by mallet percussion; the high-pitched, metallic sound of a glockenspiel stands out. The flute and glockenspiel have no connection to the American big band sound, and because the glockenspiel is often associated with children's music, Cathy is cast even further out of contemporary American teenhood or imminent adulthood, even as her character now boasts a more contemporary American look. And to nonmusicians, especially in North America, the "glockenspiel"—both the instrument and the sound of the word itself—has been bathed in comic cliché, much as "Swahili" was treated at the time.

The Patty Duke Show aired during a time when American pop culture seemed obsessed with California and west-coast culture, be it surfer music, Herb Alpert, *Sunset Magazine*, Jackson Browne, or "California Dreaming." Although the visuals of the third year credit sequence give a whiff of "California" just by virtue of Patty walking home on sidewalks lined with palm trees, the music in the revised version of "Cousins" (and in the episodes themselves) does not really partake in, or even pay to homage to, any aspect of that contemporary west coast sound, in spite of its isolated attempts to create the impression of rock and roll music to move away from the established, easy listening big band sound.

Thus, the changes of this second iteration of "Cousins" don't create an actual new sound so much as the acoustic impression of one. The tune still aligns Patty with the big band music that was asynchronous to youth music of the time—except, that is, on television. And the sound remains decidedly American. Yet one indecipherable detail persists: "Cousins" had always been reprised during each episode's closing credits, but in the last season its tempo slowed considerably, as if it were detaching itself from the zippy American energy it had previously tried to convey. Was it giving up on the upbeat optimism of the early years, as the show itself seemed to be doing with its sense of promise and expansiveness?

And so just as the new rendition of "Cousins" tried to create the impression of good old American rock and roll, the episodes of the final season keyed into the sense that Patty's American way of life was winning out, with one "matching bookend" given more weight and privilege than the other. That season, as if taking cues from the song, more or less dispensed with the twinning concept, as we have already seen. Cathy, less and less her cousin's equal, became an abstraction, an absence. In this way, "Cousins," which at first blush seemed to be introducing two identical and equal twins of differing provenance, gave musical hints of *The Patty Duke Show*'s fully Americanized outcome before the series ever really began.

Notes

Preface

1. While we realize there are problems with this, we use the term 'America' throughout the book to refer to the United States, a conflation more common to the Sixties than it is now. And speaking of the Sixties, by which we mean the "1960s," we want to clarify from the outset that most references to decades in this study are to ones from the twentieth century, unless otherwise noted.
2. Although *The Flintstones* ran from 1960 to 1966, its theme song was first employed during its third season, making it an exact contemporary of "Cousins."
3. In this study, we use the word girl instead of woman or even young women to adhere to the language of the series and its times.

Introduction

1. Tom Gliatto, "'What a Crazy Pair!' Who Can Ever Forget the *Patty Duke Show* Theme Song," People.com: https://www.yahoo.com/entertainment/crazy-pair-ever-forget-patty-214306678. html?guce_referrer=aHR0cHM6Ly93d3cuZ29vZ2xlLmNvbS88&guce_referrer_sig=AQAAAIkIdQwDDTsrJDahsBmVv7l5AxwI38eRHJVIN_K4P2r66gLpmXuE6ZTdbUrA_X3IPtrPKNu103TUeKxbnwscT2r9_eukk4ndIWEJnWtfkZbUGpHCShb6MIOFGwAuBnjNND ktYeFxG_jOuWCCmmetFiYq9ljkDUBlNNozsIO7fTaR&guccounter=2. Accessed January 2025.
2. Bill Osgerby provides a list of such shows in his essay "So Who's Got the Time for Adults!" but does not explore them individually. Renewed research helps bring out a bit more about these forgotten series. In *Too Young to Go Steady*, Brigid Bazlen starred as fifteen-year-old Pam, and film stars Joan Bennett and Donald Cook were her parents. CBS's *Peck's Bad Girl* (1959) was another short-lived series that featured Patty McCormack (best known as the murderous child in *The Bad Seed* [1956]) as Torey Peck who, at the age of 12, was on the cusp of teenagerhood with challenges that were depicted as light as gossamer. *Margie* separated itself from other sitcoms by focusing on the Twenties rather than contemporary girl practices but it still seems to have emphasized dating as its primary subject.

   Debbie Watson appeared in two teen sitcoms two years in a row. In 1965, she starred in the television spin-off of the Tammy film series; the year before she played the title role in *Karen* (whose theme song was performed by the Beach Boys). What seems to be the show's one surviving episode establishes it as an instructional sitcom with an imperious dad (Richard Denning) reminding Karen, after a disastrous ski trip, that he'd taught his errant daughter how to navigate right from wrong. https://www.youtube.com/watch?v=GFN7v6FIllY. Accessed June 1, 2025.

   Fair Exchange, which ran for a season and a half on CBS (1962-63), is interesting for a premise that overlaps a wee bit with *The Patty Duke Show*: at their fathers' behest, a British girl comes to live with a family in the United States and an American one (coincidentally named Patty) goes to the United Kingdom. While it is hard to generalize from the few surviving episodes available online, it is interesting to note that often both girls undertake initiatives for the adults rather than for themselves, something that also characterizes select episodes of *The Patty Duke Show*. https://www.youtube.com/watch?v=WzGUU1Tj4rM. Accessed June 11, 2025.

American girl culture scholar Mary Celeste Kearney examines several teen girl sitcoms from earlier in the Fifties that emerged out of radio or film (as well as novels and comic strips). Several episodes of one series she cites, *Meet Corliss Archer* (two versions, 1951 and 1954), survive on the web and suggest that some conventions that we associate with the Sixties teen sitcom were already in place earlier: for instance, like Martin Lane with regards to Richard on *The Patty Duke Show*, Corliss's dad endlessly belittles Corliss's boyfriend Dexter. And anticipating an early episode of Duke's series (S1E7: "The Babysitters"), one installment has Corliss and Dex launching an ambitious babysitting enterprise in which they use rationalized planning to tend to multiple customers simultaneously. See https://www.youtube.com/watch?v=LdGM9uCE GSU&list=PLEAKW4PcnvxmPQ9g16lgiVXR2YuYs_PJQ&index=2. Accessed June 11, 2025.

3. *The Many Loves of Dobie Gillis* is sometimes a formally innovative series—its direct address by Dobie to the television viewer is oft noted in histories of sitcom—and its experimentation can lead in some cases to violation of its own formulae and conventions, including emphatic concentration on male point of view. Thus, as early as episode 2, Dobie's dominant object of love, the money hungry Thalia Menninger (Tuesday Weld), is allowed a subjective vision in which she imagines how much money would flow in if Dobie became a successful doctor for her to marry.

4. Moya Luckett, "Girl Watchers: Patty Duke and Teen TV" in Lynn Spigel and Michael Curtin, eds., *The Revolution Wasn't Televised: Sixties Television and Social Conflict* (Taylor & Francis Group, 1997), 95.

5. See, for example, David Farber, *The Age of Great Dreams: America in the 1960s* (Hill and Wang, 1994); Todd Gitlin. *The Sixties: Years of Hope Days of Rage* (Bantam Books, 1987); Mike Davis and Jon Wiener, *Set the Night on Fire: L.A. in the Sixties* (Verso, 2020).

6. See Aniko Bodroghkozy, *Groove Tube: Sixties Television and the Youth Rebellion* (Duke University Press, 2001); Susan Douglas, *Where the Girls Are: Growing up Female with the Mass Media* (Three Rivers Press, 1994); Pamela Robertson Wojcik, *Gidget: Origins of a Teen Girl Transmedia Franchise* (Routledge, 2022); Victoria E. Johnson, *Heartland TV: Prime Time Television and the Struggle for US Identity* (New York University Press, 2008).

7. Passing discussions of *The Patty Duke Show* also appear in Kristi Rowan Humphries, *The Evil Twins of American Television: Feminist Alter Egos Since 1960* (Lexington Books, 2019); Ilana Nash, *American Sweethearts: Teenage Girls in Twentieth-Century Popular Culture* (Indiana University Press, 2006).

8. Susan Douglas, *Where the Girls Are*, 20.

9. Television Academy Foundation interviews: William Schallert.https://interviews.television academy.com/search-clips?search=Schallert+William&type=profession. Accessed February 25, 2025.

10. Gerald Jones discusses what he terms the instructional sitcoms throughout his *Honey, I'm Home! Sitcoms: Selling the American Dream* (Grove Weidenfeld, 1992), especially chapter 7.

11. Leslie Raddatz, "Any Number Can Play 'Father Image' with this Dandy Do-It-Yourself Casting Kit," *TV Guide*, May 20, 1964, 24–27(quotation from p. 24).

12. So associated were girls with escapist fan culture that when a young Angelena was spotted reading the alternative press publication *The Freep* (LA Free Press) and not something like the anticipated teen fanzine *Tiger Beat*, her choice merited a photo and a bemused article in the *LA Times*. For discussion, see Davis and Wiener, *Set the Night on Fire*, 158-59, referencing Tom Nolan, "The LA Free Press Costs 15 Cents," *LA Times*, Oct. 2, 1936, W36.

13. Paul Goodman, *Growing Up Absurd: Problems of Youth in the Organized Society* (Random House, 1960).

14. Beginning at UC Berkeley, the students' Free-Speech Movement referenced the classification of individuals by computer cards (for example, by the registrar's office) as the extreme symbol of the disciplinary tactics of a dominant power which set out to slot everyone into their assigned identity. See Steven Lubar, " 'Do Not Fold, Spindle or Mutilate': A Cultural History of the Punch Card," *Journal of American Culture*, 15, no. 4 (Winter 1992): 43–55. Early in the decade, "The Genius" episode of *The Patty Duke Show* is fully of its historical moment in depicting the vulnerabilities of computer classification of youth.

15. Susan Douglas notes the frequency of quizzes—low-tech, low-cost versions of Lynde's computer—appearing in girls' magazines in the Sixties: "So these quizzes reinforced the notion that you had to assume different roles for different occasions—that there was not a 'real' you, just an actress performing a variety of parts." Douglas, *Where the Girls Are*, 101.

16. Herbert Marcuse, *One-Dimensional Man: Studies in the Ideology of Advanced Societies* (Beacon Books, 1964), xvii.

17. Theodor Adorno, "How to Look at Television" (1954) in *The Culture Industry: Selected Essays on Mass Culture* (Routledge, 1991), 163.
18. Raymond Williams, *Problems in Materialism and Culture* (Verso, 1980). Television scholar Aniko Bodroghkozy employs Williams's concept of "structure of feeling" to discuss broadly the possibility of progressive trends in Sixties commercial television. See her *Groove Tube: Sixties Television and the Youth Rebellion*, 15.

Chapter 1

1. Hollis Alpert, "Television—The Patty Duke Show," *Woman's Day*, Sept. 12, 1963, 18.
2. "1959 Commercial for Remco Movieland Drive-in Toy": https://www.youtube.com/watch?v=vxAuHK2q0Ac and "REMCO Coney Island Penny Machine Classic TV Commercial" (1959) https://www.youtube.com/watch?v=13UjWqHUe1s. Accessed February 27, 2025.
3. Patty Duke and Kenneth Tynan. *Call Me Anna: The Autobiography of Patty Duke* (Bantam, 1997), 34.
4. Ibid., 14.
5. Ibid., 25.
6. Ibid., 23. Further references to *Call Me Anna* in this paragraph are inserted parenthetically.
7. Hollis Alpert, "Television: The Patty Duke Show," *Woman's Day*, Sept. 12, 1963, 96.
8. Duke and Tynan, *Call Me Anna*, 39.
9. Ruby Saunders, "The Two Faces of Patty Duke," *Calling All Girls,* December 1965, 70.
10. "She Looks Younger Than Her Years," *TV Guide*, Sept. 12, 1963, 96.
11. Jane Howard papers, Columbia University Rare Book and Manuscript Library, Box 3 (*Life* Magazine articles).
12. Handwritten note by David Schermer in Ibid.
13. "Miss Patty Duke," *TV Guide*, Dec. 28-Jan. 4, 1963, 8, no author given.
14. Alfred Gillespie, "The Double Life of Patty Duke," *Good Housekeeping*, Apr. 1964, 62.
15. Duke and Tynan, *Call Me Anna*, 121.
16. The performance can be seen at: https://www.youtube.com/watch?v=KGWiUci0Jas. Duke is the episode's second guest. Accessed February 26, 2025.
17. Duke and Tynan, *Call Me Anna*, 116.
18. Patty Duke and Gloria Hochman. *A Brilliant Madness: Living with Manic Depressive Illness* (Bantam, 1992), 1.
19. William Asher interview with Television Academy, https://interviews.televisionacademy.com/interviews/william-asher?clip=82176#interview-clips. (first of two interviews that address *The Patty Duke Show*). Accessed February 25, 2025.
20. Duke and Tynan, *Call Me Anna*, 156 (photo caption).
21. Paul O'Keefe, email to authors, October 19, 2024.
22. They also appeared on family- and adult-oriented variety shows; Duke, for instance, guested on CBS's *Ed Sullivan Show*, whose revue format was famous for prohibiting performers from playback or lip-synching, something that must have been terrifying for many of these untrained singers. https://www.youtube.com/watch?v=UysJ5whekKw. Accessed July 1, 2024.
23. Anonymous, "Patty Duke Film Due for Slotting in Teen-Wake of Beatles Release," *Variety,* July 21, 1965, 9.
24. Duke and Tynan, *Call Me Anna*, 178.
25. *TV Guide* listing, May 9–11, 1964.
26. Gary Gerani and Casey Bond, *Patty Duke as "Billie": Role Model or Sell-Out?* (Atlanta, GA: BearManor Media, 2015), xiv.
27. Television Academy Foundation interviews: Patty Duke. https://interviews.televisionacademy.com/search?search_api_views_fulltext=Patty+Duke&type=All. Accessed February 25, 2025.
28. Gerani and Bond, *Patty Duke as "Billie,"* 8.
29. Duke and Tynan, *Call Me Anna*, 167.
30. Ibid., 177.
31. Ibid., 179.

32. For an interesting and sympathetic account of *The Valley of the Doll*'s odd place in history, see "Be Kind Rewind" on YouTube, which speaks of the film's forcing all of the actors to play out every moment to the hilt. Part one https://www.youtube.com/watch?v=cTQJN1Xw0h8;part two https://www.youtube.com/watch?v=3rvy8Daq3OI. Accessed November 22, 2023.
33. Duke and Tynan, *Call Me Anna*, 185.
34. Similarly, in 1970's *My Sweet Charlie*, her co-lead goes so far as to call Duke's character "ugly," so ugly that a man would never touch her.
35. Duke and Tynan, *Call Me Anna*, 210.
36. Duke and Tynan, *Call Me Anna*, 214. The production outside of Galveston, Texas was interrupted by some of the racial politics depicted in the film when an unknown person planted marijuana in Duke's dressing room. Her height saved her from charges: it was placed so high that she couldn't reach it even when standing on a chair.
37. Duke and Tynan, *Call Me Anna*, 210.
38. "Ten Things I Love About Patty Duke." Eclectic Lady's list also includes Duke's post-*Valley* "cult following," "overcoming a pretty crappy childhood," and being "a fabulous [LGBTQ] ally." Eclectic Lady even goes so far as to laud "her super sweet voice" and the fact that "she sparkled." https://eclecticladylandblog.wordpress.com/2017/06/07/ten-things-i-love-about-patty-duke/. Accessed August 18, 2023.
39. Duke, *Greatness*, p. 4. Duke's acceptance speech can be viewed at: https://www.youtube.com/watch?v=Ta09S8Ws8-g. Accessed June 13, 2023.
40. Duke and Tynan, *Call Me Anna*, 12.
41. https://en.wikipedia.org/wiki/Look_What%27s_Happened_to_Rosemary%27s_Baby. Accessed August 19, 2023.
42. Notes on William Schallert. Hannah Schallert, email to authors, April 7, 2025, 1.
43. Duke and Tynan, *Call Me Anna*, 288.
44. Duke, *A Brilliant Madness*, 183.
45. Ibid., 183.
46. In another act of doubling, Duke's brother Raymond appears briefly as their father, seated at a bar.
47. Duke, *A Brilliant Madness*, 185.
48. Duke would claim that her marriage to Tell was annulled because it was "never consummated." Duke, *A Brilliant Madness*, 25.

Chapter 2

1. Ralph Rosenblum and Robert Karen, *When the Shooting Stops, the Cutting Begins: An Editor's Story* (Da Capo Press, 1996), 232.
2. Patty Duke and Kenneth Tynan, *Call Me Anna: The Autobiography of Patty Duke* (Bantam, 1997), 116.
3. Sheldon's own account of his career often comes off as self-aggrandizing and should be approached with critical caution. See Sidney Sheldon, *The Other Side of Me: A Memoir* (Warner Books, 2005).
4. Television Academy Foundation interview: William Asher. https://interviews.televisionacademy.com/interviews/william-asher?clip=82176#interview-clips (first of two interviews that address *The Patty Duke Show*). Accessed February 25, 2025.
5. Television Academy Foundation interview: Sidney Sheldon. https://interviews.televisionacademy.com/search?search_api_views_fulltext=sidney+sheldon&type=All. Accessed, March 30, 2025.
6. Television Academy Foundation, interviews with Sidney Sheldon and William Asher.
7. Sidney Sheldon Papers, USC Cinematic Arts Library and Archive, Folder 4 (UA) Box 1. Further quotations from unpublished materials from and to Sheldon are also from this collection.
8. Tino Balio treats ZIV in passing in his definitive history of UA: *United Artists, Volume 2, 1951–1978: The Company That Changed the Film Industry* (University of Wisconsin Press, 2009),

107–08. For a history of ZIV up to the UA purchase, see Morleen Getz Rouse, *A History of the F.W. ZIV Radio and Television Syndication Companies, 1930–1960*, PhD, Mass Communications, University of Michigan, 1976.

9. Peter Lawford papers, Series 1, Arizona State University Library.
10. Television Academy Foundation interview: William Schallert. https://interviews.television academy.com/search-clips?search=Schallert+William&type=profession. All of the above quotes from Schallert come from this interview. Accessed, February 25, 2025.
11. Hannah Schallert, Notes on William Schallert, Email to authors on April 7, 2025, 1.
12. Ibid., 2.
13. Ibid.
14. Ibid.
15. Television Academy Foundation interview: Patty Duke. https://interviews.televisionacademy. com/search?search_api_views_fulltext=Patty+Duke&type=All. Accessed February 25, 2025.
16. Hannah Schallert, Notes on William Schallert, 2.
17. Ibid.
18. Duke and Tynan, *Call Me Anna*, 117.
19. Patty Duke and William J. Jankowski, *In the Presence of Greatness: My Sixty Year Journey as an Actress* (BearManor Media, 2018), 53–54.
20. Anonymous, "Conversation Piece: Patty Duke's 'Parents'" (interview with William Schallert and Jean Byron), *TV Guide*, Aug. 29–Sept. 4, 1964, 16.
21. Ibid.
22. John Maynard, "Eddie Applegate: 17 Going on 30," *TV Guide*, Oct. 17–23, 1965, 12–14.
23. Television Academy Foundation interview: Patty Duke.
24. Patty Duke, *In the Presence of Greatness*, 29–30.
25. *Hollywood Reporter*, May 11, 1962, 4, no author given.
26. Bob Stahl, "*TV Teletype by Bob Stahl*," *TV Guide*, August 3–9, 1963, inside cover.
27. Donald Kirkley, "Now Will the Real Patty Duke Please Stand Up?," *Baltimore Sun*, Aug. 4, 1963, 49.
28. Contract courtesy of the Wisconsin Center for Film and Theater Research. (From the David Susskind Papers.)
29. Paul Jones, "Gallagher Report: TV's New Shows—Flops? Winners?," *The Atlanta Constitution*, Aug. 23, 1963, 12.
30. Donald Kirkley, "Look and Listen with Donald Kirkley," *The Baltimore Sun*, Oct. 21, 1963, 14.
31. Kirkley, "Now Will Real Patty Stand Up?" 49.
32. Television Academy Foundation interview: William Asher.
33. Paul O'Keefe, email with authors, October 19, 2024.
34. After the 2025 release of Ryan Coogler's "twin" movie *Sinners*, interest in how twins were filmed from a single actor was revived, and the *New York Times* published a piece covering techniques over the years. https://www.nytimes.com/2025/04/25/movies/sinners-twins-visual-effects. html?searchResultPosition=1. Accessed April 25, 2025.
35. The awkwardness of this conventional use of doubles is parodied extensively in an episode of *Newhart* (1982–90) in which the vapid Stephanie (Julia Duffy) has dreams of TV stardom and pushes her boyfriend Michael (Peter Solari) to produce a pilot for a twins sitcom, "Seeing Double." Faced with an unworkably low budget, the team can't afford optical effects so they employ a bewigged double for shared scenes. The double doesn't resemble Stephanie in the slightest and thus humorously keeps her back to the camera at all times, even if that means walking sideways around the set.
36. Herbert's parents pulled him from the series when it was announced that production would move to New York. He continued to work throughout the decade, although parts soon dried up, and he would face many of the difficulties faced by former child actors.
37. Duke and Tynan, *Call Me Anna*, 120. We'd be generous even labeling the accent "English," were we so inclined. In one episode, a plot twist calls for an English accent and Patty does the duty, as if Cathy's ambiguously "Scottish" vocals were somehow too foreign even to attempt that.
38. The brief scenes that were included in the aired show's opening credits varied across the seasons. A few, like the mirror scene, lasted all three years, while others came and went. We were at first puzzled when we saw clips in the title sequences that were taken from episodes that had not yet aired. Paul O'Keefe recalled, "My memory is that we would shoot episodes about five or six weeks before they aired. For example, we would go into production in July, but our first episode

would air in September . . . film from an upcoming episode could be included in the opening titles of the first episode of the season and probably be a 'tease' for the show's fans." (Email correspondence of October 19, 2024, with the authors; he doesn't recall whether the episodes were shot in their broadcast sequence, however.)

39. See unsigned notices, "30 Cities Appraise 31 New Shows," *Variety*, Oct. 23, 1963, 24; "It's 30 Share or Drop Dead," *Variety*, Oct. 16, 1963, 34, "Now That We've Had a Good Year, What Will We Do for an Encore?," *Variety*, Apr. 8, 1964, 36–37.
40. Moya Luckett, "Girl Watchers: Patty Duke and Teen TV," in Lynn Spigel and Michael Curtin, eds., *The Revolution Wasn't Televised: Sixties Television and Social Conflict* (Taylor & Francis Group, 1997), 99.
41. Ruby Saunders, "Two Faces of Patty Duke," *Calling All Girls*, Dec. 1965, 15.
42. Alfred Gillespie, "The Double Life of Patty Duke," *Good Housekeeping*, April 1964, 52–62.
43. Anonymous, "Nice Girls Finish First," *Variety*, Jan. 15, 1964, 37.
44. Television Academy Foundation interviews: William Schallert.
45. "Channing Will Debut Tonight with Program to Remember," *The Atlanta Constitution*, Sept. 18, 1963, 35; Sept. 25, 1963, 10.
46. Walt Dutton, "Patty's Show Triumphs over a Weak Script," *Los Angeles Times*, Sept. 20, 1963, C16.
47. "Groz," "*The Patty Duke Show*," *Variety*, Sept. 25, 1963, 35.
48. Duke and Tynan, *Call Me Anna*, 125.
49. Ad in *Women's Wear Daily*, May 20, 1964, v. 108, n. 100, p. 27.
50. In fact, the Visit to Washington genre runs across mass culture narratives of the time, particularly those geared to children. The title character of Disney's *The Absent-Minded Professor* (1961) uses Flubber to fly his car there, and, in a spin-off comic book for *Dennis the Menace* (also 1961), Dennis travels to the White House, where he accidentally meets Caroline Kennedy. Lauren Berlant discusses the significance of pilgrimages to Washington for American identity, especially for young citizens, in *The Queen of America Goes to Washington City: Essays on Sex and Citizenship* (Duke University Press, 1997).
51. Written by Doris Schroeder and published by Whitman Publishing in Wisconsin, the books had their copyrights held by the series' distributor United Artists. Schroeder had been a screenwriter of women's melodramas in the Twenties and B-Westerns in the Forties and Fifties before moving on to young-adult adventure and mystery novels. Whitman published many books (quite a number by Schroeder) that placed extant film or TV characters or the actors playing them in thriller or suspense narratives, such as casting Disney Mouseketeer Annette Funicello in *Annette and The Mystery at Moonstone Bay*. Such ready, almost eager, confusion of celebrity and character had antecedents in oddities such as Ginger Rogers or Shirley Temple mystery/thriller books in the Thirties and celebrity adventure comic books in the Fifties starring John Wayne and others.
52. Paul O'Keefe, February 2, 2023, interview with the authors.
53. Just as the show was retreating from split screens, they were becoming more common in the movies; after gaining hold in Fifties sex comedies, they were frequently used in the Sixties—recall the early montage sequence of Nellie rising to stardom in *The Valley of the Dolls*.
54. Luckett, "Girl-Watchers," see especially pp. 112–13.
55. Tricia Jenkins, "Feminism, Nationalism, and the 1960s' Slender Spies," *Journal of Popular Film and Television* 43, no. 1 (2015), 4–27.
56. "Horo," "*The Patty Duke Show*," *Variety*, Sept. 29, 1965, 34.
57. Television Academy Foundation interviews: William Schallert.
58. *The Patty Duke Show* was lucky to make it to three seasons. Revealingly, some of the other shows that boomers remember as long-lasting chunks of their childhood never even attained the three-year mark: *Gilligan's Island, F Troop*, and *The Smothers Brothers Comedy Hour* all ran for two years; *Gidget* just one. Repeated syndication only reinforced those faulty memories of these comedies. As early as 1985, the popular Nickelodeon programming block "Nick at Night" reran classic sitcoms, making it appear as if these offerings had always been around and part of one's TV viewing experience.
59. "Patty Duke Renewal Waiting on 'Batman,'" *Variety*, Jan. 26, 1966, 29.
60. Television Academy Foundation interviews: William Schallert.
61. Ray Richmond, "*The Patty Duke Show*: Still Rockin' in Brooklyn Heights," *Variety*, April 26–May 2, 1999, 33.
62. https://www.youtube.com/watch?v=6TBJJzp-TAo. For background footage about the shooting of the PSA, see https://www.youtube.com/watch?v=-Dn3quUzaUM&t=55s.

Chapter 3

1. Gerald Jones, *Honey, I'm Home! Sitcoms: Selling the American Dream* (Grove Weidenfeld, 1992); David Marc, *Comic Visions: Television Comedy and American Culture*, 2nd edition (Blackwell, 1997); Mary M. Dalton and Laura R. Linder, *The Sitcom Reader, Second Edition: America Re-Viewed, Still Skewed* (State University of New York, 2016); Joanne Morreale, *Critiquing the Sitcom: A Reader* (Syracuse University Press, 2003). It should be noted that scholar Paul Attallah pointedly takes some distance from the standard argument in his contribution to the Morreale anthology: he notes how that argument incessantly returns to *M*A*S*H*, *All in the Family*, or *The Dick Van Dyke Show* as ostensibly "quality" shows which are "seen as important precisely to the extent to which they do not resemble situation comedies, because they make significant social statements, or because of strong characterization and good scripting." Attallah, "The Unworthy Discourse: Situation Comedy in Television" in *Critiquing the Sitcom*, 92-93.
2. Patrick Keating, *Hollywood Lighting: From the Silent Era to Film Noir* (Columbia University Press, 2009).
3. John Caldwell. *Televisuality: Style, Crisis, and Authority in American Television* (Rutgers University Press, 1995), 56–57.
4. See Lynn Spigel, "From Domestic Space to Outer Space: The 1960s Fantastic Family Sitcom," *Welcome to the Dreamhouse: Popular Media and Postwar Suburbs* (Duke University Press, 2001), 107–140.
5. Aniko Bodroghkozy, *Groove Tube: Sixties Television and the Youth Rebellion* (Duke University Press, 2001).
6. Bodroghkozy, "'Is This What You Mean by Color TV'? Race, Gender, and Contested Meanings in NBC's *Julia*," in Lynn Spigel and Denise Mann, eds., *Private Screenings: Television and the Female Consumer* (University of Minnesota Press, 1992), 143–68.
7. https://beverlyhillbillies.fandom.com/wiki/Rural_purge. Accessed August 3, 1974.
8. Marc, *Comic Visions*, 143; 137.
9. Jones, *Honey, I'm Home!*, 134.
10. Marc, *Comic Visions*, 148.
11. Jones, *Honey, I'm Home!*, 4.
12. Amy Argetsinger, "I Loved the 'All in the Family' Theme Song. Now I Actually Get It." *Washington Post*, May 17, 2025.
13. Jones, *Honey, I'm Home!*, 14.
14. Theodor Adorno, "How to Look at Television" (1954) in *The Culture Industry: Selected Essays on Mass Culture* (Routledge, 1991), 169.
15. Jones, *Honey, I'm Home!*, 3.
16. Marc, *Comic Visions*, xv; 38.
17. For a basic overview, see Judy Kutulas, *Sitcom Mom: The Evolution of a Classic Television Character* (Lexington Books/Fortress Academic, 2023).
18. Jones, *Honey, I'm Home!*, 161.
19. Phuksachart's manuscript in progress, *Archives of Embarrassment*, explores the representations and labor of Asian Americans in postwar US television.
20. Betty Friedan, "Television and the Feminine Mystique," part 1, *TV Guide*, Feb. 1-7, 1964, 6–11.
21. Frank Orme, "TV for Children: What's Good? What's Bad?" *Parents' Magazine and Better Homemaking*, Feb. 1966, 54-55; 118–20.
22. Ilana Nash, "'Nowhere Else to Go': *Gidget* and the Construction of Adolescent Femininity," *Feminist Media Studies* 2, no. 1 (2002): 341-56.
23. Paul O'Keefe interview with authors. Accessed February 2, 2023.
24. Television Academy Foundation interviews: Patty Duke. https://interviews.televisionacademy.com/search?search_api_views_fulltext=Patty+Duke&type=All. Accessed February 25, 2025.
25. Paul O'Keefe interview with authors.
26. George Lipsitz, "Why Remember Mama? The Changing Face of a Woman's Narrative," in Morreale, ed., *Critiquing the Sitcom: A Reader* (Syracuse University Press, 2003), 7-24.
27. Marc, *Comic Visions*, 43.
28. Susan Douglas, *Where the Girls Are: Growing up Female with the Mass Media* (Three Rivers Press,1994), 125; a loosely paginated photo caption.
29. Jones, *Honey, I'm Home!*, 156-57.

30. Patricia Mellencamp, *High Anxiety: Catastrophe, Scandal, Age and Comedy* (Indiana University Press, 1992), 329.

31. Moya Luckett, "Girl Watchers: Patty Duke and Teen TV," in Lynn Spigel and Michael Curtin, eds., *The Revolution Wasn't Televised: Sixties Television and Social Conflict* (Taylor and Francis, 1997), 101.

32. Ibid.

33. Kelly Schrum, *Some Wore Bobby Sox: The Emergence of Teenage Girls' Culture, 1920-1945* (Palgrave MacMillan, 2004), 137.

34. In her book, *American Sweethearts*, Ilana Nash has likewise noted the entrepreneurial efforts undertaken by Patty Lane and turns to "The Tycoons" to elaborate her point. Her analysis, however, zeroes in on the ultimate failure of Patty's business, not her ingenuity or follow-through—nor does she mention that capitalism itself might be fueling the chaos that comes to dominate the enterprise. Instead, Nash maintains that its failure punishes Patty Lane for her initiative and drive, and works to restore what she calls patriarchal norms, whose "message" is one of "putting the girl in her place" (3). Nash's readings of girls popular culture at large (the focus of her study) repeatedly skew toward this negative conclusion and assume that young female consumers will take in this punitive message, consciously or not. As she puts it, mass-generated images are "instructional texts teaching young girls how to accept and properly perform the roles their society expects them to play" (14).

35. As Pamela Robertson Wojcik notes, the Frederick Kohner series of first-person Gidget novels also has its all-American teen announcing her desire to be like Sagan, both in cultural ambition and in everyday lifestyle. See Robertson Wojcik, *Gidget: Origins of a Teen Girl Transmedia Franchise* (Routledge, 2021), 18–28.

36. Bill Osgerby, "'So Who's Got the Time for Adults!': Femininity, Consumption, and the Development of Teen TV—From Gidget to Buffy," in G. Davis and K. Dickinson, eds., *Teen TV: Genre, Consumption, Identity* (British Film Institute, 2004), 71–98.

37. Sophia Rosenfeld, *The Age of Choice: A History of Freedom in Modern Life* (Princeton University Press, 2025).

38. Cleveland Amory, "*The Patty Duke Show*: Review" *TV Guide*, Jan. 24, 1964, inside cover.

39. Lynn Spigel, *Make Room for TV: Television and the Family Ideal in Postwar America* (University of Chicago Press, 1992), 60.

40. David Grote, *The End of Comedy: Sit-Com and the Comedic Tradition* (Archon Books, 1983).

41. Melissa Phruksachart, "The Promise of Asian Children: Cold War Television's Oriental Enchantments." Paper delivered at the Association for Asian American Studies conference, April 15, 2022, Denver, CO.

42. Patty Duke and Kenneth Tynan, *Call Me Anna: The Autobiography of Patty Duke* (Bantam, 1997), 131.

43. Susan Sontag, *Against Interpretation and Other Essays* (Farrar, Straus and Giroux, 1966), 10.

44. Nash, "Nowhere Else to Go," 27.

Chapter 4

1. Unlike studies that periodize the American Sixties or US sitcoms, discourses on twinning typically downplay historical context and assess the function of twins in an almost ontological fashion. Fine exceptions exist, to be sure, and the effort to provide historical and cultural contexts is increasing in recent accounts of twinning, such as those by William Viney and Hillel Schwartz. At the same time, and in those two cases in particular, the authors march through so many historical and cultural periods that "twinship" is made into an overwhelming, almost open-ended category.

2. William Viney, *Twinkind: The Singular Significance of Twins* (Princeton University Press, 2023), 24.

3. To be sure, many studies and memoirs written by twins also follow well-worn conventions about each twin relating to their "other." These are not salient for *The Patty Duke Show*, because being a twin doesn't seem to matter much to Patty or Cathy. Additionally, our exploration concentrates on media-generated twins, rather than actual, biological ones.

4. Viney, *Twinkind*, 116. Genetic research in the sciences started to peak in the Sixties, when researchers often turned to twins as propitious test cases in exploring ideas about nature or nurture.

5. Hillel Schwartz, *The Culture of the Copy: Striking Likenesses, Unreasonable Facsimiles* (Zone Books, 2014), 239.

6. A more benign tradition reworks the good-evil dichotomy as ordinary/extraordinary. For example, in Disney's series *Liv and Maddie* (2013-17), discussed later in this chapter for its debts to *The Patty Duke Show*, one sister is an average high school student while the other is a very famous celebrity who's come home for a break from life in the fast lane. Even earlier, another Disney girl culture sitcom, *Hannah Montana* (2006-11) chronicles how a pop star Hannah relies on her anodyne alter identity Miley to retreat into when fame becomes too unnerving (e.g., overbearing fans). These sorts of doublings, not always about twins, no doubt bear connections to those sorts of films in which a superhero shields him- or herself via a bland double: most famously, Superman and Clark Kent (where a mere doffing of eyeglasses transforms a turn-off into an object of desire for Lois Lane). In passing, it's worth noting that one *Hannah Montana* episode does deal with twins (rather than a girl doubling herself) and seems specifically to take its plot from an episode of *The Patty Duke Show*. The installment ("Torn Between Two Hannah's") has Miley's Southern cousin show up and wreak havoc just as Cousin Betsy does in S2E18, "The Perfect Hostess," of *The Patty Duke Show*.

7. Sigmund Freud, "The Psychogenesis of a Case of Homosexuality in a Woman" (1920) in James Strachey, ed. and trans., *The Standard Edition of the Complete Psychological Works of Sigmund Freud*, volume 18 (London: Hogarth Press, 1955) 159; Freud, "The Uncanny" (1919) in James Strachey, ed. and trans., *The Standard Edition of the Complete Psychological Works of Sigmund Freud*, volume 17 (London: Hogarth Press, 1955), 217–56.

8. James Meyer, "The Double: Identity and Difference in Art since 1900" in *The Double: Identity and Difference in Art Since 1900* (National Gallery of Art/Princeton University Press, 2022), 13.

9. Lisa Gitelman. *Paper Knowledge: Toward a Media History of Documents*. (Duke University Press, 2014).

10. Schwartz, *The Culture of the Copy*, 189.

11. Theodor Adorno, "How to Look at Television" (1954) in *The Culture Industry: Selected Essays on Mass Culture* (Routledge, 1991), 227.

12. In *Teenage Tyranny*, a widely quoted book published during the time of *The Patty Duke Show*, a husband-and-wife team lamented how "American society is growing down rather than growing up" by catering to "teenage standards of thought, culture, and goals." See Grace and Fred M. Hechinger, *Teenage Tyranny* (William Morrow, 1963), x. The idea of "growing down" curiously complements Paul Goodman's exclusion of girls from any potential for growing *up*, absurdly or not. See Goodman, *Growing Up Absurd: Problems of Youth in the Organized Society* (Random House, 1960).

13. Paul Mayersberg, *Hollywood: The Haunted House* (Allen Lane, 1967).

14. As early as 1950, *Sunset Boulevard* turns former silent screen star Norma Desmond into a ghostly double of herself, poignantly but ghoulishly played out in a scene in which she watches her silent films that were actually early movies of Gloria Swanson, the actor who plays the aging Desmond.

15. For a fuller discussion, see the Introduction to Andrew Ross, *No Respect: Intellectuals and Popular Culture* (Routledge, 1989), 5 especially.

16. Tricia Jenkins, "Feminism, Nationalism, and the 1960s' Slender Spies: A Look at *Get Smart* and *The Girl from U.N.C.L.E.*," *Journal of Popular Film and Television* 43, no. 1 (2015): 14–27. Curiously, and despite the article's focus on female representation, Jenkins fails to mention the white woman-led *Honey West*, a spy show that ran for one year—also premiering in 1965.

17. Susan Sontag, "Notes on Camp," in *Against Interpretation and Other Essays* (Farrar, Straus and Giroux, 1966), 277–93.

18. Reba A. Wissner "Can TV Music Be Camp? Notes from the 1960s," in Isabel Pinedo and W.D. Phillips, eds., *Camp TV of the 1960s: Reassessing the Vast Wasteland* (Oxford University Press, 2023), 215–35.

19. Quinlan Miller, *Camp TV: Trans Gender Queer Sitcom History* (Duke University Press, 2019).

20. Impersonations—another form of doubling—by iconic performers like Frank Gorshin and Rich Little were ubiquitous in nightclubs, radio, television, and even LP recordings of the time. Vaughn Meader's uncanny imitation of President Kennedy helped the comedy LP "The First Family" win a Grammy for Album of the Year. But when Kennedy was assassinated, Meader's career came to an abrupt end.

21. Helena de Bres, *How to Be Multiple: The Philosophy of Twins* (Bloomsbury, 2023), 47.
22. Randy Rainbow, https://www.youtube.com/watch?v=kDB5b5aYef4. Accessed July 22, 2024.
23. One wonders if this is a nod to Maddy, the twin cousin to Laura Palmer in David Lynch's acclaimed *Twin Peaks*. (Maybe, in addition, both Maddies have a longer-term legacy in *Vertigo*'s Madeleine, the ethereal blonde double of earthy and ordinary Judy, both played by Kim Novak. Significantly, as a work focused on male obsession, *Vertigo* is not directly about a woman willfully taking over another identity—so it's not really about the smothering twin or double: Judy is twice pushed by men to pretend to be Madeleine and the result is a double death for the woman, originally symbolic, later real.)
24. In "Sisters Are Two of a Kind, Like Those 1960s Cousins," *New York Times*, September 13, 2023, *Times* culture critic Neil Genzlinger argued that Liv and Maddie improved on *The Patty Duke Show* by allowing Maddie to be a star basketball player, thereby claiming advances in gender opportunity. Clearly, the critic was unaware of Duke's film *Billie*. https://www.nytimes.com/2013/09/14/arts/television/liv-and-maddie-offers-shades-of-the-patty-duke-show.html.
25. Ray Richmond, "*The Patty Duke Show*: Still Rockin'," *Variety*, April 26-May 2, 1999, 33.
26. Constantine Verevis. "Trading Places: *Das Doppelte Lottchen* and *The Parent Trap*," in Iain Robert Smith and Constantine Verevis, eds., *Transnational Film Remakes* (Edinburgh University Press, 2017), 130–43.
27. Natasha Shimon, "On 'Mickey 17,' 'The Substance,' Coercive Consent and Splitting the Self," *The Michigan Dailey*, June 3, 2025. https://www.michigandaily.com/arts/film/on-mickey-17-the-substance-coercive-consent-and-splitting-the-self/, Accessed June 11, 2025.

Chapter 5

1. Lynn Spigel, "From Domestic Space to Outer Space: The 1960s Fantastic Family Sitcom," *Welcome to the Dreamhouse: Popular Media and Postwar Suburbs* (Duke University Press, 2001), 107–40.
2. Tom Hayden goes so far as to assert that the famous youth manifesto of 1962 The Port Huron Statement (which he authored the first draft of) got the attention of the White House and that some of its positions, such as students as a new motor of history (over an older working class—older in time but also in age of its constituents) started to influence Kennedy administration sentiments, but then was cut short by the assassination. See Hayden's preface to a new edition of the statement, *The Port Huron Statement: The Visionary Call of the 1960s Revolution* (Thunder's Mouth Press, 2005), 15–18.
3. Spigel, "From Domestic Space to Outer Space," 113–14.
4. For Mailer's infamous take-down of Kennedy as a commodified showman version of a presidential candidate for a commodified county, see his "Superman Comes to the Supermarket," in *Mind of an Outlaw: Selected Essays* (Random House, 2014): 109–44.
5. Theodore White, "For President Kennedy: An Epilogue," *Life*, Dec. 6, 1963. https://www.jfklibrary.org/asset-viewer/archives/THWPP/059/THWPP-059-009. Accessed April 2, 2023.
6. Ibid.
7. Carl Sferrazza Anthony. *Camera Girl: The Coming of Age of Jackie Bouvier Kennedy* (Gallery Books, 2023).
8. See Michael Curtin, *Redeeming the Wasteland: Television Documentary and Cold War Politics* (Rutgers University Press, 1995).
9. Gerald Jones, *Honey, I'm Home! Sitcoms: Selling the American Dream* (Grove Weidenfeld, 1992), 147.
10. Susan Douglas, *Where the Girls Are: Growing up Female with the Mass Media* (Three Rivers Press, 1994). See her discussion on 112-21.
11. Patty Duke and Kenneth Tynan. *Call Me Anna: The Autobiography of Patty Duke* (Bantam, 1997), 124. (A more mature Duke worked on Robert F. Kennedy's Presidential campaign.)
12. Douglas, *Where the Girls Are*, 13.
13. Ibid., 110.
14. Jones, *Honey, I'm Home!*, 145.
15. Ibid., 157.

16. David Farber, *The Age of Great Dreams: America in the 1960s* (Hill and Wang, 1994), 10–11.
17. See Dana Polan, *Julia Child's The French Chef* (Duke University Press, 2011).
18. For further discussion, see Alice Yeager Kaplan, *Dreaming in French: The Paris Years of Jacqueline Bouvier Kennedy, Susan Sontag, and Angela Davis* (University of Chicago Press, 2012).
19. Mary Desjardins, *Father Knows Best* (Wayne State University Press, 2015).
20. In an interview with Kenneth Jackson on New York historiography, the *Wall Street Journal* offers the following: "New York historian Kenneth Jackson identifies Brooklyn Heights as the oldest true commuter town. Starting in 1814, daily steamboat service to Manhattan let thousands of people plant themselves outside the city. . . Sleepy suburbs like Brooklyn were a kind of respite from the city . . ." *Wall Street Journal*, Sep. 17, 2018, A13.
21. Paul O'Keefe email to authors, Oct. 19, 2024.
22. Victoria E. Johnson, *Heartland TV: Prime Time Television and the Struggle for US Identity* (New York University Press, 2008).
23. Another episode (S3E17) is entitled "Ross Runs Away, But Not Far."
24. Nominally, the program is devoted to classical music, tellingly deejayed by none other than Cathy, whom Patty locks in a closet to give the blokes a chance.
25. Moya Luckett, "Girl Watchers: Patty Duke and Teen TV," in Lynn Spigel and Michael Curtin, eds., *The Revolution Wasn't Televised: Sixties Television and Social Conflict* (Taylor and Francis, 1997), 108–12.
26. Not unlike the lanky basketball player who, in "The Conquering Hero" (S1E8), is invited to stay with the Lanes while his family is away. There he knocks over Natalie's beloved, expensive *imported* sculpture, once again confirming the destruction wreaked by outsiders.
27. David Marc, *Comic Visions: Television Comedy and American Culture*, 2nd edition (Blackwell, 1997), 64.
28. Alan Nadel, *Television in Black-and-White America: Race and National Identity* (University Press of Kansas, 2005), 17.
29. Mary Celeste Kearney, "'Against a Sharp White Background': Toward Race-Based Intersectional Approach in Youth Media Studies," *Cinema Journal* 57, no. 1 (Fall 2017): 119–24.
30. Arnold Horwitt's script (dated Jan. 11, 1965) includes a resonant but passing moment where Patty declares herself ready to cancel the show when she can't get a celebrity and instead hold a "protest rally! To show we're against all the wars and uprisings and poverty in the world!" The line did not make it into the episode as filmed. The script is in the Sidney Sheldon papers, box 1, folder 10, at the USC Cinematic Arts Library and Archives.
31. Jones, *Honey, I'm Home!*, 157.
32. Farber, *The Age of Great Dreams*, 34.
33. Norman Mailer, "Superman Comes to the Supermarket."
34. Heather Hendershot, *When the News Broke: Chicago 1968 and the Polarizing of America* (University of Chicago Press, 2024).
35. Douglas, *Where the Girls Are*, 143–44.

Coda

1. Josh Morrison, email correspondence with Caryl Flinn, Mar. 2024.
2. Ibid.
3. Ibid.
4. A colleague who watched the two versions of "Cousins" noted that the Beatlemania that emerged after the group's 1964 US debut could easily have given Season 3's reference to hot dogs causing Patty to "lose control" a more intense libidinal resonance.

Bibliography

Adorno, Theodor. "How to Look at Television." In *The Culture Industry: Selected Essays on Mass Culture*, eds., J. M. Bernstein. Routledge, 1991, 158–77. (Originally published 1954.)

Barile, Louise A. "Patty Duke's Son: 'She Was the Bravest Person I've Ever Known,'" *Closer* 12, no. 6 (February 12, 2024): 14–16.

Baughman, James L. *Same Time, Same Station: Creating American Television 1948–1961.* John Hopkins University Press, 2007.

Bodroghkozy, Aniko. *Groove Tube: Sixties Television and the Youth Rebellion.* Duke University Press, 2001.

Caldwell, John. *Televisuality: Style, Crisis, and Authority in American Television.* Rutgers University Press, 1995.

Dalton, Mary M. and Laura R. Linder, eds. *The Sitcom Reader: America Viewed and Skewed.* State University of New York Press, 2005.

Davis, Mike and Jon Wiener. *Set the Night on Fire: L.A. in the Sixties.* Verso, 2020.

De Bres, Helena. *How to be Multiple: The Philosophy of Twins.* Bloomsbury, 2023.

Desjardins, Mary. *Father Knows Best.* Wayne State University Press, 2015.

Douglas, Susan J. *Where the Girls Are: Growing up Female with the Mass Media.* Three Rivers Press, 1994.

Douglas, Susan J. "1964," "The American Experience." PBS. https://video.alexanderstreet.com/watch/1964-interview-with-susan-j-douglas-historian-part-1-of-2; https://search.alexanderstreet.com/preview/work/bibliographic_entity%7Cvideo_work%7C3485169#/embed/object (part 2 of 2) Accessed February 21, 2025.

DuCille, Ann. *Technicolored: Reflections on Race in the Time of TV.* Duke University Press, 2018.

Duke, Patty and Kenneth Tynan. *Call Me Anna: The Autobiography of Patty Duke.* Bantam, 1987.

Duke, Patty and Gloria Hochman. *A Brilliant Madness: Living with Manic Depressive Illness.* Bantam, 1992.

Duke, Patty and William J. Jankowski. *In the Presence of Greatness: My Sixty Year Journey as an Actress.* BearManor Media, 2018.

Farber, David. *The Age of Great Dreams: America in the 1960s.* Hill and Wang, 1994.

Freud, Sigmund. "The Uncanny." In *The Standard Edition of the Complete Psychological Works of Sigmund Freud*, volume 17, ed. and trans. James Strachey. Hogarth Press, 1955, 217–56. Originally published 1919.

Friedan, Betty. "Television and the Feminine Mystique, Part One: Television's Image of the American Woman," *TV Guide* 12, no. 5 (February 1–7, 1964): 6–11.

Friedan, Betty. "Television and the Feminine Mystique, Part Two: The Monsters in the Kitchen," *TV Guide* 12, no. 6 (February 8–14, 1964): 19–24.

Gerani, Gary and Casey Bond. *Patty Duke as "Billie": Role Model or Sell-Out?* BearManor Media, 2015.

Gitlin, Todd. *The Sixties: Years of Hope, Days of Rage.* Bantam Books, 1987.

Goodman, Paul. *Growing Up Absurd: Problems of Youth in the Organized Society.* Random House, 1960.

Grote, David. *The End of Comedy: Sit-Com and the Comedic Tradition.* Archon Books, 1983.

Hamamoto, Darrell Y. *Nervous Laughter: Television Situation Comedy and Liberal Democratic Ideology*. Praeger, 1989.

Harrington, Michael. *The Other America: Poverty in the United States*. Macmillan, 1962.

Hechinger, Grace and Fred M. *Teenage Tyranny*. William Morrow, 1963.

Himmelstein, Hal. *Television Myth and the American Mind*, 2nd edition. Praeger, 1994.

Humphreys, Kristi Rowan. *The Evil Twins of Television: Feminist Alter Egos Since 1950*. Lexington Books, 2019.

Jenkins, Tricia. "Feminism, Nationalism, and the 1960s' Slender Spies," *Journal of Popular Film and Television* 43, no. 1 (2015): 4–27.

Johnson, Victoria E. *Heartland TV: Prime Time Television and the Struggle for US Identity*. New York University Press, 2008.

Jones, Gerald. *Honey, I'm Home! Sitcoms: Selling the American Dream*. Grove Weidenfeld, 1992.

Kaplan, Alice. *Dreaming in French: The Paris Years of Jacqueline Bouvier Kennedy, Susan Sontag, and Angela Davis*. University of Chicago Press, 2012.

Kearny, Mary Celeste. "Recycling Judy and Corliss: Transmedia Exploitation and the First Teen-Girl Production Trend," *Feminist Media Studies* 4, no. 3 (November 2004): 265–95.

Kearny, Mary Celeste. "De la bobby-soxer à Gidget: La première vague de programmes télévisés adolescents aux États-Unis," trans. Laure Parsemain, *Télévision: Le moment expérimental*, eds., Gilles Delavaux and Denis Marechal. Rennes: Apogée/INA, 2011: 208–19.

Kearny, Mary Celeste. "'Against a Sharp White Background': Toward Race-Based Intersectional Approach in Youth Media Studies," *Cinema Journal* 57, no. 1 (Fall 2017): 119–24.

Klein, Naomi. *Doppelganger: A Trip into the Mirror World*. Farrar, Straus and Giroux, 2023.

Leighton, Frances Spatz. *Patty Goes to Washington*. Ace Books, 1964.

Luckett, Moya. "Girl Watchers: Patty Duke and Teen TV." In *The Revolution Wasn't Televised: Sixties Television and Social Conflict*, eds., Lynn Spigel and Michael Curtin. Taylor and Francis, 1997, 95–116.

Marc, David. *Comic Visions: Television Comedy and American Culture*, 2nd edition. Blackwell, MA, 1997.

Marcuse, Herbert. *One-Dimensional Man: Studies in the Ideology of Advanced Societies*. Beacon Books, 1964.

Marcuse, Herbert. *Eros and Civilization: A Philosophical Inquiry into Freud*, 1st edition, 1955. Beacon Books, 1966.

Mayersberg, Paul. *Hollywood: The Haunted House*. Allen Lane, 1967.

Mellencamp, Patricia. *High Anxiety: Catastrophe, Scandal, Age and Comedy*. Indiana University Press, 1992.

Meyer, James *et al.*, eds. *The Double: Identity and Difference in Art since 1900*. National Gallery of Art/Princeton University Press, 2022.

Miller, Quinlan. *Camp TV: Trans Gender Queer Sitcom History*. Duke University Press, 2019.

Mills, Brett. *Television Sitcom*. British Film Institute, 2005.

Morreale, Joanne, ed. *Critiquing the Sitcom: A Reader*. Syracuse University Press, 2003.

Nadel, Alan. *Television in Black-and-White America: Race and National Identity*. University Press of Kansas, 2005.

Nash, Ilana. "'Nowhere Else to Go': *Gidget* and the Construction of Adolescent Femininity," *Feminist Media Studies* 2, no. 1 (2002): 341–56.

Nash, Ilana. *American Sweethearts: Teenage Girls in Twentieth-Century Popular Culture*. Indiana University Press, 2006.

Osgerby, Bill. "'So Who's Got the Time for Adults!': Femininity, Consumption, and the Development of Teen TV—from Gidget to Buffy." In *Teen TV: Genre, Consumption, Identity*, eds., G. Davis and K. Dickinson. London: British Film Institute, 2004: 71–98.

Pinedo, Isabel Cristina and Wyatt D. Phillips, eds. *Camp TV of the 1960s: Reassessing the Vast Wasteland*. Oxford University Press, 2023.

Ross, Andrew. *No Respect: Intellectuals and Popular Culture*. Routledge, 1989.

Saunders, Ruby. "The Two Faces of Patty Duke," *Calling All Girls*, no. 62 (December 1965): 64–71.

Schroeder, Doris. *Patty Duke and Mystery Mansion*. Whitman Publishing, 1964.

Schroeder, Doris. *Patty Duke and the Adventure of the Chinese Junk*. Whitman Publishing, 1966.

Schwartz, Hillel. *The Culture of the Copy: Striking Likenesses, Unreasonable Facsimiles*. Zone Books, 2014.

Sheldon, Sidney. *The Other Side of Me: A Memoir*. Warner Books, 2005.

Sontag, Susan. *Against Interpretation and Other Essays*. Farrar, Straus and Giroux, 1966.

Spigel, Lynn. *Make Room for TV: Television and the Family Ideal in Postwar America*. University of Chicago Press, 1992.

Spigel, Lynn. "From Domestic Space to Outer Space: The 1960s Fantastic Family Sitcom." In Spigel, *Welcome to the Dreamhouse: Popular Media and Postwar Suburbs*. Duke University Press, 2001, 107–40.

Spigel, Lynn. *TV by Design: Modern Art and the Rise of Network Television*. University of Chicago Press, 2023.

Verevis, Constantine. "Trading Places: *Das Doppelte Lottchen* and *The Parent Trap*." In *Transnational Film Remakes*, eds., Iain Robert Smith and Constantine Verevis. Edinburgh University Press, 2017, 130–43.

Viney, William. *Twinkind: The Singular Significance of Twins*. Princeton University Press, 2023.

Watson, Mary Ann. *The Expanding Vista: American Television in the Kennedy Years*. Oxford University Press, 1990.

Wojcik, Pamela Robertson. *Gidget: Origins of a Teen Girl Transmedia Franchise*. Routledge, 2021.

Index

For the benefit of digital users, indexed terms that span two pages (e.g., 52–53) may, on occasion, appear on only one of those pages.

Figures are indicated by an italic *f* following the page number